Lecture Notes of the Institute for Computer Sciences, Social Informatics and Telecommunications Engineering   132

More information about this series at http://www.springer.com/series/8197

Pavel Gladyshev · Andrew Marrington
Ibrahim Baggili (Eds.)

Digital Forensics and Cyber Crime

Fifth International Conference, ICDF2C 2013
Moscow, Russia, September 26–27, 2013
Revised Selected Papers

 Springer

Editors
Pavel Gladyshev
School of Computer Science
    and Informatics
University College Dublin
Dublin
Ireland

Ibrahim Baggili
Tagliatela College of Engineering
University of New Haven
West Haven
USA

Andrew Marrington
College of Technical Innovation
Zayed University
Dubai
United Arab Emirates

ISSN 1867-8211   ISSN 1867-822X (electronic)
Lecture Notes of the Institute for Computer Sciences, Social Informatics
and Telecommunications Engineering
ISBN 978-3-319-14288-3   ISBN 978-3-319-14289-0   (eBook)
DOI 10.1007/978-3-319-14289-0

Library of Congress Control Number: 2014958660

Springer Cham Heidelberg New York Dordrecht London

Printed on acid-free paper

Springer International Publishing AG Switzerland is part of Springer Science+Business Media
(www.springer.com))

Preface

With every passing year, our reliance on information technology and cyber infrastructure continues to increase at an incredible pace. This fact is not lost on those who wish to use technology for criminal activities. Industry white papers and media reports suggest that the annual cost of cybercrime to the global economy is in the vicinity of four hundred billion dollars—greater than the gross domestic product of most countries. Cybercrime is undoubtedly a transnational criminal activity without boundaries or borders.

This volume contains papers presented at the 5th Annual International ICST Conference on Digital Forensics and Cybercrime (ICDF2C 2013), held during September 26–27, 2013, in Moscow, Russia. ICDF2C is unique in that it brings together representatives from academia, government, law enforcement, and industry together for multidisciplinary presentations and discussions. The focus of the conference is on the applied nature of digital forensics, and it provides an opportunity for researchers and practitioners to interact and discuss the various challenges and potential solutions in the field.

Nineteen papers were accepted through a double-blind peer-review process for presentation at ICDF2C 2013 out of 38 submissions received. This year, ICDF2C collaborated with the *Journal of Digital Investigation*, the leading international journal in the area of digital forensics and incident response. Two papers from the conference appear in these proceedings only in extended abstract form, as they were selected to be published in *Digital Investigation*. The remaining 17 papers appear in full in these proceedings. They cover diverse topics, ranging from regulation of social networks to file carving and many topics inbetween, representing an excellent cross section of the current work in the field of digital forensics and cybercrime.

On behalf of the whole Organizing Committee, I would like to sincerely thank the individuals who volunteered their time to be on the Technical Program Committee. I especially want to thank our keynote speakers, Mr. Kunwon Yang, the Assistant Director of INTERPOL Digital Forensics Laboratory, and Mr. Alexey Yakolev, Assistant Director of the Digital Forensic Service of the Investigative Committee of the Russian Federation. The success of the conference was in large part due to the efforts of the staff at EAI, in particular Erica Polini, whose tireless efforts and cheerful smile saw us through many adversities.

Andrew Marrington

Organization

Steering Committee

Pavel Gladyshev	University College Dublin, Ireland
Marcus Rogers	Purdue University, USA
Ibrahim Baggili	University of New Haven, USA
Sanjay Goel	University at Albany, State University of New York, USA

Organizing Committee

Conference Co-chairs

Pavel Gladyshev	University College Dublin, Ireland
Ibrahim Baggili	University of New Haven, USA

Program Chair

Andrew Marrington	Zayed University, UAE

Technical Program Committee

Frank Adelstein	GrammaTech, USA
Irfan Ahmed	University of New Orleans, USA
Ali Ismail Awad	Al Azhar University, Egypt
Ibrahim Baggili	University of New Haven, USA
Mark Branagan	Queensland University of Technology, Australia
Murray Brand	Edith Cowan University, Australia
Fred Cohen	Management Analytics, USA
Kim-Kwang Raymond Choo	University of South Australia, Australia
Glenn Dardick	Longwood University, USA
Barbara Endicott-Popovsky	University of Washington, USA
Ernest Foo	Queensland University of Technology, Australia
Katrin Franke	Gjøvik University College, Norway
Felix Freiling	Friedrich-Alexander-Universität Erlangen-Nürnberg, Germany
Zeno Geradts	Nederlands Forensisch Instituut, The Netherlands
Pavel Gladyshev	University College Dublin, Ireland
Yuri Gubanov	Belkasoft, Russia
Farkhund Iqbal	Zayed University, UAE
Thomas Kemmerich	University of Bremen, Germany

Gary Kessler	Embry-Riddle Aeronautical University, USA
Valery Koniavsky	PVTI
Samuel Liles	Purdue University, USA
James Lyle	National Institute of Standards and Technology, USA
Andrew Marrington	Zayed University, UAE
Fadi Al-Masalha	Applied Science Private University, Jordan
Stig Mjølsnes	Norwegian University of Science and Technology, Norway
Bruce Nikkel	UBS AG, Switzerland
Owen O'Connor	Cernam Pty Ltd, Austria
Marcus Rogers	Purdue University, USA
Vassil Roussev	University of New Orleans, USA
Kathryn Seigfried-Spellar	University of Alabama, USA
Eugene Spafford	Purdue University, USA
Craig Valli	Edith Cowan University, Australia

Sponsors

Sponsor	InfoSecurity Russia 2013
Technical Sponsor	CREATE-NET, Trento, Italy
Media Partner	Digital Investigation

Extended Abstracts

Evaluating Detection Error Trade-offs for Bytewise Approximate Matching Algorithms?

Frank Breitinger[1], Georgios Stivaktakis[1], and Vassil Roussev[2]

[1] da/sec - Biometrics and Internet Security Research Group
Hochschule Darmstadt, Darmstadt, Germany
{ frank.breitinger,georgios.stivaktakis} @cased.de
[2] Department of Computer Science
University of New Orleans, New Orleans, LA, USA
vassil@roussev.net

Extended Abstract. *Bytewise approximate matching* is a relatively new area within digital forensics, but its importance is growing quickly as practitioners are looking for fast methods to analyze the increasing amounts of data in forensic investigations. The essential idea is to complement the use of cryptographic hash functions to detect data objects with *bytewise identical* representation with the capability to find objects with *bytewise similar* representations.

Unlike cryptographic hash functions, which have been studied and tested for a long time, approximate matching ones are still in their early development stages, and have been evaluated in a somewhat ad-hoc manner. Recently, the FRASH testing framework [1] has been proposed as a vehicle for developing a set of standardized tests for approximate matching algorithms; the aim is to provide a useful guide for understanding and comparing the absolute and relative performance of different algorithms.

In this work, we are concerned only with bytewise approximate matching algorithms and their evaluation. Currently the best-known algorithms are ssdeep [2] and sdhash [3] and we will use them as a case study. Prior work [4] has argued that sdhash outperforms ssdeep in terms of a variety of metrics. This work is an effort to standardize such evaluation and make it possible for researchers and practitioners to easily reproduce the test results and compare tools, both current and future. Indeed, there are already other efforts, such as mrsh-v2 [5], to develop approximate matching tools, which reinforces the need for having an open and extensible platform for testing and evaluation.

The specific aim of this work is to extend FRASH [1] by developing precision and recall tests that enable us to characterize the behavior of approximate matching algorithms using a detection error trade-off (DET) curve (a.k.a. ROC). For these tests, we use controlled (pseudo-)random data that allows us to precisely generate and manipulate the test targets and know the exact ground truth.

By special arrangement between ICDF2C and the *Digital Investigation* Journal, this paper appears here in abstract form only. The full paper appears in the journal as: Frank Breitinger, Georgios Stivaktakis, and Vassil Roussev, Evaluating Detection Error Trade-offs for Bytewise Approximate Matching Algorithms, Digital Investigation, Volume 11, Issue 2, June 2014, pp. 81–89. doi:10.1016/j.diin.2014.05.002.

The overall proceeding is simple: generate a synthetic test set, copy this set and manipulate the copied files where we applied the following modifications:

Fragment detection: f_2 is a fragment of f_1 where the size of f_2 is one out of $X = \{50\ \%,$ 40 %, 30 %, 20 %, 10 %, 5 %, 4 %, 3 %, 2 %, 1 %}.

Single-common-block correlation: f_1 and f_2 have equal size and share a common byte string (block) of size $X = \{50\ \%, 40\ \%, 30\ \%, 20\ \%, 10\ \%, 5\ \%, 4\ \%, 3\ \%, 2\ \%, 1\ \%\}$. The position of the block is chosen randomly for each file.

Alignment robustness: f_2 is a copy of f_1, prefixed with a random byte string of length $X = \{1\ \%, 5\ \%, 10\ \%, 20\ \%\}$.

Random-noise resistance: f_2 is an obfuscated version of f_1, i.e., X % of f_2's bytes are edited, where $X = \{0.5\ \%, 1.0\ \%, 1.5\ \%, 2.0\ \%, 2.5\ \%\}$ of the file size.

Our test examines the performance of the algorithms as a function of file size. For that purpose we consider the behavior at six fixed file sizes −1, 4, 16, 64, 256 and 1024KiB.

The results are broadly in agreement with prior efforts, however, our work shows in more detail the tools' performance under different scenarios and allowed us to *quantify* the relationship between tool design and real-world performance. Further, we showed that each of the algorithms has a distinct operational range and analysts must understand the relationships between input parameters and result significance in order to operate the tools correctly. Therefore, having a rigorous testing framework, such as FRASH, is critical to evaluating and calibrating various approximate matching algorithms.

We expect that further tools in the approximate matching family will be developed, and the presented framework is designed to accommodate them with minimal effort allowing for fast, objective, and repeatable evaluation.

Acknowledgments. This work was partly funded by the EU (integrated project FIDELITY, grant number 284862) and supported by CASED (Center for Advanced Security Research Darmstadt).

References

1. Breitinger, F., Stivaktakis, G., Baier, H.: FRASH: a framework to test algorithms of similarity hashing. In: 13th Digital Forensics Research Conference (DFRWS'13), Monterey, August 2013
2. Kornblum, J.: Identifying almost identical files using context triggered piecewise hashing. Digital Invest. **3**, 91–97 (2006). http://dx.doi.org/10.1016/j.diin.2006.06.015
3. Roussev, V.: Data fingerprinting with similarity digests. In: Chow, K.-P., Shenoi, S. (eds.) Advances in Digital Forensics VI. IFIP AICT, vol. 337, pp. 207–226. Springer, Heidelberg (2010). http://dx.doi.org/10.1007/978-3-642-15506-2_15
4. Roussev, V.: An evaluation of forensic similarity hashes. Digital Invest. **8**, 34–41 (2011). http://dx.doi.org/10.1016/j.diin.2011.05.005
5. Breitinger, F., Baier, H.: Similarity preserving hashing: eligible properties and a new algorithm MRSH-v2. In: Rogers, M., Seigfried-Spellar, K.C. (eds.) ICDF2C 2012. LNICST, vol. 114, pp. 167–182. Springer, Heidelberg (2012)

Distinguishing the Viewers, Downloaders, and Exchangers of Internet Child Pornography by Individual Differences: Preliminary Findings

Kathryn C. Seigfried-Spellar

The University of Alabama, 410 Farrah Hall, Tuscaloosa AL, 35487, USA
kseigspell@as.ua.edu

The consumers of child pornography are a heterogeneous population, meaning there is no "typical" profile that will allow someone to easily identify a child pornography user. Not only are the individuals who commit child pornography offenses different, the crimes committed are different as well. Individuals who engage in child pornography do so at varying degrees, with some offenders engaging in more offenses than others. Statistics on the number of child pornography cases in the United States suggest there are differences in the offenders' level of engagement with child pornography. For example, some child pornography cases only involve the possession of child pornography whereas other cases involve offenders who are actively networking and trafficking the pornographic images. In addition, research suggests there is personality traits associated with the preference or intentional use of Internet child pornography. However, research has yet to determine if personality characteristics and cognitive traits discriminate between individuals who engage in different child pornography-related offenses (searching for/viewing, downloading, and exchanging).

Therefore, the current study explored the personality differences between self-reported consumers of Internet child pornography based on their level of engagement (i.e., searching for/viewing, downloading, or exchanging pornographic materials featuring individuals under the age of 18 years). Individuals were classified as viewers, downloaders, or exchangers of Internet child pornography based on their responses to an anonymous online survey, which also measured various personality and cognitive characteristics (e.g., extraversion). "Viewers" referred to individuals who did not intentionally or knowingly download any pornographic images of minors; instead, these individuals admitted to searching for and accessing websites in order to view online child pornography. "Downloaders" were individuals who self-reported that they knowingly and intentionally downloaded pornographic images of minors. Finally, those individuals who self-reported that they knowingly and intentionally shared and exchanged pornographic images of minors were labeled as "Exchangers."

Respondents were voluntarily recruited via the Internet by publicizing or advertising the study using various online resources including chat rooms, bulletin boards, discussion forums, and social media websites. This sampling methodology met the

---

By special arrangement between ICDF2C and the *Digital Investigation* Journal, this paper appears here in abstract form only. The full paper will appear in a future issue of Digital Investigation.

current needs of this study, which desired to: (1) sample respondents from the "general population of Internet child pornography users" rather than the forensic or clinical population, and (2) increase the respondents' confidence in self-disclosure of sensitive topics. 273 respondents completed the anonymous online survey; 257 respondents (94 %) were classified as non-child pornography consumers, and 16 respondents (6 %) were classified as Internet child pornography consumers. When only considering the child pornography users, 63 % ($n = 10$) were categorized as searchers/viewers, 18.5 % ($n = 3$) were categorized as downloaders, and 18.5 % ($n = 3$) were categorized as exchangers.

Individuals' self-reporting more severe child pornography offenses (e.g., exchanging) scored higher on conscientiousness, impulsive-seeking, and extraversion compared to the lower offense levels (e.g., searching for). The author investigated which facets of conscientiousness (i.e., competence, order, dutifulness, achievement, self-discipline, and deliberation) were correlated with CP Level. CP Level was significantly correlated with dutifulness and self-discipline. Post Hoc analyses suggested a significant difference between the "Viewers" and "Exchangers" for the self-discipline item. Overall, the significant correlation in conscientiousness scores, specifically on self-discipline, between the "Viewers" and "Exchangers" may reflect the level of sophistication necessary for distributing child pornography via the Internet. In addition, there was a significant positive correlation between impulsive-seeking and level of child pornography engagement. Future research should continue to assess if there is a difference in the level of excitement-seeking, yet self-disciplined nature, associated with viewing, downloading, or exchanging Internet child pornography.

Finally, exploratory analyses suggested a significant mean difference, on average, between child pornography group membership and extraversion. Specifically, those individuals who reported exchanging child pornography were more extraverted than those individuals who reported only searching for and viewing Internet child pornography. Higher scores on extraversion may reflect the offender's ability to socially network on the Internet in order to gain access to child pornography (i.e., exchanging/sharing).

Despite the small number of child pornography users, significant findings warrant future studies assessing the relationship between individual differences and the different nonproduction child pornography offenses. Research suggests there are different levels of child pornography use – some individuals are closet collectors while others are active traders – and the current study suggests there may be differences in personality as well. These differences may assist law enforcement and therapeutic programs in identifying those offenders who are at risk for engaging in the more serious forms of non-production child pornography offenses. In addition, certain offenders may be less likely to recidivate than others, and personality characteristics may predispose individuals to become engaged in certain Internet child pornography behaviors (browsing versus trading). Overall, future research should continue to use Internet-based research designs to assess why some individuals search for, view, download, and/or exchange Internet child pornography when others do not.

Contents

Digital Forensics - Technical

Robust Copy-Move Forgery Detection Based on Dual-Transform   3
    Munkhbaatar Doyoddorj and Kyung-Hyune Rhee

Forensic Decryption of FAT BitLocker Volumes   17
    P. Shabana Subair, C. Balan, S. Dija, and K.L. Thomas

Forensic Artifacts of the flareGet Download Manager   30
    Prachi Goel and Babu M. Mehtre

Amazon Kindle Fire HD Forensics   39
    Asif Iqbal, Hanan Alobaidli, Andrew Marrington, and Ibrahim Baggili

Resurrection: A Carver for Fragmented Files   51
    Martin Lambertz, Rafael Uetz, and Elmar Gerhards-Padilla

Taxonomy of Data Fragment Classification Techniques   67
    Rainer Poisel, Marlies Rybnicek, and Simon Tjoa

Identifying Forensically Uninteresting Files Using a Large Corpus   86
    Neil C. Rowe

FaceHash: Face Detection and Robust Hashing.   102
    Martin Steinebach, Huajian Liu, and York Yannikos

**Information Warfare, Cyber Terrorism, and Critical
Infrastructure Protection**

Regulating Social Network Services for Lawful Interception.   119
    Esti Peshin

Determining When Conduct in Cyberspace Constitutes Cyber Warfare in Terms
of the International Law and *Tallinn Manual on the International Law
Applicable to Cyber Warfare*: A Synopsis   130
    Murdoch Watney

Digital Forensics - Standards, Certification and Accreditation

Measuring Accuracy of Automated Parsing and Categorization Tools
and Processes in Digital Investigations.   147
    Joshua I. James, Alejandra Lopez-Fernandez, and Pavel Gladyhsev

Towards a Process Model for Hash Functions in Digital Forensics   170
  Frank Breitinger, Huajian Liu, Christian Winter, Harald Baier,
  Alexey Rybalchenko, and Martin Steinebach

Automation in Digital Forensics

An Automated Link Analysis Solution Applied to Digital
Forensic Investigations.   189
  Fergal Brennan, Martins Udris, and Pavel Gladyshev

Computer Profiling for Preliminary Forensic Examination   207
  Andrew Marrington, Farkhund Iqbal, and Ibrahim Baggili

Digital Forensics and the Cloud

Determining Training Needs for Cloud Infrastructure Investigations
Using I-STRIDE.   223
  Joshua I. James, Ahmed F. Shosha, and Pavel Gladyhsev

Cloud Forensic Readiness: Foundations   237
  Lucia De Marco, M-Tahar Kechadi, and Filomena Ferrucci

Poster Presentation

Mozilla Firefox Browsing Artifacts in 3 Different Anti-forensics Modes   247
  Deepak Gupta and Babu M. Mehtre

Author Index   253

Digital Forensics - Technical

Robust Copy-Move Forgery Detection Based on Dual-Transform

Munkhbaatar Doyoddorj[1] and Kyung-Hyune Rhee[2]([⊠])

[1] Department of Information Security, Pukyong National University,
Busan, Republic of Korea
d_mbtr@pknu.ac.kr
[2] Department of IT Convergence and Application Engineering,
Pukyong National University, 599-1, Daeyeon3-Dong, Nam-gu,
Busan 608-737, Republic of Korea
khrhee@pknu.ac.kr

Abstract. With the increasing popularity of digital media and the ubiquitous availability of media editing software, innocuous multimedia are easily tampered for malicious purposes. Copy-move forgery is one important category of image forgery, in which a part of an image is duplicated, and substitutes another part of the same image at a different location. Many schemes have been proposed to detect and locate the forged regions. However, these schemes fail when the copied region is affected by post-processing operations before being pasted. To rectify the problem and further improve the detection accuracy, we propose a robust copy-move forgery detection method based on dual-transform to detect such specific artifacts, in which a cascade of Radon transform (RT) and Discrete Cosine Transform (DCT) is used. It will be shown that the dual-transform coefficients well conform the efficient assumption and therefore leads to more robust feature extraction results. Experimental results demonstrate that our method is robust not only to noise contamination, blurring, and JPEG compression, but also to region scaling, rotation and flipping, respectively.

Keywords: Passive image forensics · Copy-move forgery · Dual-transform · Duplicated region detection · Mixture Post-processing

1 Introduction

With the ever increasing diffusion of simple and powerful software tools for digital source editing, image tampering is becoming more common, stimulating an intense quest for algorithms, to be used in the forensics field, which help deciding about the integrity of digital images. Furthermore, it is necessary for us

This research was supported by Basic Science Research Program through the National Research Foundation of Korea (NRF) funded by the Ministry of Education (NRF-2013R1A1A4A01009848) and a Research Grant of Pukyong National University (2013-0472).

© Institute for Computer Sciences, Social Informatics and Telecommunications Engineering 2014
P. Gladyshev et al. (Eds.): ICDF2C 2013, LNICST 132, pp. 3–16, 2014.
DOI: 10.1007/978-3-319-14289-0_1

to develop automatic methods to authenticate the images and indicate potential forgeries.

In order to protect the integrity and reveal the manipulation of digital media, two types of countermeasures, active and passive approaches, are extensively investigated in previous studies. Active approach, including digital signature, watermarking, and *etc.*, relies on pre-processing before distribution, which requires additional and shared information. However, there is no universally recognized standard, and the complexity greatly restricts its application. On the other hand, the passive approach only requires digital media without any supplemental information.

Due to the variety of manipulations and the diversity of individual characteristics of media, passive approach usually faces difficulties at a larger scope, and suffers from complicated and time consuming problems [11].

One of the most common types of image forgeries is the copy-move forgery [12], where a region from one part of an image is copied and pasted onto another part in same image, thereby concealing the image content in the latter region. Such concealment can be used to hide an undesired object or increase the number of objects apparently present in the image. Although a simple translation may be sufficient in many cases, additional operations are often performed in order to better hide the tampering. These include rotation, scaling, lossy compression, noise contamination, blurring, and among others. Also, the copied part comes from the same image, all of its properties and statistic information are the same as the rest of the image. Thus, it is difficult to detect forgeries by techniques that compare statistics of different part of an image to each other. Hence, in order to be able to reliably detect such forgeries, a several techniques have been recently proposed which try to be robust to some of these transformations.

In the literature, researchers have developed various techniques. Huang *et al.* [1] proposed improved robustness using a discrete cosine transform (DCT) to noise addition, global blurring and lossy compression, but does not deal with geometrical transformations of the tampered region. The method of Khan *et al.* [2] reduces the time complexity of the PCA-based approach by using a discrete wavelet transform (DWT), but also does not address geometrical transformations. In [3], Mahdian *et al.* took advantage of the blur invariant moments to extract the block features. Though these methods can detect the copy-move forgery in most cases, they may fail if the copied regions are rotated or flipped. Ryu *et al.* [4] employed Zernike moments to extract the features for block matching. This method achieved an average detection precision rate of 83.59 % in the case of region rotation. In [5], Liu *et al.* proposed a method using Hu moments to extract the features of the blocks. This method is robust not only to noise contamination, JPEG compression and blurring, but also to moderate rotation.

Our contributions. The aim of this paper is to demonstrate a robust copy-move forgery detection method for passive image forensics through a construction of the invariant features from dual-transform, such as Radon and discrete cosine transforms. The key insight of our work is that the copied region concealed with post-processing operations before being pasted in same image, the invariant image features are detectable by using the ability of such transform even if the feature strength is weakened. When the position of the copied part is unknown, we able to detect the exact pasted position that using the extracted invariant features, under the assumption that the pasted regions will yield similar features with the copied regions.

In the proposed method, Radon transform is utilized to project the image onto directional projection space, and then 1-D DCT is used to extract significant frequency features from the Radon space. Dual-transform largely reduces the influence of geometrical and image processing operations, and the invariant feature of the dual-transform coefficients is found to be stable. Extensive comparative studies show the superiority and robustness of the proposed method.

The remainder of the paper is organized as follows. Section 2 introduces the concept of the dual-transform, which includes Radon and DCT transforms. The proposed method is presented in Sect. 3. The experimental results are provided in Sect. 4. Conclusion is drawn in Sect. 5.

2   The Concept of the Dual-Transform

2.1   Radon Transform (RT)

Applying Radon transform on an image $f(x, y)$ for a given set of angles can be thought of as computing the projection of the image along the given angles [6]. The resulting projection is the sum of the intensities of the pixels in each direction, *i.e.* a line integral. For an image $f : \mathbb{R} \times \mathbb{R} \rightarrow [0, 255]$ containing an object, the result g of Radon transform is a function $\mathcal{R} : \mathbb{R} \times [0, 2\pi] \rightarrow \mathbb{R}_+$ defined as:

$$g(s, \vartheta) = \mathcal{R}(f(x, y)) = \int_{-\infty}^{\infty} f(s \cos \vartheta - t \sin \vartheta, s \sin \vartheta + t \cos \vartheta) dt \qquad (1)$$

$$\begin{bmatrix} s \\ t \end{bmatrix} = \begin{bmatrix} \cos \vartheta & \sin \vartheta \\ -\sin \vartheta & \cos \vartheta \end{bmatrix} \begin{bmatrix} x \\ y \end{bmatrix} \qquad (2)$$

Radon transform of the translated, rotated and scaled images exhibits interesting properties, which can be employed to construct a method for invariant object recognition. Therefore, the behavior of the transform for these three variations in the input image should be defined. Any translation in spatial domain leads in the Radon domain to translation in the s direction. The amount of the translation varies with the ϑ dimension. The scaling of the original image along both axes results in the scaling along the s axis in the Radon domain. The value of the transform is also scaled. The rotation in spatial domain leads to circular translation along the ϑ axis in the Radon domain. The behaviour of Radon transform is summarized in Table 1, and depicted in Fig. 1.

2.2   Discrete Cosine Transform (DCT)

Discrete cosine transform is used to know frequency components present in a image [7]. DCT mainly reduces the redundant information present in the image

Table 1. Behavior of Radon transform for rotated, scaled and translated images.

Behavior	Image function, f	Radon transform, $g = \mathcal{R}(f)$.
Original	$f(x, y)$	$g(s, \vartheta)$
Rotated	$f_{polar}(r, \vartheta_0 + \varphi)$	$g(s, (\vartheta + \vartheta_0) mod 2\pi)$
Scaled	$f(\alpha x, \alpha y)$	$\frac{1}{|\alpha|} g(\alpha s, \vartheta)$
Translated	$f(x - x_0, y - y_0)$	$g(s - x_0 \cos \vartheta - y_0 \sin \vartheta, \vartheta)$

(a)   (b)   (c)

Fig. 1. Radon transform. (a) Image projection, (b) Test image, and (c) Its projection on Radon space.

by omitting the undesired parts of the image. Orthogonality, symmetry, separability, and decorrelation are important properties of DCT. The most common DCT definition of a 1D sequence of length N is

$$C(u) = \alpha(u) \sum_{x=0}^{N-1} f(x) \cos \left[\frac{\pi(2x + 1)u}{2N} \right], \qquad (3)$$

for $u = 0, 1, ..., N - 1$. In Eq. (3), $\alpha(u)$ is defined as

$$\alpha(u) = \begin{cases} \sqrt{\frac{1}{N}} & \text{for} \quad u = 0 \\ \sqrt{\frac{2}{N}} & \text{for} \quad u \neq 0. \end{cases} \qquad (4)$$

The DCT coefficients for the transformed output image $C(u)$ with an input image $f(x)$ can be calculated by using the Eq. (3). N is the pixel dimensions of the input image $f(x)$. The intensity value of the pixel N of the image is given by $f(x)$ and $C(u)$ is the DCT coefficients in u of the DCT matrix.

3   Robust Copy-Move Forgery Detection

In this section, we present the proposed robust copy-move forgery detection method based on dual transform. At first, we describe a model for copy-move forgery in digital images, and then introduce our proposed method to detect such specific artifact.

3.1   Model for Copy-Move Forgery

The task of finding the copy-move forgery is that of finding at least two large similar regions. Given an image $f(x, y)$, the tampered image $f'(x, y)$, must subject to: $\exists$ regions D_1 and D_2 are subsets of D and a shift vector $d = (dx, dy)$, (we assume that $|D_1| = |D_2| > |D| * 0.85\%$ and $|d| > L$), $f'(x, y) = f(x, y)$ if $(x, y) \notin D_2$ and $f'(x, y) = f(x - dx, y - dy)$ if $(x, y) \in D_2$, where D_1 is the source and D_2 is the target region, $D_2 = D_1 + d$. We consider that the similarity of the target region is larger than 0.85% of the image size. It would be easy to detect above forgery via exact match. However, to make the tampered image harder to detect, the attacker may perform various processing on $f'(x, y)$. Then the tampered image becomes $f''(x, y) = \xi(f'(x, y))$, where ξ is the post-processing operator, which includes geometrical and image processing operations. The post-processing attack makes the task of detecting forgery significantly harder. In the next section, we present an efficient method for detecting copy-move forgery which is also robust against various forms of post-processing operations.

3.2   The Proposed Method

Our proposed method is based on dual-transform, which includes Radon and discrete cosine transformations. This set of transformations were designed for an efficient and robust approach. The main issue in directly applying these tools to image forgery detection is that these tools were designed to find duplicate but separate, images, whereas we are trying to find identical regions in same image. We perform modifications in the feature extraction and matching processes to efficiently detect such forgery. Firstly, we apply Radon transform on each divided blocks to project the image into a directional projection space, then perform 1-D DCT to derive the frequency features from the Radon space. Following we select the DCT coefficients with low frequency by using a dimension reduction. Finally, an invariant robust features are extracted. The details of the proposed method is given as the following:

1. **Pre-processing.** Image is tiled by overlapping blocks of $b \times b$ pixels. Blocks are horizontally slid by one pixel rightwards starting with upper left corner and ending with the bottom right corner. The total number of overlapping blocks for an image of $M \times N$ pixels is $S_{blocks} = (M - b + 1) \times (N - b + 1)$, for each block $B_l(l = 1, ..., S_{block})$. For instance, an image with the size of 640×480 with blocks of size 8×8 yields $299,409$ overlapping blocks.
2. **Feature extraction.** Each block is applied Radon transform, the space is projected on the Radon space. The results of Radon transform are contained in the columns of a matrix with the number of projections generated being equal to the number of the defined angles, $(\vartheta_1, \vartheta_2, ..., \vartheta_n)$. Then, delete the rows in projection matrix, which are composed of 0. This will remove the redundancy data generated by Radon transform.

   On each projection (represented by column of the projection matrix) according to projection angles, we apply 1-D DCT to derive the frequency features from the Radon space. We quantize the coefficients according to the JPEG quantization table using a predetermined quality factor Q. The quantized coefficients can be denoted as $c_k = \{c_1, c_2, ..., c_k\}$. The dimension reduction can make the sorting and matching faster. The frequency features are the nature of 1-D DCT that the energy of transformed DCT coefficients will be focused on the first several values (lower frequency values). Thus, those higher frequency coefficients can be truncated. The truncation can be done by saving only a part of vector components. Here, we define a factor $p, (0 < p \leq 1)$, that only first $\lceil p \times k \rceil$ DCT coefficients are saved for further processing. $c_r = \{c_1, c_2, ..., c_r\}$, $(r = \lceil p \times k \rceil, r < k)$, where p denotes a saved the percentage of DCT coefficients and k denotes the number of coefficients on the projections according to angles ϑ_n. For example, we select the projection angle $\vartheta = 8$, and derived the 1-D DCT coefficients (column matrix 15×1) from the projection space. Five coefficients are deleted, which are composed of 0. The concentration of energy in 80 % is calculated as, $\lceil p * k \rceil = \lceil 0.8 * 10 \rceil = 8$ coefficients.

The truncated DCT coefficients in projection matrix are sorted by a lexicographically order. Let the matrix C denote the sorted vectors, the size of the matrix will be C_r^m.

$$C = \begin{bmatrix} C_1^1 & C_2^1 & ... & C_r^1 \\ C_1^2 & C_2^2 & ... & C_r^2 \\ . & . & ... & . \\ C_1^m & C_2^m & ... & C_r^m \end{bmatrix}_{(M-b+1)(N-b+1)} \tag{5}$$

By using a lexicographic sorting, similar features will locate at the neighboring rows and the feature matching can be achieved in a small range.

3. **Similarity matching.** The feature matching is to find out the corresponding similar rows from between m rows of the C matrix. In order to detect the forged region correctly, the similarity threshold τ_s and the distance threshold τ_d should be predetermined, respectively. In our method, we search for the corresponding rows by estimating the Euclidean distance of feature vectors, as follows:

$$D(C_r^m, C_r^{m+v}) = \sqrt{\sum_{r=1}^u C_r^m - C_r^{m+v})^2} < \tau_s \tag{6}$$

If $D(C_r^m, C_r^{m+v})$ is smaller than a threshold τ_s, the corresponding features will be regard as correctly matched. Then the locations of two features are stored. The matching will be repeated for all rows of C. Since the feature vectors of the rows are quite similar with each other which have the overlapping pixels, only the rows with the actual distance between two similar features are compared as follows:

$$L(C_r^m, C_r^{m+v}) = \sqrt{(x_i - x_{i+j})^2 + (y_i - y_{i+j})^2} > \tau_d \tag{7}$$

where x and y are the coordinates of the corresponding features.

Fig. 2. Image forgery detection. (a) Original image, (b) Forged image, (c) Detected forgery with similar features, and (d) Results after filtering.

4. **Detection.** When all the matched feature pairs are saved, which is achieved by marking the copied and forged regions, respectively. Generally speaking, the regions are stamped on a binary image. That is to say, all the detected features including the forged and un-forged features are marked to generate a detection map. Fig. 2 shows an example of the proposed method for marking. In general, there are some falsely detected features marked on the initial detection map in Fig. 2(c), and these falsely detected features should be removed by filtering in Fig. 2(d). For the filtering, we generate a sliding window with the size of 8 × 8 pixels, and move it from left to right and up to bottom. Each time, the window moves forward by 8 pixels to make sure all the pixels of the image will be filtered and each pixel will be filtered only once. If the number of white pixels are less than 60 in the window, all pixels of the window are marked as black. Otherwise, keep the number of the white pixels and do nothing. After filtering, some small isolated false matches can be removed. Figure 2(d) shows the detection result after the filtering operation.

4   Experimental Results

In this section, we present the experimental results of our proposed method. We simulated our method under a PC with 3.2G Hz Core i5 CPU, 8G RAM, and Windows 8 platform. The simulation was carried out using Matlab version R2008a. We test our method on Benchmark data for image copy-move detection dataset including 120 authentic and 124 forged color images of size 3888 × 2592 pixels with different outdoor scenes, as shown in Fig. 3. The authentic images were taken by different digital cameras. All tampered images in this dataset are generated from the authentic images by crop-and-paste operation using Adobe Photoshop CS3 version 10.0.1 on Windows XP. The tampered regions are from the same authentic image.

Fig. 3. Examples of test images.

4.1 Robustness Test for Feature Vectors

We extracted the features, which expressed by DCT coefficients of 1-D DCT based on the Radon space. These features will not change a lot after some post-processing operations. We have defined the model for copy-move forgery in Sect. 3.1. If an image is contaminated by additive Gaussian noise operation (AWGN), then the pixel value will be changed, for each pixel, we define $f(x,y) = \lfloor f(x,y) \rfloor + \xi_{noise}, (0 < \xi < 1)$, where $f(x,y)$ is the corresponding pixel value that contaminated by signal noise, $\lfloor f(x,y) \rfloor$ is the nearest value less than or equal to the original pixel value, ξ_{noise} is the random noise which is independent identically distributed. For instance, each noisy block $B'_i = B_i + \xi_{noise}$, and the extracted features $c'_r = c_r + \xi'_{noise}$, since $E(\xi'_{noise}) = 0$, $D(\xi'_{noise}) = \sum_{i=1}^{b^2} \xi'_{noise}/b^2$, generally $\sum_{i=1}^{b^2} (\xi')^2_{noise} \ll b^2$. Since we get $c'_r \approx c_r$. For the Gaussian blurring only affects in some high frequency components of each blocks, but changes in the low frequency components are a little. The robustness against

Table 2. The correlation coefficients for the feature vectors, $\vartheta = 8$, (8×8).

Vectors	Extracted, c_r	Post-processed, c_ξ					
		AWGN	AWGN	Blurring	Blurring	JPEG	JPEG
		SNR	SNR	w, σ	w, σ	Q	Q
		$25dB$	$50dB$	3, 1	5, 0.5	5	10
c_1	958.75	959.26	962.31	957.45	959.07	958.26	962.12
c_2	886.37	893.63	896.25	884.16	886.36	884.69	887.02
c_3	875.12	885.02	894.89	873.52	874.85	873.81	878.29
c_4	801.50	820.75	828.20	799.21	802.80	798.68	796.93
c_5	745.25	753.39	761.62	744.03	746.68	748.52	736.84
Correlation coefficients		0.9980	0.9804	1.0000	1.0000	1.0000	1.0000

the geometrical operations are provided by the property of Radon transform. In order to show the robustness of the feature vectors, we chose a size of block 8×8, 16×16, and 32×32, respectively, from the natural images. Then we applied some post-processing operations with different parameters. The results of robustness test are presented in Table 2. c_r and c_ξ are feature vectors that the extracted and post-processed vectors, respectively. After some post-processing, we calculate the correlation coefficients between them, if the result is close to 1, which implies the feature vector is robust and the invariance is more stable. The correlation coefficient is used as a measure of correlation, as it is invariant to intensity change. (Here we note that the extracted feature vectors are reduced by dimension reduction.)

4.2 The Evaluation of the Detection Performance

In order to quantify the accuracy of detection, the true positive ratio (TPR) and the false positive ratio (FPR) are employed, as follows:

$$TPR = \frac{|\Omega_1 \cap \Omega_2| + |\overline{\Omega_1} \cap \overline{\Omega_2}|}{|\Omega_1| + |\overline{\Omega_2}|}, \qquad FPR = \frac{|\Omega_1 \cup \Omega_2| + |\overline{\Omega_1} \cup \overline{\Omega_2}|}{|\Omega_1| + |\overline{\Omega_1}|} - 1 \qquad (8)$$

where Ω_1 and Ω_2 are the original copied region and the detected copied region, while $\overline{\Omega_1}$ and $\overline{\Omega_2}$ are the forged region and the detected forged region, respectively. In order to set the threshold parameters, we randomly chose 50 images from the dataset and then make a series of forgeries. After that, we use different the projection angles ranging from 8 to 64 degree with 8 increment, then a set of values for $\tau_s = 0.005$ and $\tau_d = 4$, respectively, from the number of testing results. The threshold parameters are chosen by highest true positive ratio with corresponding lowest false positive ratio. In order to decide the block size, we tested

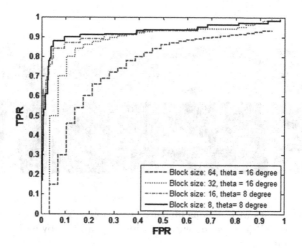

Fig. 4. Detection results for varying block sizes.

the TPR and FPR curves for various block sizes with a selection of different directional projection angles.

As shown in Fig. 4, we notice that smaller block size is resulted higher detectability property. But, large block size is indicated lowest detection performance. Therefore, we set the block size of 8×8 pixels in all our following experiments.

Table 3. The feature matching accuracies with various post-processing operations.

Operations		*Compression*			*Additive Gaussian noise*		
		JPEG 30	JEG 60	JPEG 90	SNR 10	SNR 20	SNR 30
Rotation	10°	0.979	0.982	0.987	0.969	0.971	0.975
	30°	0.971	0.974	0.985	0.950	0.956	0.969
	45°	0.963	0.966	0.976	0.936	0.938	0.948
Scaling	5	0.984	0.984	0.987	0.974	0.975	0.978
	10	0.982	0.983	0.988	0.968	0.971	0.979
	15	0.965	0.976	0.978	0.956	0.964	0.966
Blurring	3 × 3	0.970	0.972	0.976	0.931	0.948	0.951
	5 × 5	0.962	0.968	0.971	0.920	0.927	0.939
	7 × 7	0.927	0.931	0.935	0.901	0.917	0.919
Contrast	10	0.975	0.976	0.976	0.970	0.973	0.976
changing	30	0.973	0.970	0.974	0.960	0.966	0.968
	45	0.967	0.966	0.966	0.947	0.956	0.957
Rot. + Flip	10°, Hor.	0.889	0.898	0.897	0.836	0.847	0.848
Sc. + Flip	10, Ver.	0.885	0.890	0.893	0.825	0.826	0.825
Rot. + Sc.	10°, 10	0.738	0.768	0.787	0.704	0.731	0.747

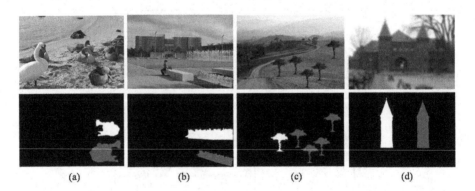

(a)   (b)   (c)   (d)

Fig. 5. Detection results with various mixture operations. (a) Object scaling with horizontally flipping, (b) Object scaling with rotation, (c) Multi-copy with JPEG, and (d) Blurring with scaling.

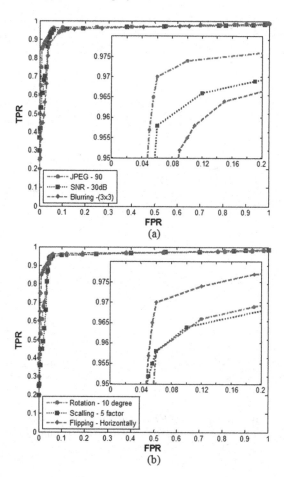

Fig. 6. Detection results with various attacks. (a) Image processing operations, and (b) Geometrical operations.

(a) The performance of the feature matching. We evaluated the feature matching process that the copied regions have been subjected to various geometrical operations (rotation, scaling and flipping) and image processing operations (blurring and contrast changing). Additionally varying the levels of lossy compression (JPEG) and the additive Gaussian noise (AWGN) were performed with mixture operations. The purpose of this testing is to highlight the performance of features that we have employed. The accuracies of the feature matching are determined by proportion of true positives in the matching feature pairs. The obtained results are reported in Table 3.

In Table 3, the mixture operations tend to have somewhat lower accuracy than other operations, which is shown at low quality factors and signal noise ratio (SNR). Especially, the accuracies for blurring and contrast changing indicate lower layer among of individual operations, respectively. Nevertheless, TPR and

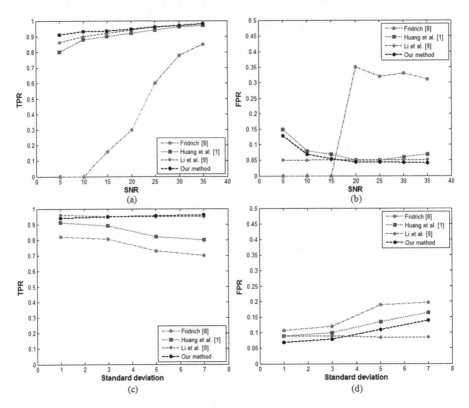

Fig. 7. Detection results with TPR/FPR curves. The performance comparisons (a–b) with different the SNR levels ($5dB \leq SNR \leq 35dB$), and (c–d) with Gaussian blurring (w = 5, σ = 1 to 7).

FPR are quite acceptible even with low quality factors and signal noise ratio (SNR).

(b) The robustness against post-processing operations. The advantage of the proposed method is that it can resist against geometrical and image processing operations. In order to test the efficiency and robustness of our method further, we test all images from Benchmark dataset. For each image, a random sized region was copied then pasted onto a non-overlapping position, while the copied regions are distorted by different mixture post-processing operations. For instance, as shown in Fig. 5, the copied region is distorted by scaling with horizontal flipping, rotation with scaling, multi-copy with JPEG, and blurring with scaling, respectively. From the results we show that the forged regions can be detected accurately. Figure 6 presents the detection results of our method on various kind of individual post-processing operations. As can be seen, we are able to attain quite high accuracies at low false positive rates in selection of higher rate values. In the case of blurring, it can be seen that the resistance of such operation is lower than other post-processing operations.

(c) **The performance comparisons.** The overall average performance comparisons of our method with other related work are performed more precisely in this section. Some invariant feature extraction methods for copy-move forgery are presented in Fridrich [8], Huang *et al.* [1], and Li *et al.* [9]. As shown in Fig. 7(a–b), the forged images are contaminated with additive Gaussian noise ($5dB \leq SNR \leq 35dB$). Fridrich's method has the lowest TPR than other methods, when less than $10dB$, the TPR is approximate to zero. Observation of TPR in our method achieves higher TPR among other methods. For FPR, Fridrich's method has lower FPR value, that cannot detect any forged region, when the FPR is less than $15dB$. However, such method quickly leads to higher FPR when the SNR level is higher, which indicates it is sensitive to noise adding. Our method have a better performance with Li *et al.*'s method, however with lower FPR.

In case of blurring, the forged regions are blurred by a Gaussian blurring filter ($w = 5$, $\sigma = 1$ to 7). Figure 7(c–d) shows the TPR curve of our method has better performance followed by Li *et al.*'s method, however, the TPR curves of Fridrich and Huang *et al.* are drop significantly, when the blurring radius increased. In FPR, our method has the lowest value, even increased the larger blurring radius.

5 Conclusion

In this paper, we proposed a robust copy-move forgery detection method for a suspicious image. To extract an invariant robust features of a given image, we applied dual-transform. The extracted features are represented by lexicographically ordered DCT coefficients on the frequency domain from the Radon space, that each overlapped image blocks are projected by the columns of a matrix with the number of the defined angles ϑ_n on the Radon domain. Experimental results supported that the proposed method was appropriated to identify and localize the copy-move forgery even when though the forged region had been manipulated intentionally. The main contribution of our work is a method capable of easily detecting traces of various attacks. We concerned the geometrical and image processing operations, and any of their arbitrary combinations. The detection performance of our method is satisfactory enough and meets the robustness criteria.

References

1. Huang, Y., Lu, W., Sun, W., Long, D.: Improved DCT-based detection of copy-move forgery in images. J. Forensic Sci. Int. **206**(13), 178–184 (2011)
2. Khan, S., Kulkarni, A.: Reduced time complexity for detection of copy-move forgery using discrete wavelet transform. Int. J. Comput. Appl. **6**(7), 31–36 (2010)
3. Mahdian, B., Saic, S.: Detection of copy-move forgery using a method based on blur moment invariants. J. Forensic Sci. Int. **171**(27), 180–189 (2007)

4. Ryu, S.-J., Lee, M.-J., Lee, H.-K.: Detection of copy-rotate-move forgery using zernike moments. In: Böhme, R., Fong, P.W.L., Safavi-Naini, R. (eds.) IH 2010. LNCS, vol. 6387, pp. 51–65. Springer, Heidelberg (2010)
5. Liu, G.J., Wang, J.W., Lian, S.G., Wang, Z.Q.: A passive image authentication scheme for detecting region duplication forgery with rotation. J. Netw. Comput. Appl. **34**(5), 1557–1565 (2011)
6. Fiffy, M.A.: The radon transform and some of its applications. J. Mod. Optics. **32**(1), 3–4 (1985)
7. Khayam, S.A.: The Discrete Cosine Transform (DCT): Theory and Application. J. Inf. Theor. Coding, 1–31 (2003)
8. Fridrich, A.: Detection of copy-move forgery in digital images. In: Proceedings of the Digital Forensic Research Workshop, Cleveland OH, USA (2003)
9. Li, L., Li, S., Zhu, H.: An efficient scheme for detecting copy-move forged images by local binary patterns. J. Inf. Hiding Multimedia Signal Process. **4**(1), 46–56 (2013)
10. Christlein, V., Riess, R., Angelopoulou, E.: On rotation invariance on copy-move forgery detection. In: IEEE International Workshop on Information Forensics and Security, pp. 1–6 (2010)
11. Farid, H.: A survey of image forgery detection. IEEE Signal Process. Mag. **26**(2), 16–25 (2009)
12. Chrislein, V., Riess, R., Jordan, J., Angelopoulou, E.: An evaluation of popular copy-move forgery detection approaches. IEEE Trans. Inf. Forensics Secur. **7**(6), 1841–1854 (2012)

Forensic Decryption of FAT BitLocker Volumes

P. Shabana Subair, C. Balan[✉], S. Dija, and K.L. Thomas

Centre for Development of Advanced Computing, PO Box 6520,
Vellayambalam, Thiruvananthapuram 695033, Kerala, India
{shabana, cbalan, dija, thomaskldija}@cdac.in

Abstract. New versions of Windows come equipped with mechanisms, such as EFS and BitLocker, which are capable of encrypting data to an industrial standard on a Personal Computer. This creates problems if the computer in question contains electronic evidence. BitLocker, for instance, provides a secure way for an individual to hide the contents of their entire disk, but as with most technologies, there are bound to be weaknesses and threats to the security of the encrypted data. It is conceivable that this technology, while appearing robust and secure, may contain flaws, which would jeopardize the integrity of the whole system. As more people encrypt their hard drives, it will become harder and harder for forensic investigators to recover data from Personal Computers. This paper documents the Bitlocker Drive Encryption System (version 2) in Windows 7. In particular it describes how to forensically decrypt and load a FAT disk or image which is bitlocked, if the keys are provided.

Keywords: Bitlocker To Go · Bitlocker keys · Full volume encryption key · Volume master key · AES-CCM · Elephant diffuser · AES-CBC

1 Introduction

Volumes encrypted with BitLocker will have a different signature than the standard NTFS header. Instead, they have in their volume header (first sector): 2D 46 56 45 2D 46 53 2D or, in ASCII, -FVE-FS-.

These volumes can be identified by the BitLocker GUID/UUID: 4967d63b-2e29-4ad8-8399-f6a339e3d00.

The actual data on the encrypted volume is protected with either 128-bit or 256-bit AES or optionally diffused using an algorithm called Elephant. The key used to do the encryption, the Full Volume Encryption Key (FVEK) and/or TWEAK key, is stored in the BitLocker metadata on the protected volume. The FVEK and/or TWEAK keys are encrypted using another key, namely the Volume Master Key (VMK). Several copies of the VMK are also stored in the metadata. Each copy of the VMK is encrypted using another key; also know as key-protector key. Some of the key-protectors are:

- TPM (Trusted Platform Module)
- Smart card
- recovery password

© Institute for Computer Sciences, Social Informatics and Telecommunications Engineering 2014
P. Gladyshev et al. (Eds.): ICDF2C 2013, LNICST 132, pp. 17–29, 2014.
DOI: 10.1007/978-3-319-14289-0_2

- start-up key
- clear key; this key-protector provides no protection
- user password

BitLocker has support for partial encrypted volumes.

1.1 BitLocker To Go

BitLocker To Go is a full-disk encryption protection technology for removable storage devices. Though it is based on BitLocker technology, BitLocker To Go significantly enhances the technical capabilities of BitLocker. For example, it is compatible with all FAT (FAT32, exFAT, etc.) file systems in addition to NTFS, dramatically increasing its compatibility with existing devices.

Volumes encrypted with BitLocker To Go will have a hybrid encrypted volume, meaning that part of the volume is unencrypted and contains applications to unlock the volume and the other part of the volume is encrypted. The "discovery drive" volume contains BitLocker To Go Reader to read from encrypted volumes on versions of Microsoft Windows without BitLocker support.

BitLocker To Go is designed primarily for enterprises, where there is serious risk of a user bringing an unprotected storage device into the environment, copying important corporate information (inadvertently or not) to it, and then losing the device outside of the workplace. USB memory keys, in particular, are small and convenient, and quite popular, but they're also easily lost. With BitLocker To Go enabled on the device, one can help protect sensitive corporate–or, for that matter, personal–data in the event of loss or theft.

BitLocker To Go works completely independently of BitLocker, so you do not need to enable BitLocker on the PC, or utilize any TPM hardware, in order to use BitLocker To Go. In use, however, it is similar to BitLocker, and can also be enabled via a simple right-click menu choice.

This paper contains the details necessary to access Bitlocker protected FAT volumes. It describes the Bitlocker recovery information like the BitLocker keys, the encryption methods, the details of volume header, the metadata block and about the metadata header and metadata entries. Finally this paper presents the steps to unlock a BitLocker FAT32 volume.

2 Bitlocker Recovery Information

2.1 Bitlocker Keys

The BitLocker key management system uses a series of keys to protect the data at rest. This section describes the various keys that are used in the BitLocker encryption process as they have been documented by Microsoft.

2.1.1 Full Volume Encryption Key (FVEK)

The key used to protect the data i.e. the sector data is the Full Volume Encryption Key. It is stored on the protected volume and is stored encrypted. To prevent unauthorized access the FVEK is encrypted with the Volume Master Key (VMK). The size of the FVEK is dependent on the encryption method used i.e. FVEK is 128-bit of size for AES 128-bit and FVEK is 256-bit for AES 256-bit.

2.1.2 Volume Master Key (VMK)

The key used to encrypt the FVEK is the Volume Master Key (VMK). It is also stored on the protected volume. The VMK is 256-bit. In fact several copies of the VMK are stored on the protected volume. Each copy of the VMK is encrypted using a different key such as the recovery key, external key, or the TPM. If the volume is bitlocked using both external key as well as the recovery password, then there will be two metadata entries for VMK where each metadata entry stores the VMK encrypted with recovery key and the external key respectively. When decrypted, both the VMK will be the same. If the VMK differ then it means that the decryption has failed.

It is also possible that the VMK is stored unencrypted which is referred to as clear key.

2.1.3 TWEAK Key

The TWEAK is part of the FVEK stored encrypted with the Volume Master Key (VMK). The size of the TWEAK key depends on the encryption method used. The key is 128-bit for AES 128-bit and the key is 256-bit for AES 256-bit.

The TWEAK key is present only when the Elephant Diffuser is enabled. The TWEAK key is stored in the metadata entry that holds the FVEK which is always 512-bit. The first 256-bits are reserved for the FVEK and the other 256-bits are reserved for the TWEAK key. Only 128-bit of the 256-bits are used when the encryption method is AES 128-bit i.e. when the Elephant Diffuser is disabled.

2.1.4 Recovery Key

BitLocker stores a recovery (or numerical) password to unlock the VMK. This recovery password is stored in a {%GUID %}.txt file.

Example recovery password: 471207-278498-422125-177177-561902-537405-4680 06-693451.

The recovery password is valid only if it consists of 48 digits where every 6 numbers are grouped into a block thus consisting of 8 blocks. Here each block should be divisible by 11 yielding a remainder 0. The result of a division by 11 of a block is a 16-bit value. The individual 16-bit values make up a 128-bit key.

2.1.5 External Key

The External key is stored in a file named {%GUID %} .BEK. The GUID in the filename equals the key identifier in the BitLocker metadata entry. The BEK file contains the external key identifier and a 32 byte external key.

The different keys allow different mechanisms to be used to access the stored data. Each access mechanism can be used to decrypt a copy of the VMK which in turn is used to decrypt the FVEK which in turn is used to decrypt the protected data.

2.2   Encryption Methods

BitLocker uses two encryption methods to encrypt the data. First it uses the AES-CBC with or without Elephant Diffuser to encrypt the sector data i.e. the main data. Second it uses the AES-CCM to encrypt the keys like the VMK and FVEK.

2.3   Unencrypted Sector(s)

In BitLocker the sectors that are stored as unencrypted sectors are

- The unencrypted volume header
- The BitLocker metadata

Both BitLocker Windows 7 and To Go store an encrypted version of the first sectors in a specific location. This location is found in the FVE metadata block header. It is the location where the original boot sector starts.

At this point we shall describe the important offsets that are of interest to a forensic examiner in the volume header, metadata block header, metadata header and the content of the metadata entries. Specifically the paper explains how to decrypt a bit-locked drive.

We'll begin with the Bitlocker Volume Header, and then explain the details of the metadata block, the metadata header and the metadata entries. Finally the last section explains the steps to decrypt the sectors of the bitlocked volume and replace them so that the original volume is recovered.

2.4   Volume Header

The BitLocker Windows To Go volume header for a FAT volume is similar to FAT32 boot sector. Let us refer this duplicate boot sector as the volume header from now on. This volume header is 512 bytes of size. If a FAT volume (i.e. it is either FAT12 or FAT16 or FAT32 or exFAT) is bitlocked, the volume header is same as that of the FAT32 boot sector. The important information that the volume header consists of is the offsets of the three FVE metadata blocks [4].

From the volume header we get the offsets of the three FVE metadata blocks which contain the offset of the original boot sector which is stored encrypted in some location.

2.5   FVE Metadata Block

A Bitlocker protected volume contains three identical metadata blocks for redundancy. Even though the first metadata block gets damaged, the second and third metadata block can be used to get the original boot sector offset. As shown in the Fig. 1, the volume header contains the offsets of the three metadata blocks.

To find metadata blocks on a damaged volume, the examiner can search the volume for the metadata signature -FVE-FS-. Because each metadata block can only begin at offsets that are a multiple of the bytes per sector and sectors per cluster, the examiner could speed up the search by only searching for the string at these offsets. To be safe,

424	16		BitLocker identifier contains a GUID
440	8		FVE metadata block 1 offset Contains an offset relative to the start of the volume
448	8		FVE metadata block 2 offset Contains an offset relative to the start of the volume
456	8		FVE metadata block 3 offset Contains an offset relative to the start of the volume

Fig. 1. The data showing the metadata block offsets in the Volume header [4]

the examiner should assume the smallest legal values and thus search for the BitLocker signature at multiples of 512 bytes.

Each FVE metadata block consists of:

1. A FVE metadata block header
2. A FVE metadata header.
3. An array of FVE metadata entries

2.6   FVE Metadata Block Header

The FVE metadata block header consists of the signature "-FVE-FS". The metadata block is valid only if the signature is present. The size field indicates the size of the metadata block:

Offset	Size	Value	Description
16	8		Encrypted volume size Contains the number of bytes
24	4		
28	4		Number of volume header sectors Contains the number of sectors
32	8		FVE metadata block 1 offset Contains an offset relative to the start of the volume
40	8		FVE metadata block 2 offset Contains an offset relative to the start of the volume
48	8		FVE metadata block 3 offset Contains an offset relative to the start of the volume
56	8		Volume header offset Contains an offset relative to the start of the volume

Fig. 2. Structure of FVE metadata block header [4]

Each Bitlocker metadata block begins with a variation length header followed by a variable number of entries. The FVE metadata block header contains the offset of the original boot sector. When decrypting, BitLocker will decrypt from the back to the front. The encrypted volume size at offset 16 contains the number of bytes of the volume that are encrypted or need to be decrypted (Fig. 2).

2.7 FVE Metadata Header

The FVE metadata header is 48 bytes. There are several pieces of forensically valuable data in the metadata header. First, the volume's Global unique Identifier (GUID) is stored at offset 16. This GUID should be included on any access device that unlocks this device such as USB sticks. Examiners can search for this GUID on USB devices to find possible Bitlocker access devices. The date and time Bitlocker was enabled is recorded at the offset 40. Finally the next counter value to be used for key encryption nonce is stored at the offset 32. As mentioned earlier, this could be useful in deter-mining how many access devices have been created for a volume. Also, the encryption method at offset 36 describes the type of encryption that has been used to encrypt the volume.

2.8 FVE Metadata Entry

There is an array of FVE metadata entries and each metadata entry is variable size and consists of entry size, entry type and so on. If the volume is bitlocked using both recovery password and external key, then there will be metadata entries for both the recovery key and the external key. The Fig. 3 shows the FVE metadata entry structure as taken from [4].

Offset	Size	Value	Description
0	2		Entry size
2	2		Entry type
4	2		Value type
6	2	1	Version
8	...		Data

Fig. 3. FVE metadata entry values

2.9 FVE Metadata Entry Types

Each value in the entry type filed indicates which type of key the metadata entry stores.

2.10 FVE Metadata Value Types

The metadata value types indicate whether the key is erased, or whether it is a stretch key, or volume master key.

The Bitlocker metadata header is followed by a series of metadata entries. These entries contain the encrypted FVEK and several copies of the VMK. Each copy of the VMK is encrypted with a different key. If for example a volume is bitlocked using only the recovery key then the VMK will be encrypted using the recovery key whereas if the volume is bitlocked using both recovery key and external key then the VMK will be encrypted with the two keys and stored separately.

Each metadata entry consists of data concerning where the key in question is stored and has at least two encrypted key protectors. The first key protector structure contains a copy of the VMK encrypted with the key and the second key protector structure contains a copy of the key encrypted using the VMK. The timestamps are identical in both the key protectors. The same is applicable for VMK and FVEK. The first key protector contains a copy of the FVEK encrypted using the VMK and the second key protector contains a copy of the VMK encrypted using FVEK. Now as all the details are explained, the next section deals with the steps of decrypting and loading a FAT Bitlocker volume.

3 Loading a Bitlocked Volume

In this section we describe the steps needed to decrypt and load a FAT bitlocked volume. Here an evidence file that has two partitions has been taken where one is FAT32 volume that is bitlocked. The.txt file having the recovery password and a.bek file having the external key which is generated are stored on some external drive. Both these files are used for the recovery process and using these keys, the VMK and FVEK are derived. The process is same for all the other FAT file systems.

3.1   Derivation of Keys

Here the first sector of the bitlocked volume does not contain the original boot sector. Instead it contains the bitlocked volume header which is similar to the FAT32 boot sector. Though it is similar some values are changed and provide other valuable information as shown in the Table 1. The important information that the volume header contains is the offsets of the three metadata blocks. So by getting the offset of the first metadata block, the metadata block header is read and the signature –FVE-FS is checked so that a valid metadata block is read.

The metadata block consists of two important information. One is the original boot sector starting sector information and the second is the encrypted volume size. There are important while recovering the bitlocked volume.

Next the metadata header and metadata entries are read and the key protector structures are stored. The key protector structures contain the encrypted keys which have to be decrypted, the protection type, GUID and the last modification time.

3.1.1   Decryption of the VMK Using Recovery Password
The recovery password is the 48-digit key that is taken from the.txt file. The Fig. 4 shows the text file containing the 48-digit recovery key and the GUID highlighted.

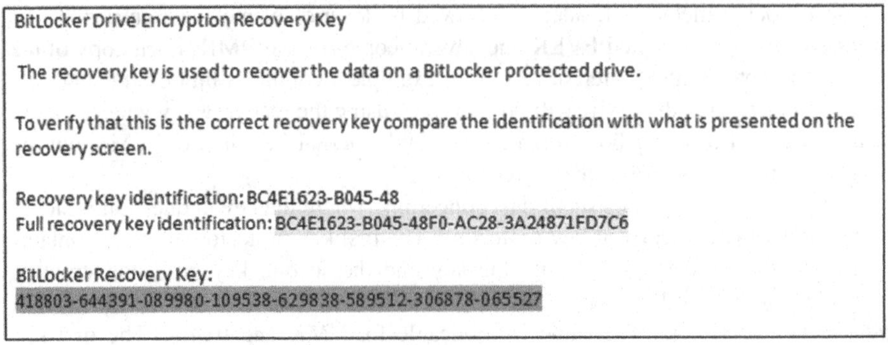

BitLocker Drive Encryption Recovery Key

The recovery key is used to recover the data on a BitLocker protected drive.

To verify that this is the correct recovery key compare the identification with what is presented on the recovery screen.

Recovery key identification: BC4E1623-B045-48
Full recovery key identification: BC4E1623-B045-48F0-AC28-3A24871FD7C6

BitLocker Recovery Key:
418803-644391-089980-109538-629838-589512-306878-065527

Fig. 4. The .txt file showing the GUID and the 48 digit recovery key

As described in Sect. 2, the individual 16-bit values make up a 128-bit key. The corresponding recovery key is calculated using the following approach:

```
Initialize a structure consisting of:
uint8_t last_sha256 [32 ];
uint8_t initial_sha256 [32 ];
uint8_t salt[ 16 ];
uint64_t count;
```

Initialize both the last SHA256 and the count to 0. Calculate the SHA256 of the 128-bit key and update the initial SHA256 value. The salt is stored on disk in the stretch key which is stored in the recovery key protected Volume Master Key (VMK). Loop for 1048576 (0 × 100000) times:

- calculate the SHA256 of the structure and update the last SHA256 value
- increment the count by 1

The last SHA256 value contains the 256-bit key which is recovery key that can unlock the recovery key protected Volume Master Key (VMK).

3.1.2 Decryption of the VMK Using Startup Key
The generated .bek file is used along with the metadata entry. Both the bek file and the metadata entry contain the same Globally Unique Identifier (GUID). This allows for the correct matching of the BEK with the metadata entry and also for checking the validity of the BEK file.

The external key from the .bek file is extracted and the data from the key protector structure is decrypted using this external key which unlocks the VMK. The Fig. 5 shows the external key highlighted in the BEK file.

3.1.3 Decryption of FVEK
The encrypted FVEK is stored in the key protector structure of the metadata entry which is highlighted as shown in the Fig. 6.

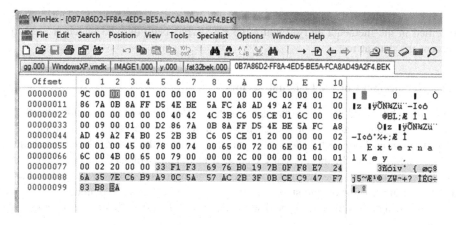

Fig. 5. The BEK file of the Bitlocker volume

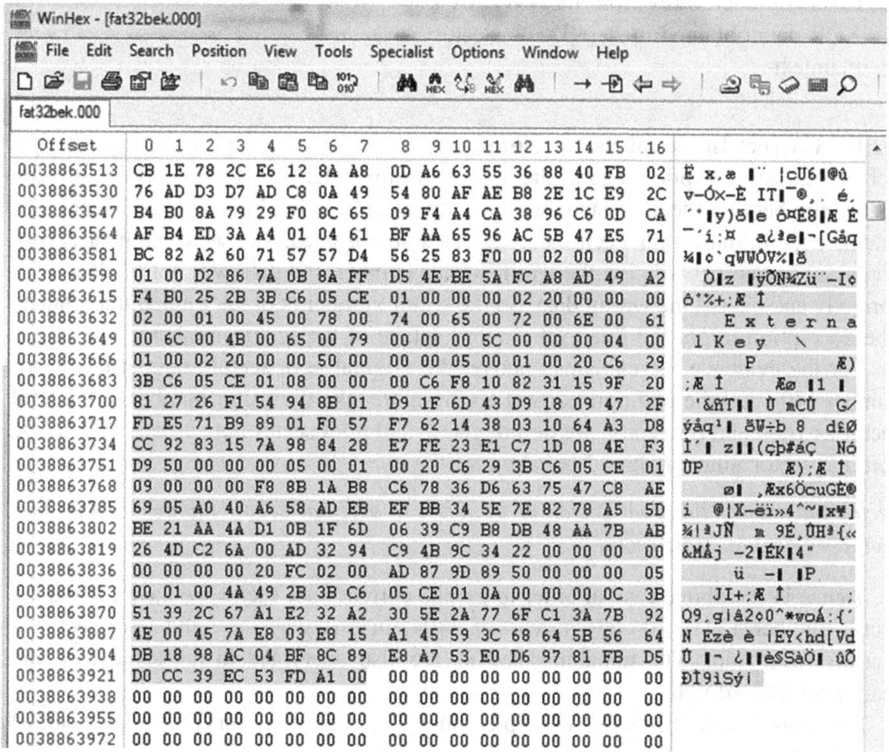

Fig. 6. The metadata entry showing the external key

The encrypted data is decrypted using the VMK and the type of algorithm as specified in the metadata entry. Finally the FVEK has been derived which is used to decrypt the data at rest.

3.2 Replacement of the Original Sectors

Though the bitlocked volume contains a volume header it is not the correct boot sector. The original boot sector is stored encrypted somewhere in the volume. So we have to find the original boot sector, decrypt it and then replace the volume header with the original boot sector. In the previous section it has been explained that the metadata block header contains the original boot sector starting offset. So by getting the offset and by having the sector, the steps for decrypting the sector are explained.

Here the data has to be decrypted sector by sector. The steps in decrypting a sector of data are:

1: Decrypt the data with FVEK in AES-CBC mode
2: Run Diffuser B in decryption direction 3 times
3: Run Diffuser A in decryption direction 5 times
4: Calculate Sector key from the TWEAK key
5: XOR data obtained in step 3 with Sector Key
6: Plaintext

3.2.1 Correct Intake of Sector Number

For successful decryption, one of the important things that should be considered is the sector number. In the first step, we have to calculate the Initialization Vector. To calculate the Initialization Vector, the sector number is used. The sector number is very important because if we give the wrong sector number, the data will not be decrypted correctly and we get the wrong data. So the sector number is of very much importance. The decryption might fail due to the wrong intake of the sector number.

For the evidence file explained above, the original boot sector starts at the sector number 1404 and the partition starts at 63. So if we take the sector number of the boot sector as 1404 and decrypt it, we do not get a valid boot sector but some junk data. So here the sector number should be taken as:

Sector number of the boot sector to be taken = original sector number of the boot sector − partition start sector.

Hence in the above case in order to get the correct boot sector we have to take the sector number 1341(1404-63) instead of 1404. In this way the valid boot sector is placed at the front. The remaining sectors are also decrypted in the same way and rearranged accordingly.

The Figs. 7 and 8 show the encrypted boot sector and the decrypted boot sector of the bitlocked volume.

3.2.2 Decryption of Sectors After Encrypted Volume Size is Reached

The next important issue to be considered is the decryption of the sectors after the encrypted volume size is reached. Starting from the encrypted boot sector offset, all the

```
0748498848  50 E5 98 B1 75 9E 28 E4   82 36 1A 4D 51 36 4C 87   3C  Paìtu|(aìb MQbLì<
0748498865  5A 9B 67 D6 32 19 29 62   2A 90 83 C6 C1 1A B9 7D   1B  Z|gÖ2 )b* |ÆÁ ¹}
0748498882  C6 6D CC AD D7 A9 50 B9   26 75 0A 2B 13 EF EC F9   8E  ÆmÌ-×®P¹&u + ìiù|
0748498899  7B 2B A0 B4 C5 F3 CB 6C   63 4F 3F F9 F5 C5 8C E0   76  {+ ´ÁóËlcO?ùõÁ|àv
0748498916  FC D5 F4 23 7B A2 A1 E5   01 03 C4 A0 96 4D F0 59   CF  üÕõ#{o¡å Ä ¡M8ŸÏ
0748498933  3C 6B 1E AD 4B FA B4 9C   5A C6 85 05 5F EC 52 EB   7F  <k -Kú´|ZÆ| _ìRë
0748498950  D4 07 4A 9B 5E 0A 9D CC   68 A7 87 DE D9 F7 50 FD   E4  Ô J|^ Ih$|þÙ÷Pýä
0748498967  6C A8 4C 64 A9 B7 32 E0   E0 87 30 5A 0F E5 DE 68   E7  l¨Ld©·2à à‡0Z åÞhç
0748498984  10 82 41 CF C0 28 BC 3E   58 BB E3 AC 49 FB E7 92   C5  |AÏÀ(¼>X»ã¬Iûç' Å
0748499001  00 4C 0D 55 91 A4 F4 C7   A6 8E CB 2A B5 E6 07 B2   05  L U'¤õÇ|¦Ë*µæ ²
0748499018  2E 13 94 44 67 43 BE 5C   80 64 9B CF 2E 8B B7 15   2E  .|DgC¾\|d|Ï.|·|.
0748499035  EB A9 E9 0C D7 C6 E6 9B   FE 32 45 B8 CA F7 F8 91   F9  ë©é xÆæ|þ2E¸Ê÷ø'ù
0748499052  B9 2B 93 B5 31 5A EE 11   CC 52 C6 C5 A6 7F 91 DD   DF  ¹+|µ1Zî ÌRÆÅ| 'Ýß
0748499069  0A 6B 7D 1B 99 C9 9D 83   05 2E 5B 9E 09 F3 2D 85   94  k} |É | .[| ó-||
0748499086  13 8C 79 5C D5 40 44 D7   E7 BA 4B 06 7C B7 EA EE   00  |y\Õ@D×çºK |·êî
0748499103  D7 9D AD BD 52 D0 BD 18   9F DC 7B 22 03 3F 1B 81   8B  × -½RÐ½ |Ü{" ? |
0748499120  D7 20 0F FC B7 37 23 64   37 F3 53 8B 73 8A 5A 65   FF  × ü·7#d7óS|s|Zeÿ
0748499137  C7 59 FF 3B 9F D1 75 E8   80 F9 75 1C 11 3B 82 DB   80  ÇYÿ;|Ñuè|ùu ;|Û|
0748499154  5A 73 98 A3 18 F0 DF 74   57 93 E9 64 A7 7C 56 3F   C0  Zs|£ ðßt|éd$|V?À
0748499171  D6 D5 87 24 84 1B B5 CA   8E B3 2E FF 53 17 05 E2   C5  ÖÕ|$| µÊ|³.ÿS âÅ
0748499188  2A 27 88 BA 20 77 8E 7E   09 1D A1 36 E7 29 1F 48   74  *'|º w|~ |¡6ç) Ht
0748499205  6C 31 55 4A 45 C0 EE 0D   C4 3A 2E 4E CD 3A 58 68   AA  l1UJEÀî Ä:.NÍ:Xhª
0748499222  52 11 5C 67 2A F6 EA D4   6C 25 19 D6 6E 65 4F 4A   95  R \g*öêÔl% ÖneOJ|
0748499239  8E 24 9E 96 1C 77 A9 1E   EC BD B5 72 BE 88 87 93   6A  |$|| w© ì½µr¾|‡|j
0748499256  A9 C9 74 55 90 2E 2A DA   6C 51 40 ED 97 65 21 A0   CF  ©ÉtU .*ÚlQ@íel Ï
0748499273  BF 22 EA 3D 15 CD 3B AC   29 88 CD 72 C2 9C 87 FA   7B  ¿"ê=.Í;¬)|ÍrÂ||ú{
0748499290  35 58 99 2A 87 7E 08 60   62 5D 00 94 B5 25 85 95   46  5X|*|~ `b] |µ%|F
0748499307  9B C1 16 75 4A 1D 94 FB   48 A4 96 82 E0 0E F8 F5   F6  |Á uJ |ûH¤||à øõö
0748499324  37 A1 20 F3 D0 24 70 08   61 3C 99 63 95 44 4E 19   FE  7¡ óÐ$p a<|c|DN þ
0748499341  5D 73 C0 8D 43 2A BA 45   AB D7 44 F6 74 BD 5C 1C   22  ]sÀ C*ªE«×Döt½\ "
0748499358  18 C5 C0 11 3E 9D 4E 1D   BA 8E 7F 8E 4A 88 E0 B0   DA  ÅÀ >|N º|J|à°Ú
0748499375  DF 26 94 CD D6 34 15 51   6F C7 14 E6 81 5A 3D A3   4F  ß&|ÍÖ4 QoÇ æ Z=£O
0748499392  CD 6F 97 E5 F7 95 24 A8   0E FB C5 D8 0F 49 8C FD   86  Ío|å÷|$¨ ûÅØ I|ý|
0748499409  F7 58 F1 A4 22 1C 1E F4   EA 22 0E B5 AC F9 D1 2E   E5  ÷Xñ¤" ô" ôê" µ¬ùÑ.å
0748499426  E3 07 88 2B 37 FF 46 65   4C 7F 3C D4 F7 2A 70 C4   24  ã |+7ÿFeL <Ô÷*pÁ$
0748499443  F6 DA B2 CE DF 1E 1A 8E   D1 AF C2 B7 DB FC BD 6C   1F  öÚ²Î ß |Ñ¯Â·Ûü½l
```

Fig. 7. Boot sector before decryption

sectors are decrypted and written in the same order starting from the boot sector until the encrypted size limit is reached. If the total number of sector is less than the encrypted volume size then there will be no problem. But if the total number of sectors is greater than the encrypted volume size, then the next corresponding sector should be the corresponding sector from the start of the volume header and so on.

For example, for the above evidence, if the volume header starts at sector 63, the original sector starts at sector 1404, the total number of sectors as 2506 and the encrypted volume size is 1009 sectors. Then while decrypting the sector 1404 (the original boot sector becomes the 63 sector), sector 1405 becomes sector 64 and so on up to sector 2413 since the encrypted volume size has reached. Then to get the sector 2414, we start at sector 63 and add up to the number of sectors covered (i.e. 1009). So the sector 1072 becomes the 2414 sector (63 (volume header sector) + 1009 (encrypted volume size)). In this manner, the sectors are decrypted and arranged to get the un-bitlocked drive.

Offset	0	1	2	3	4	5	6	7	8	9	10	11	12	13	14	15	16	
00000000	EB	58	90	4D	53	44	4F	53	35	2E	30	00	02	08	1A	10	02	ëX MSDOS5.0
00000017	00	00	00	00	F8	00	00	3F	00	FF	00	80	00	00	00	00	E8	ø ? ÿ ı è
00000034	1F	00	F3	07	00	00	00	00	00	00	02	00	00	00	01	00	06	ó
00000051	00	00	00	00	00	00	00	00	00	00	00	00	00	80	00	29	5A	ı)Z
00000068	7F	58	2C	4E	4F	20	4E	41	4D	45	20	20	20	20	46	41	54	X,NO NAME FAT
00000085	33	32	20	20	20	33	C9	8E	D1	BC	F4	7B	8E	C1	8E	D9	BD	32 3ÉÑ¼ô{ Á Ù½
00000102	00	7C	88	4E	02	8A	56	40	B4	41	BB	AA	55	CD	13	72	10	|N IV@´A»ªUÍ r
00000119	81	FB	55	AA	75	0A	F6	C1	01	74	05	FE	46	02	EB	2D	8A	ûUªu öÁ t þF ë-
00000136	56	40	B4	08	CD	13	73	05	B9	FF	FF	8A	F1	66	0F	B6	C6	V@´ Í s ¹ÿÿ ñf ¶Æ
00000153	40	66	0F	B6	D1	80	E2	3F	F7	E2	86	CD	C0	ED	06	41	66	@f ¶Ñ â?÷â Í Àí Af
00000170	0F	B7	C9	66	F7	E1	66	89	46	F8	83	7E	16	00	75	38	83	·Éf÷áf Fø ~ u8
00000187	7E	2A	00	77	32	66	8B	46	1C	66	83	C0	0C	BB	00	80	B9	~* w2f F f À » ¹
00000204	01	00	E8	2B	00	E9	2C	03	A0	FA	7D	B4	7D	8B	F0	AC	84	è+ é. ú}´} ð¬
00000221	C0	74	17	3C	FF	74	09	B4	0E	BB	07	00	CD	10	EB	EE	A0	Àt <ÿt ´ » Í ëî
00000238	FB	7D	EB	E5	A0	F9	7D	EB	E0	98	CD	16	CD	19	66	60	80	û}ëå ù}ëà Í Í f`
00000255	7E	02	00	0F	84	20	00	66	6A	00	66	50	06	53	66	68	10	~ f fj fP Sfh
00000272	00	01	00	B4	42	8A	56	40	8B	F4	CD	13	66	58	66	58	66	´B V@ ô Í fXfXf
00000289	58	66	58	EB	33	66	3B	46	F8	72	03	F9	EB	2A	66	33	D2	XfXë3f;Fø r ù앀f3Ò
00000306	66	0F	B7	4E	18	66	F7	F1	FE	C2	8A	CA	66	8B	D0	66	C1	f ·N f÷ñþÂ Êf ÐfÁ
00000323	EA	10	F7	76	1A	86	D6	8A	56	40	8A	E8	C0	E4	06	0A	CC	ê ÷v Ö V@ èÀä Ì
00000340	B8	01	02	CD	13	66	61	0F	82	75	FF	81	C3	00	02	66	40	, Í fa uÿ Ã f@
00000357	49	75	94	C3	42	4F	4F	54	4D	47	52	20	20	20	20	00	00	Iu ÃBOOTMGR
00000374	00	00	00	00	00	00	00	00	00	00	00	00	00	00	00	00	00	
00000391	00	00	00	00	00	00	00	00	00	00	00	00	00	00	00	00	00	
00000408	00	00	00	00	00	00	00	00	00	00	00	00	00	00	00	00		
00000425	00	00	00	0D	0A	52	65	6D	6F	76	65	20	64	69	73	6B	73	Remove disks
00000442	20	6F	72	20	6F	74	68	65	72	20	6D	65	64	69	61	2E	FF	or other media.ÿ
00000459	0D	0A	44	69	73	6B	20	65	72	72	6F	72	FF	0D	0A	50	72	Disk errorÿ Pr
00000476	65	73	73	20	61	6E	79	20	6B	65	79	20	74	6F	20	72	65	ess any key to re
00000493	73	74	61	72	74	0D	0A	00	00	00	00	00	AC	CB	D8	00	00	start ¬ËØ
00000510	55	AA	94	D8	D5	BD	8A	02	B8	51	C0	68	14	6B	C9	3A	22	Uª ØÕ½ ,QÀh kÉ:"

Fig. 8. Boot sector after decryption

4 Conclusion

BitLocker To Go is a full-disk encryption protection technology for removable storage devices. Though it is based on BitLocker technology, BitLocker To Go significantly enhances the technical capabilities of BitLocker. A forensic examiner can use the recovery key or start key to access the FVEK and thus the protected data. These can be used to decrypt the series of keys protecting the FVEK like VMK. Some pieces of the metadata surrounding these keys could be useful to a forensic examiner, including the order in which keys were generated, the number of keys generated, and the types of those keys. Additionally, some features of the key management system allow access to all of the access devices protecting a volume provided the user has a valid access device.

References

1. Kumar, N., Kumar, V.: Bitlocker and Windows Vista, May 2008. http://www.nvlabs.in/node/9
2. Microsoft Corporation. Bitlocker drive encryption technical overview. Technical report, Microsoft Corporation, May 2008. http://technet2microsoft.com/WindowsVista/en/library/ce4d5a2e-59a5-4742-89cc-ef9f5908b4731033.mspx?mfr=true

3. Kornblum, J.D.: Implementing Bitlocker Drive Encryption For Forensic Analysis, ManTech International Corporation. jessekornblum.com/publications/di09.pdf
4. Metz, J.: Bitlocker Drive Encryption (BDE) format specification: Analysis of the BitLocker Drive Encryption (BDE) volume
5. Kornblum, J.D.: Bitlocker To Go, ManTech International Corporation. http://jessekornblum.com/presentations/dodcc10-1.pdf

Forensic Artifacts of the flareGet Download Manager

Prachi Goel[1] and Babu M. Mehtre[2(✉)]

[1] School of Computer and Information Sciences, University of Hyderabad,
Hyderabad, India
prachi_8dec@rediffmail.com
[2] Institute for Development and Research in Banking Technology (IDRBT)
Established by Reserve Bank of India, Hyderabad, India
bmmehtre@idrbt.ac.in

Abstract. There is an increasing interest in finding artifacts (digital evidence)
created by various software tools. flareGet is an advanced multi-threaded and
multi-segment download manager for Linux. This is the only download manager
for Linux that integrates with almost all the browsers. In this paper, we examine
(from a digital forensics angle) the artifacts created by flareGet for Linux,
specifically on Ubuntu 12.04 distribution. The flareGet artifacts include download path, URL address, settings of flareGet, date and time of the activity performed, the encryption technique used by flareGet, etc. This is useful for the
digital forensic investigator to search and interpret the artifacts created or left in
the process of using flareGet.

Keywords: Artifacts · Digital forensics · Investigation · flareGet

1 Introduction

There is an increasing interest in finding artifacts (digital evidence) created by various
software tools. There are a number of software tools which have been examined for
artifacts on Windows and Linux platform. Relatively, the number of such tools
examined for artifacts on Windows platform is more than those on Linux platform.
flareGet is a native Linux application written in C++, using the Qt framework. For
installing flareGet, the system should meet the following minimum dependencies:

1. Qt libraries with version >=4.8.1
2. glibc (C library) with version >=2.13.

flareGet is a full featured, advanced, multi-threaded, multi-segment download
manager and accelerator on Linux [1]. It supports all 32 and 64 bit 'Debian' and 'Red
Hat Package Manager'-based Linux distributions. flareGet is proprietary software
however; it is also available freely with limited features. The following features are not
present in the freely available flareGet version 1.4-7:

1. Up to 16 parallel connections per download.
2. Browser Integration with all the browsers.

© Institute for Computer Sciences, Social Informatics and Telecommunications Engineering 2014
P. Gladyshev et al. (Eds.): ICDF2C 2013, LNICST 132, pp. 30–38, 2014.
DOI: 10.1007/978-3-319-14289-0_3

3. Support for download speed limits.
4. Support for auto-refreshing of URL and cookies.

Freely available, flareGet can support up-to 8 parallel connections per download and provides the integration with Mozilla Firefox via FlashGot (a third party add-on). flareGet supports HTTP, HTTPS and FTP for downloading the files from Internet. It also supports Meta links. It uses a robust dynamic file segmentation algorithm which splits the download into segments to accelerate the process of downloading. In addition to dynamic file segmentation, it uses HTTP-pipelining in which multiple requests are sent on a single TCP connection without waiting for the corresponding responses. This further accelerates each segment up to six times. It uses intelligent file management to automatically categorize the downloaded files based on their extensions. The downloaded files are grouped into different folders as per their categories.

This paper focuses on the artifacts created in the process of using flareGet (freely available version 1.4-7) on Linux (Ubuntu 12.04 distribution). Even though the examination is done by using the free version of flareGet, the same type of artifacts are applicable to professional flareGet (because the features which are not available in the free version would not affect the artifacts created by flareGet). It is found that flareGet creates the artifacts in the location: '/home/< user >/.config' with different folder names. The important folders created by flareGet from the forensics point of view are discussed in the following sections. All the traces created by flareGet are traced by using Strace (a debugging utility for Linux).

The GUI of the flareGet download manager is shown in Fig. 1. The Left Panel of flareGet contains two main tabs: 'All Downloads' and 'Finished'. Under the 'All Downloads' tab there are various status tabs which include *Completed, Running, Paused, Failed* and *Cancelled*. Under the 'Finished' tab there are various categories tab which include *Compressed, Application, Documents, Videos, Audio, Images* and *Others*. The Right Panel displays the information of the corresponding tab on the left panel when clicked by the user. For example, in Fig. 1, the right panel shows the information of all the files including their states like *completed, running, paused, failed* and *cancelled*, shown when the 'All Downloads' tab on left panel gets clicked.

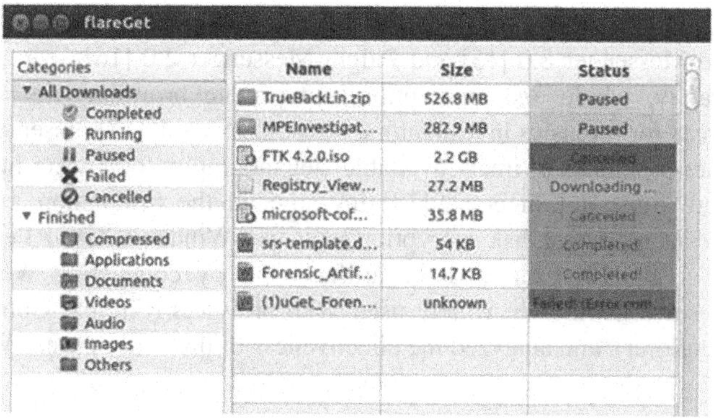

Fig. 1. The GUI of flareGet.

This paper is organized into 5 sections. The first section gives a brief introduction of the flareGet. The second section discusses the related work done by others. The third section details the artifacts of flareGet in five sub-sections. Sections 3.1, 3.2 and 3.3 describe from where the forensic investigator can find the downloaded/downloading files, proxy settings and paused file information. Section 3.4 describes from where the forensic investigator can find the information about websites requiring authentication during the download process, and it also describes the encryption technique used by flareGet to store the user's passwords for these websites. Section 3.5 shows the installation and un-installation artifacts of the flareGet. The summary of flareGet artifacts is given in Sect. 4. Finally the paper concludes in Sect. 5.

2 Related Work

Numerous researchers have worked to find the artifacts left behind by different software applications from the digital forensics perspective. In the literature there are many papers for detecting software application artifacts on the Windows platform but less research has been done to find software application artifacts on the various Linux platforms. The Windows Registry provides essential information from forensics point of view [2]. Vivienne Mee et al. [3] examined the use of the Windows Registry as a source of forensic evidence in digital investigations, especially related to Internet usage.

Bit Torrent is a peer-to-peer file sharing protocol used for distributing large amounts of data. It has been seen that usage of Bit Torrent client application leaves the traces in the registry [4]. Increase of the Gnutella network (peer-peer network) usage lead researchers to find the artifacts left behind after the use of Limewire [5] and FrostWire [6] software tools.

Geoffrey Fellows [7] presented WinRAR temporary folder artifacts which provide the essential evidence to the investigator to prove which files were viewed or extracted using WinRAR program. Muhammad Yasin et al. [8, 9, 10] analyzed the 'Download Accelerator Plus', 'Free Download Manager' and 'Internet Download Manager' for collection of digital forensic artifacts.

Many Instant messenger software applications have been examined which provide exchange of text messages in real-time. These include Yahoo Messenger 7.0 [11], Trillian basic 3.x [12], MSN Messenger 7.5 [13], AOL Instant Messenger 5.5 [14], Windows Live Messenger 8.0 [15] and Pidgin Messenger 2.0 [16].

Steganography, whole disk encryption and private browsing are some of the challenging areas for forensics investigators. Rachel Zax et al. [17] presented the traces left behind after a number of freely available steganography tools were installed, run, and uninstalled. Sungsu Lim et al. [18] investigated the installation, runtime, and deletion behaviors of virtual disk encryption tools in a Windows XP SP3 environment. Huwida Said et al. [19] examined the artifacts left by conducting Web browsing privacy mode sessions in three widely used Web browsers (Firefox, Google Chrome and Internet Explorer), and analyzed the effectiveness of this tool in each Web browser.

3 flareGet Artifacts

3.1 Downloaded Files Information

The important question during investigation of a download manger is what are the files that were downloaded or are still being downloaded by the user. There are two ways to find this information. The first way is to look at flareGet.conf file which is located in the directory '/home/<user>/.config/flareGet_ALLDOWN'. This file contains the entire downloaded and downloading file information. Figure 2 is showing the portion of flareGet.conf file. The *CurrLength* in this file indicates the total number of files which is the count of *downloaded, downloading, cancelled, failed, paused* and *queued*, provided the user has selected to remember the *finished, cancelled* and *failed* downloads in settings page of flareGet. If the user has not selected to remember the *finished, cancelled* and *failed* downloads then the *CurrLength* indicates the total number of files which are paused or queued. Even if the user has *unchecked* to remember the *finished, cancelled* and *failed* downloads then the investigator can also find this information in the file 'flareGet.conf', provided it is not over-written by another file information because flareGet overwrites the whole flareGet.conf file at the time of exit. The same is applicable to the files which get deleted by the user from flareGet, i.e., the file information remains until overwritten by the flareGet. Each down-loaded file information record starts with an integer. For example, in Fig. 2 the file having the name 'TrueBackLin.zip' indicated by 'fname' started with integer '0'. All the attributes of this file start with integer '0'. Similarly the next file attribute starts with integer '1' and so on. The important attributes from the forensic point of view are explained below:

furl: shows where the downloaded file is stored.

fsize: shows the size of the downloaded file in string format.

durl: shows the web address from where the file gets downloaded.

flocation: shows where the downloaded file gets stored.

fdownloaded: shows how much file gets downloaded.

filesize: shows the size of the downloaded file in bytes.

referrer: holds the website from which the download started (required for auto refreshing of URL).

hash: holds the hash value given by the user

hashType: whether the hash is MD5 or SHA1.

cstatus: an integer which takes different values for different states of the file which is shown in Table 1.

dateStarted: stores the date and time when the downloading process started in plain text.

dateFinished: stores the date and time when the downloading process gets finished in plain text. If the downloading process was not finished then it would not show any value.

The second way is to look at folder 'flareGet_FINDOWN' which is located at '/home/<user>/.config/'. This folder contains the file 'flareGet.conf' which stores all the file information whose downloading gets completed. This file contains the same attri-butes as explained for the file located at folder 'home/<user>/.config/flareGet_ALL-DOWN'. Even if the user has unchecked to remember the finished downloads then also

Table 1. Different *cstatus* values for different *states* of file.

cstatus	States of the file
0	Downloading of file gets finished
2	File is downloading
3	Downloading file is in paused state
4	Downloading of file gets failed
5	Downloading file gets cancelled by the user
6	file is queued by the flareGet
8	file is queued by the user
9	Downloading of file gets failed and paused by the user
11	File downloaded using Metalink

```
flareGet.conf  ×
[General]
currLength=6
0fname=TrueBackLin.zip
0furl=/home/pgoel/Downloads/flareGet/Compressed/TrueBackLin.zip
0fsize=526.8 MB
0durl=http://www.cyberforensics.in/Uploads/Downloads/TrueBackLin.zip
0flocation=/home/pgoel/Downloads/flareGet/Compressed
0tsegs=1
0tsegsInit=4
0segsUsed=0
0filesize=552440325
0percent=1%
0referrer=unknown
0downId=08-05-2013 14:24:38TrueBackLin.zip
0oldfname=TrueBackLin.zip
0cstatus=9
0fdownloaded=5.3 MB
0postData=
0cookie=
0dateStarted=08-05-2013 14:41:45
0dateFinished=---
0userAgent=MozillaMozilla
0hash=
0hashType=0
0isScheduled=false
```

Fig. 2. The portion of 'flareGet.conf file' located at '/home/<user>/.config/flareGet_ ALLDOWN'.

the investigator can find this information in file 'flareGet.conf', provided it is not overwritten because flareGet overwrites the whole 'flareGet.conf' file at the time of exit.

3.2   Proxy Settings Information

The investigator can find the proxy setting by looking at the folder 'flareGet Settings' which is located at '/home/<user>/.config/'. If the manual proxy is set by the user then 'proxy_addr' and 'port_num' contain the address and port number respectively. The 'username' and 'pwd' holds the user name and password if required for the proxy setting respectively. The password is stored in plain text which accelerates the process of investigation. For manual proxy setting it provides 3 options:

1. HTTP/HTTPS
2. SOCKS v5
3. FTP.

The 'proxyType' can takes three values, i.e., 0, 1 and 2 for HTTP/HTTPS, SOCKS v5 and FTP respectively. Since this file contains the universal settings of flareGet, it can also give the following information:

1. Where are the files stored by default?
2. Which browsers are integrated with flareGet?
3. Scheduled activities which are configured by the user etc.

3.3 Information of Paused Files

The paused file information is present in two folders. The investigator can look at the folder 'flareGet_ALLDOWN' (explained in Sect. 3.1) or 'flareGet'. The 'flareGet' folder is located at '/home/<user>/.config/'. The file 'datasegment.conf' in this folder is essentially used to provide resume capabilities for file downloads if the download is paused by the user or the Internet connection is not available. flareGet also provides resume capabilities for downloading files after closing flareGet or shutting down the PC. The 'datasegment.conf' file keeps the name of the paused file with a record of how many bytes have been downloaded by each thread of the download. Records of threads of each download are also located at this location. If the paused file is subsequently downloaded or deleted by the user then the 'datasegment.conf' file would not contain any information about that file, and the thread records created by flareGet get deleted.

3.4 Information About Websites that Require Authentication During Download

There is a facility given by flareget to store the username and password for websites which require authentication during the download in the 'site manager' setting page. The website name with the corresponding username and password provided by the user in the 'site manager' setting page is stored in file 'flareGet.conf', which is located at '/home/<user>/.config/flareSBase'. All the passwords are stored in encrypted form. Figure 3 shows the content of this file. The fields 'sites', 'small' and 'good' store the website name, username and password respectively. The site names, usernames and passwords are separated by commas. For example, for the website 'www.premium.com', the user name is 'prachi' and password is 'mmmnnnooo', which is in encrypted form.

To find the encryption technique used by flareGet, the following experiment is performed by taking 3 types of password samples which are described below:

1. Sequence of repeated letters.
2. Combination of letters with numbers.
3. Alphanumeric characters.

```
[flareGet.conf  ✕

[General]
sites=www.premium.com, www.download.com

small=prachi, spandana
good=mmmnnnooo, ioduh456Jhw
```

Fig. 3. The content of 'flareGet.conf' file located at '/home/<user>/.config/flareSBase'.

Table 2 shows the three different samples of passwords with the corresponding encrypted password stored by flareGet. It is clear from Table 2 that flareGet uses a simple additive cipher technique whose key is equal to 3. flareGet first converts the characters entered by the user as a password into ASCII code and then adds 3 to the corresponding ASCII code.

Table 2. Analysis of encrypted password.

Password in plain text	ASCII code	Password in encrypted form	ASCII code
jjjkkklll	106 106 106 107 107 107 108 108 108	mmmnnnooo	109 109 109 110 110 110 111 111 111
flare123Get	102 108 97 114 101 49 50 51 71 101 116	ioduh456Jhw	105 111 100 117 104 52 53 54 74 104 119
flare@! $Get*	102 108 97 114 101 64 33 36 71 101 116 42	ioduhC$'Jhw-	105 111 100 117 104 67 36 39 74 104 119 45

Since ASCII is defined for 128 (ASCII code from 0-127) characters, in boundary cases, the addition of '3' to the ASCII code exceeds the 126th ASCII code (127 is reserved for DEL). So to handle these boundary cases, flareGet uses the additive modulo 94 (127 - 33). The first 32 ASCII characters are reserved for control characters and the 33rd ASCII character is for space. flareGet uses the additive modulo 94 if the resultant ASCII code of a character + 3 is greater than 126. Table 3 shows the cases where modulo 94 comes into the picture. It is clear from the Table 3 that flareGet uses the escape character '\' for '"'.

3.5 Installation and Un-installation Artifacts

Ubuntu stores the installation and un-installation information in dpkg.log which is located in '/var/log/'. Un-installing flareGet does not remove any directory created by flareGet at location '/home/<user>/.config/'. This provides important evidence for the investigator even if the flareGet application is un-installed.

Table 3. Analysis of boundary cases.

Password in plain text	ASCII code	Password in encrypted form	ASCII code
pass|}rd	112 97 115 115 124 125 114 100	sdvv!\"ug	115 100 118 118 33 92 34 117 103
pass~ord	112 97 115 115 126 111 114 100	sdvv#rug	115 100 118 118 35 114 117 103
pass~ }rd	112 97 115 115 126 125 114 100	sdvv#\"ug	115 100 118 118 35 92 34 117 103

4 flareGet Artifacts Summary

flareGet creates the artifacts at the location '/home/<user>/.config/' which is summarized as follows:

1. All the downloaded/downloading file information is stored in the folder 'flareGet_ALLDOWN'.
2. All the finished/cancelled file information is stored in the folder 'flareGet_FINDOWN'.
3. The universal setting information of flareGet is stored in the folder 'flareGet Settings'.
4. Data for resumption of paused files is stored in the folder 'flareGet'.
5. Data for websites that require passwords for authentication is stored in the folder 'flareSBase'.

Installation and un-installation artifacts of the flareGet application on Ubuntu are found in the folder '/var/log/' and the file name is dpkg.log.

5 Conclusion

All the folders created by flareGet are located in one single directory, i.e., '/home/<user>/.config/'. This helps the investigator to collect the evidence easily from a single location. The artifacts, like username and password for proxy settings, date and time, etc., are found in the plain text (not encrypted) which accelerates the process of investigation. Hence, this eases the task of the forensic investigator. flareGet uses encryption only for storing the password of websites which require authentication for downloading. The encryption technique is explained in Sect. 3.4 and is quite simple. Even after the un-installation of the flareGet application on Ubuntu, the directory '/home/<user>/.config/uGet' remains intact and contains valuable evidence for the investigator.

References

1. Flareget. http://flareget.com/
2. Carvey, H.: The windows registry as a forensic resource. Digit. Invest. **2**, 201–205 (2005)

3. Mee, V., Tryfonas, T., Sutherland, I.: The windows registry as a forensic artefact: illustrating evidence collection for internet usage. Digit. Invest. **3**, 166–173 (2006)
4. Lallie, H.S., Briggs, P.J.: Windows 7 registry forensic evidence created by three popular BitTorrent clients. Digit. Invest. **7**, 127–134 (2011)
5. Lewthwaite, J., Smith, V.: Limewire examinations. Digit. Invest. **5**, S96–S104 (2008)
6. Lewthwaite, J.: Frostwire P2P forensic examinations. Digit. Invest. **9**, 211–221 (2013)
7. Fellows, Geoffrey: WinRAR temporary folder artefacts. Digit. Invest. **7**, 9–13 (2010)
8. Yasin, M., Wahla, MA., Kausar, F.: Analysis of download accelerator plus (DAP) for forensic artefacts. In: 5th International Conference on IT Security Incident Management and IT Forensics, pp. 235–238. Fraunhofer Gesellschaft Institutszentrum Stuttgart, Germany (2009)
9. Yasin, M., Wahla, MA., Kausar, F.: Analysis of free download manager for forensic artefacts. In: First International ICST Conference on Digital Forensics and Cyber Crime, pp. 59–68. Albany, NY, USA (2009)
10. Yasin, M., Cheema, A.R., Kausar, F.: Analysis of internet download manager for collection of digital forensic artefacts. Digit. Invest. **7**, 90–94 (2010)
11. Dickson, M.: An examination into yahoo messenger 7.0 contact identification. Digit. Invest. **3**, 159–165 (2006)
12. Dickson, M.: An examination into trillian basic 3.x contact identification. Digit. Invest. **4**, 36–45 (2007)
13. Dickson, M.: An examination into MSN messenger 7.5 contact identification. Digit. Invest. **3**, 79–83 (2006)
14. Dickson, M.: An examination into AOL instant messenger 5.5 contact identification. Digit. Invest. **3**, 227–237 (2006)
15. van Wouter, S.: Dongen, forensic artefacts left by windows live messenger 8.0. Digit. Invest. **4**, 73–87 (2007)
16. van Wouter, S.: Dongen, forensic artefacts left by pidgin messenger 2.0. Digit. Invest. **4**, 138–145 (2007)
17. Zax, R., Adelstein, F.: FAUST: forensic artifacts of uninstalled steganography. Digit. Invest. **6**, 25–38 (2009)
18. Lim, S., Park, J., Lim, K., Lee, C., Sangjin, L.: Forensic artifacts left by virtual disk encryption tools. In: 3rd International Conference on Human-Centric Computing (HumanCom), pp. 1–6. Cebu, Philippines (2010)
19. Said, H., Al Mutawa, N., Al Awadhi, I., Guimaraes, M.: Forensic analysis of private browsing artifacts. In: International Conferences on Innovations in Information Technology, pp. 197–202. United Arab Emirates, Abu Dhabi (2011)

Amazon Kindle Fire HD Forensics

Asif Iqbal[1,3(⊠)], Hanan Alobaidli[1,2], Andrew Marrington[3],
and Ibrahim Baggili[4]

[1] Athena Labs, Dubai, UAE
asif@babariqbal.com
[2] University of Sharjah, Sharjah, UAE
[3] Zayed University, Dubai, UAE
marrington@computer.org,
[4] University of New Haven, Connecticut, USA
ibaggili@newhaven.edu

Abstract. This research presents two developed approaches for the forensic acquisition of an Amazon Kindle Fire HD. It describes the forensic acquisition and analysis of the Amazon Kindle Fire HD device. Two developed methods of acquisition are presented; one requiring a special cable to reflash the boot partition of the device with a forensic acquisition environment (Method A), and the other exploiting a vulnerability in the device's Android operating system (Method B). A case study is then presented showing the various digital evidence that can be extracted from the device. The results indicate that Method A is more favorable because it utilizes a general methodology that does not exploit a vulnerability that could potentially be patched by Amazon in future software updates.

Keywords: Amazon Kindle Fire HD · Digital · Forensics · Analysis · Acquisition · Android forensics · Forensic flashing

1 Introduction

Tablets, also considered to be mobile devices, are the new computers of this decade. The portability of mobile devices provide users with the ability to use them anywhere and anytime in a variety of ways such as organizing their contacts, appointments, electronic correspondence, playing games etc. Over time, mobile devices accumulate a wealth of information about their users and their behavior, which is valuable in a course of an investigation. According to Fabio Marturana et al. [1] and NIST (National Institute of Standards and Technology) [2] it is more likely that law enforcement will encounter a suspect with a mobile device in his/her possession than a PC or laptop.

Scientific literature discusses various forensic research into small scale devices such as iDevices [3–6] and Android devices [7, 8, 20] from mobiles to tablets because of their importance in any investigation. Although there are many tablets that have been released in recent years, the competitive price of the Amazon Kindle Fire HD makes it attractive for consumers in the tablet sector.

The aim behind this research was to investigate forensically sound methodologies that could be used to acquire and analyze an Amazon Kindle Fire HD.

© Institute for Computer Sciences, Social Informatics and Telecommunications Engineering 2014
P. Gladyshev et al. (Eds.): ICDF2C 2013, LNICST 132, pp. 39–50, 2014.
DOI: 10.1007/978-3-319-14289-0_4

This paper is divided into several sections – Sects. 1 and 2 contain an introduction and a literature review, while Sects. 3 and 4 discuss the developed acquisition methods and the analysis of the acquired Amazon Kindle Fire HD image to identify the possible sources of evidence respectively. Finally, in Sect. 5 we conclude and give direction for future work.

2   Literature Review

Small Scale Digital Device (SSDD) forensics appeared alongside the invention of mobile devices such as PDAs, mobiles, smartphones and now tablets such as the iPad and Amazon Kindle Fire HD. The main reason for the forensic community's interest in SSDD research the valuable digital evidence that can be found on these devices. The SDDD forensics field can be defined as a sub-field of digital forensics that is concerned with the acquisition and analysis of evidence found on mobile devices such as cell phones, smartphones and now tablets like the iPad and Amazon Kindle Fire HD.

In 2011 the Amazon Kindle Fire e-reader was released as a new version of the long established Kindle e-reader. The Kindle Fire device contained new features compared to the older e-reader devices, as it included web browsing and applications – moving the Kindle out of the e-reader market segment into the tablet space. Despite the success of the various Amazon Kindle devices, and the appearance of the Amazon Kindle Fire tablet, there has been little published forensics research on these devices. With respect to the older e-reader Amazon Kindle devices, some blogs discussed the forensic investigation of these e-readers in order to provide insight into the inner working of the device and the possible evidence that can be found on it.

A blogger by the name Allyn Stott provided a brief discussion about the forensic investigation of one of the older Kindle devices, the Kindle Touch 3G. The blog identified the imaging method used along with a set of valuable information found on the device [9]. Another blog written by Marcus Thompson attempted to provide a baseline for the forensic study of the Amazon Kindle, the blog represented data acquired after imaging and analyzing the data on a Kindle device. Thompson has identified that the device image included fifty-nine books, three games, forty-five converted .pdf files, sixteen Kindle screenshots, two audio books, two book samples, one blog subscription, one magazine subscription, and one newspaper subscription. There are several other valuable information has been identified such as the browser cookies, settings and bookmarks along with information regarding the last book being read and the last time an audio book was listened to [10]. There are other blogs that tried to provide information about Amazon Kindle forensics such as [11, 12] along with these blogs MacForensicsLab have identified that its software can be used to image and analyze an Amazon Kindle keyboard [13].

The first notable published research on Kindle Forensics was by Peter Hannay at Edith Cowan University [14]. His research offered insight into forensically examining the various partitions on a Kindle by enabling the debug mode and then enabling usb networking – thus treating the Kindle like a network device to acquire data from it.

Iqbal et al. [15] conducted a study that discussed the forensic acquisition and analysis of the Amazon Kindle Fire, the first such study on an Amazon Kindle Fire.

In this research, the acquisition process required the Kindle Fire Device to be connected to a forensic workstation that contains a payload to be injected into the device using ADB (Android Debug Bridge) to a temporary location. This Payload is then executed on the device in order to reboot the device with a temporary root access using an exploit in Android Gingerbread. A bitwise image of the data partition is acquired using the Linux "dd" utility. The analysis of this image produced valuable digital artifacts, similar to the possible evidence that can be found on iDevices and any powered Android device. The research showed that the Amazon Kindle Fire is a potential source of more digital evidence (both in terms of variety and quantity) than the older Kindle e-reader devices because besides being an e-reader this version of the Amazon Kindle Fire provided tablet functionality.

In 2012 Oxygen Forensics, which offers forensic data examination tools for smartphones and mobile devices, released Oxygen Forensic Suite 2012 providing forensic support for the new Kindle Fire HD. The Oxygen team investigated the specifics of the new device, analyzed the new and unique apps, and determined types and locations of user data that can be stored by these apps [16]. However, proprietary software like Oxygen is effectively, a "blackbox" which obscures the process of acquisition and analysis of digital evidence from the examiner. Consequently questions may be raised as to the reliability of scientific testimony provided to a court by that examiner.

Currently, there has been no published research that investigated the forensic analysis and acquisition of a Kindle Fire HD. This work aims to fill this gap with regards to Kindle Fire HD forensics.

3 Acquisition Methodologies

While investigating the Amazon Kindle Fire HD, the researchers found two viable acquisition methodologies. These methodologies are discussed in the sections that follow.

3.1 Acquisition Methodology A

The first acquisition methodology required the creation of a "Factory Cable" also known as "Active Power Cable" see Fig. 1. A factory cable boots the Kindle Fire HD device to bootloader (u-boot) and awaits for commands from a host PC. For the creation of the "Factory Cable" a USB Micro-B to A cable used for Android data transfer was modified to provide +5 V to unused pin #4 on the Micro-B connector side.

Later on a custom boot image was sent to the device (overwriting the boot partition) and is booted by executing "fastboot -i 0x1949 flash boot boot.img", "fastboot -i 0x1949 flash system boot.img" and "fastboot -i 0x1949 reboot", where boot.img is a boot disk image containing a minimal Linux forensic acquisition environment, and the "i" switch is the manufacturer unique ID. Initially, we had intended to employ an approach based on that of Vidas et al., where the recovery partition is reflashed with a forensic acquisition environment [8], however, we found that the recovery partition was not available on the Kindle Fire HD device. The implementation of specific partitions can vary between different Android devices. However, the reasoning which motivated the selection of the recovery partition in the work of Vidas et al. [8] equally applies to the boot partition – the normal boot sequence of the device is still interrupted, and the user data partitions have not been overwritten. The difference is that the device would need to be reflashed after the examination in order to restore its original boot partition (which would apply equally to the recovery partition in Vidas et al. [8], only changes to that partition are less likely to be noticed by end users). In both cases, the use of the recovery partition in Vidas et al. [8] and the use of the boot partition in this work, the Android device is booted into a known "safe" acquisition environment, roughly analogous to the use of a forensic boot CD such as Helix in computer forensics.

After the recovery has finished booting, the ADB (Android Debug Bridge) server is started on the host PC. Android Debug Bridge (ADB) is a command line tool that facilitates the communication with an emulator instance or connected Android device [18] such as the Amazon Kindle Fire. ADB is used from the host PC to connect to the ADB client running on the Kindle Fire HD device. Using adb the following commands are executed on the Kindle Fire HD device to acquire an image of the "userdata" partition:

- adb shell -c "chmod 777/dev/block/"
- adb pull/dev/block/mmcblk0p13

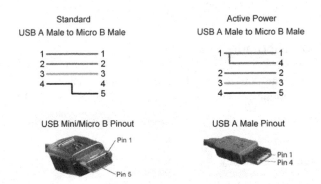

Fig. 1. The difference between a standard and an Active power cable

3.2   Acquisition Methodology B

Another method of acquisition is to use a known exploit in the Kindle Fire HD software to gain root access. In order for this method to work USB Debugging must be enabled on the Kindle Fire HD device from the setting menu (Menu-> More>Security-> Android Debugging). This acquisition methodology is dependent on the software version of the Android Kindle Fire HD device - we employed software version 7.2.3 (the latest at time of writing). Future Kindle software versions may address the vulnerability which permits this form of acquisition to work. This method works by making it seem as though the system is running in a virtualized qemu environment which enables debugging and root access in ADB (Android Debug Bridge). This exploit known as "qemu automated root" was, to our best knowledge, discovered by "sparkym3", a member of xda-developers.com forums [17].

In order to gain root access to the Amazon Kindle Fire HD device, the following commands are executed from the host workstation after connecting ADB to the device:

- adb shell mv/data/local/tmp/data/local/tmp.bak
- adb shell ln -s/data/data/local/tmp
- adb reboot
- adb wait-for-device
- adb shell rm/data/local.prop > nul
- adb shell "echo ro.kernel.qemu=1 > /data/local.prop"
- adb reboot

After the device has finished rebooting ADB will be running with root privileges. Following commands are executed to acquire an image of the user data partition:

- adb shell -c "chmod 777/dev/block/"
- adb pull/dev/block/mmcblk0p13

3.3   Discussion of the Acquisition Methodologies

Of the two acquisition methodologies we have employed, acquisition methodology A is preferred since it is independent of the software version and does not interfere with the partitions which are most likely to contain valuable digital evidence. Acquisition methodology B worked in our own experiment, but future software changes (to address the vulnerability which permits the qemu automated root exploit [17], for example) may make methodology B non-viable. Another advantage of acquisition methodology A as we see is that the examiner provides a known safe minimal Linux-based forensic acquisition environment and does not depend on any software installed on the device. Acquisition methodology B may be subject to interference from malware or an otherwise modified kernel on the Amazon Kindle Fire HD device. The downside of acquisition methodology A is that it requires specialized hardware (in the form of the factory cable), but this is not unique in digital forensics, especially with respect to small scale digital devices.

In investigations concerned with only with the primary storage of the Amazon Kindle Fire HD device, like Vidas et al. [8] we have a clear preference for avoiding the use of root kits to modify the device. However, we note that for live memory acquisition, neither of the acquisition methodologies we have described above are suitable, as they require the rebooting of the Kindle Fire HD device. In cases where live memory acquisition is necessary, it remains necessary to root the device [19]. In our analysis, described in Sect. 4 below, we have constrained ourselves to the examination of images acquired from the Kindle Fire HD device's secondary storage.

4   Case Study

The aim of the case study was to simulate the activities done by a regular user of this device and study the possible traces of evidence. In the case study the user uses the

Table 1. Amazon Kindle Fire HD Partition Table

No.	Start	End	Size	File system	Name
1	131 kb	262 kb	131 kb		Xloader
2	262 kb	524 kb	262 kb		Bootloader
3	524 kb	590 kb	65.5 kb		Idme
4	590 kb	606 kb	16.4 kb		Crypto
5	606 kb	608 kb	294 b		Misc
6	1049 kb	11.5 mb	10.5 mb		Dkernel
7	11.5 mb	213 mb	201 mb	Ext4	dfs
8	213 mb	230 mb	16.8 mb	Ext4	Efs
9	230 mb	238 mb	8389 kb		recovery
10	238 mb	246 mb	8389 kb		boot
11	246 mb	1175 mb	929 mb		system
12	1175 mb	1857 mb	682 mb	Ext4	cache
13	1857 mb	15.6 gb	13.8 gb	Ext4	userdata

device to log into his/her Amazon Account, after getting the access the user performs several activities which were as follows:

- Downloaded the book "Siddhartha by Herman Hesse" and read 10 %, then we downloaded book "SQL Server Forensic Analysis", placed a bookmark at 72 % and added several annotations.
- Downloaded and listened to some Music Albums from Amazon MP3.
- Accessed Amazon audio book service Audible.
- Accessed email from built-in email application. Several emails with attachments were accessed.
- Took a picture using the device's camera.
- Browsed slashdot.org > pcpro.com and zu.ac.ae > abpoutzu in a different tab.zu.ac. ae tab was left open.
- Installed and logged into recommended "Skype Kindle Fire Edition" app. Initiated a few videos and text chat sessions with some contacts.

After performing these activities the Amazon Kindle Fire HD device was imaged using the developed acquisition methods. The acquired image was studied and analyzed to identify the possible sources of evidence.

4.1   Acquired Data

The array of information provided by a device such as Amazon Kindle Fire HD can provide the investigator with valuable evidence. To study any device the first step was to identify the device structure in order to understand and analyze the possible sources of evidence see Table 1.

All application data is stored in the data directory of "userdata" partition, which is mounted at "/data". Every application has a directory with a unique identifier, which itself has the following sub-directories 'files', 'database', 'shared_prefs' and 'cache'. With exception of few cases most database files are stored in the database sub - directory of application data.

All user data (Documents, Books etc.) are stored on media directory of the "userdata" partition. The media directory is mounted as "/sdcard" using a fuse virtual file-system. This virtual file-system is also made available to the PC when the device is connected via a USB cable for data transfer.

Along with that all system apps, the Kindle Fire HD has a database file "cmsapi.db" with table "sync_hashes" that indicates the cloudsync status of the applications. Cloudsync status indicates that the device syncs to Amazon cloud servers either to store data or make use of the computational resources provided by the cloud.

Photos taken by the device can be recovered from "data/media/Pictures" in the "userdata' partition. The photo taken in the case study was found in that directory.

In the case of browsing history, all the browsing history from our case study was recovered from the device. History was stored in the data directory "com.amazon. cloud9" specifically in the pages table of the browser.db database file (see Fig. 2). All open tabs were stored in tabs table of browser.db (see Fig. 3). Page thumbnails and preview images were stored in the files directory of the application data with a unique id (see Fig. 4).

Table: pages							
	i	title	url	visits	visited on	boo	thumbnail	touch icon url
1	1	Amaz	http://www.amazon.com/			1	content://com.an	
2	2	Googl	http://www.google.com/			0	content://com.an	
3	3	Faceb	http://www.facebook.com/			0	content://com.an	
4	4	Yahoc	http://www.yahoo.com/			0	content://com.an	
5	5	Wikip	http://www.wikipedia.org/			0	content://com.an	
6	6	YouTu	http://youtube.com/			0	content://com.an	
7	7	Slashi	http://slashdot.org/	1	1360621813547	0	content://com.an	http://slashdot.org/
8	8	Zayec	http://www.zu.ac.ae/main/en/	1	1360621822723	0	content://com.an	http://www.zu.ac.a
9	9	Can y	http://www.pcpro.co.uk/features	1	1360621839759	0	content://com.an	
10	10	Abou	http://www.zu.ac.ae/main/en/exp	1	1360621861355	0	content://com.an	http://www.zu.ac.a

Fig. 2. com.amazon.cloud9/browser.db – pages Table contains browsing History on Amazon Kindle Fire HD

Table: tabs							
	i	app	url	positio	selected	hist	is home	title
1		1		0	0		1)	
2	3		http://www.zu.ac.ae/main/en/exp	1	1	1	0)	

Fig. 3. com.amazon.cloud9/browser.db – tab Table list open tabs

Another valuable source of potential evidence may relate to Kindle Books. The Kindle ebook library data was recovered from the "com.amazon.kindle" data directory. Library information was stored in the "KindleContent" table of the "kindle_library.db" database file; while Books themselves were stored in "/sdcard/Books/{id}" (see Fig. 5). The current position of the book was from the information recovered regarding the ebooks along with all annotation data that were recovered from "annotations.db" (see Fig. 6).

The music player history may also provide information for certain investigations. Analyzing the Amazon Kindle Fire HD structure showed that Music player history was stored in the recent table of "NowPlaying.db" database file in the "com.amazon.mp3" data directory. The history was stored with a unique id and a timestamp. Along with Music player history streaming music cache was also recovered with the metadata of cache being stored in the "PlaybackStreamCache.db" database file. This information is valuable in an investigation as it can provide a source for profiling the user behavior and habits.

Other applications such as Skype left traces on the device. These traces included all Skype contacts, text chats and video chats, and were recovered from the "com.skype. raider" data directory.

All relevant information to an investigation were being stored in the "main.db" database file in "files/{screenname}" sub-directory. Some chat excerpts were also recovered from "files/chatsync" and its sub-directories (see Fig. 7).

Kindle Fire HD uses a standard Android 4 email application; email messages sent or accessed on the device were located in the "com.android.email" data directory as expected. These Email messages were being stored in the "EmailProvider.db" database file in the databases sub-directory (see Fig. 8), while Attachments were cached in the databases/1.db_att directory.

Name	Date modified
pages_thumbnail_13c07ad7-ad12-492c-ba1f-9dd71fd4dd03	2/12/2013 3:55 AM
pages_thumbnail_14d804af-bc64-435a-9531-c9dada2a46dc	2/12/2013 3:55 AM
pages_thumbnail_0414be77-0526-42c6-8464-e61815fc3b2b	2/12/2013 3:55 AM
pages_thumbnail_9921c789-8a36-4bad-87e2-bbbff690b60f	2/12/2013 3:55 AM
pages_thumbnail_c85ba4b8-6a02-421e-871f-4abda07f6b86	2/12/2013 3:55 AM
pages_thumbnail_cbdfec91-1fb0-471d-a143-63a6a58b6068	2/12/2013 3:55 AM
pages_thumbnail_e8e021d5-b989-4608-9d3d-e486466b142f	2/12/2013 3:55 AM

Fig. 4. com.amazon.cloude9/files - Page thumbnails and preview images stored in files directory of the application data with a unique id

Table: LocalContent ▼ 🔍   New

	KEY	FILE PATH	GUID
1	AMZNID0/B003WUYRGI/0/	/system/etc/labdictionary/ODE_KCP.mobi	ODE_2010:0299D4A3
2	AMZNID0/B003ODIZL6/0/	/system/etc/labdictionary/NOAD_KCP.mobi	noad_2008:6F662540
3	AMZNID0/PSNL!KISIT!bWFrZVdl	/mnt/sdcard/Documents/PSNL!KISIT!bWFrZ	Welcome_r:C738...
4	AMZNID0/B002RKRV4Y/0/	/mnt/sdcard/Books/B002RKRV4Y_EBOK.prc	Siddhartha:BD39AA46
5	AMZNID0/B001O4IIWS/0/	/mnt/sdcard/Books/B001O4IIWS_EBOK.prc	SQL_Server_F-ensic_Analysis:B227B7A4

Fig. 5. Books stored in "/sdcard/Books/{id}"

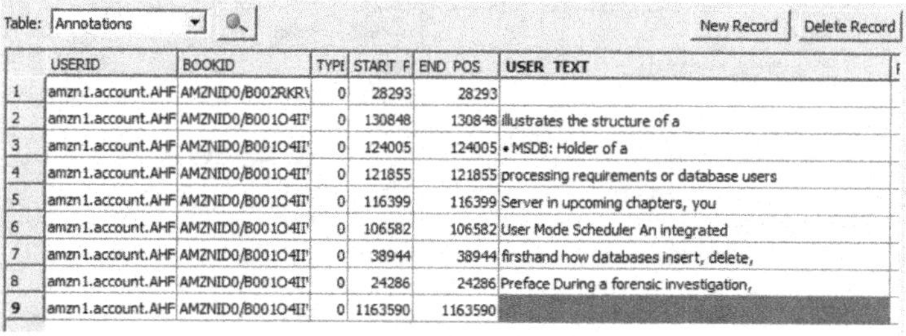
Table: Annotations | New Record | Delete Record

	USERID	BOOKID	TYPE	START P	END POS	USER TEXT
1	amzn1.account.AHF	AMZNID0/B002RKR\	0	28293	28293	
2	amzn1.account.AHF	AMZNID0/B001O4II'	0	130848	130848	illustrates the structure of a
3	amzn1.account.AHF	AMZNID0/B001O4II'	0	124005	124005	• MSDB: Holder of a
4	amzn1.account.AHF	AMZNID0/B001O4II'	0	121855	121855	processing requirements or database users
5	amzn1.account.AHF	AMZNID0/B001O4II'	0	116399	116399	Server in upcoming chapters, you
6	amzn1.account.AHF	AMZNID0/B001O4II'	0	106582	106582	User Mode Scheduler An integrated
7	amzn1.account.AHF	AMZNID0/B001O4II'	0	38944	38944	firsthand how databases insert, delete,
8	amzn1.account.AHF	AMZNID0/B001O4II'	0	24286	24286	Preface During a forensic investigation,
9	amzn1.account.AHF	AMZNID0/B001O4II'	0	1163590	1163590	

Fig. 6. Annotation data that were recovered from "annotations.db"

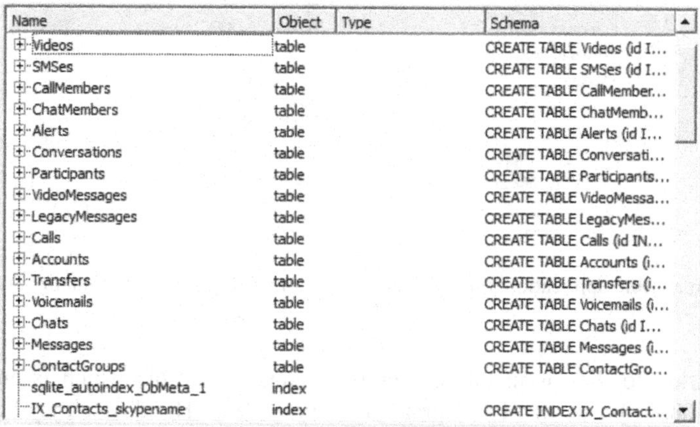

Name	Object	Type	Schema
Videos	table		CREATE TABLE Videos (id I...
SMSes	table		CREATE TABLE SMSes (id I...
CallMembers	table		CREATE TABLE CallMember...
ChatMembers	table		CREATE TABLE ChatMemb...
Alerts	table		CREATE TABLE Alerts (id I...
Conversations	table		CREATE TABLE Conversati...
Participants	table		CREATE TABLE Participants...
VideoMessages	table		CREATE TABLE VideoMessa...
LegacyMessages	table		CREATE TABLE LegacyMes...
Calls	table		CREATE TABLE Calls (id IN...
Accounts	table		CREATE TABLE Accounts (i...
Transfers	table		CREATE TABLE Transfers (i...
Voicemails	table		CREATE TABLE Voicemails (i...
Chats	table		CREATE TABLE Chats (id I...
Messages	table		CREATE TABLE Messages (i...
ContactGroups	table		CREATE TABLE ContactGro...
sqlite_autoindex_DbMeta_1	index		
IX_Contacts_skypename	index		CREATE INDEX IX_Contact...

Fig. 7. main.db/files/chatsync - Some chat excerpts recovered from files/chatsync and its sub-directories

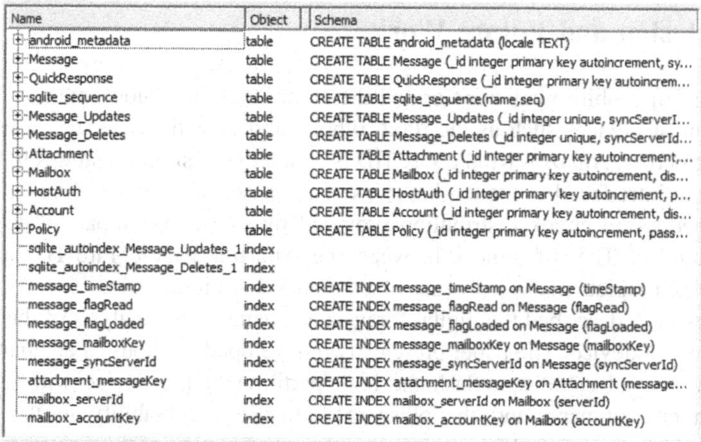

Name	Object	Schema
android_metadata	table	CREATE TABLE android_metadata (locale TEXT)
Message	table	CREATE TABLE Message (_id integer primary key autoincrement, sy...
QuickResponse	table	CREATE TABLE QuickResponse (_id integer primary key autoincrem...
sqlite_sequence	table	CREATE TABLE sqlite_sequence(name,seq)
Message_Updates	table	CREATE TABLE Message_Updates (_id integer unique, syncServerI...
Message_Deletes	table	CREATE TABLE Message_Deletes (_id integer unique, syncServerId...
Attachment	table	CREATE TABLE Attachment (_id integer primary key autoincrement,...
Mailbox	table	CREATE TABLE Mailbox (_id integer primary key autoincrement, dis...
HostAuth	table	CREATE TABLE HostAuth (_id integer primary key autoincrement, p...
Account	table	CREATE TABLE Account (_id integer primary key autoincrement, dis...
Policy	table	CREATE TABLE Policy (_id integer primary key autoincrement, pass...
sqlite_autoindex_Message_Updates_1	index	
sqlite_autoindex_Message_Deletes_1	index	
message_timeStamp	index	CREATE INDEX message_timeStamp on Message (timeStamp)
message_flagRead	index	CREATE INDEX message_flagRead on Message (flagRead)
message_flagLoaded	index	CREATE INDEX message_flagLoaded on Message (flagLoaded)
message_mailboxKey	index	CREATE INDEX message_mailboxKey on Message (mailboxKey)
message_syncServerId	index	CREATE INDEX message_syncServerId on Message (syncServerId)
attachment_messageKey	index	CREATE INDEX attachment_messageKey on Attachment (message...
mailbox_serverId	index	CREATE INDEX mailbox_serverId on Mailbox (serverId)
mailbox_accountKey	index	CREATE INDEX mailbox_accountKey on Mailbox (accountKey)

Fig. 8. com.android.email/EmailProvider.db/databases - Email messages were being stored in "EmailProvider.db" database file in databases sub-directory

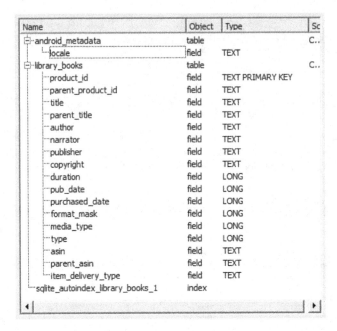

Name	Object	Type	Sc
⊟ android_metadata	table		C..
locale	field	TEXT	
⊟ library_books	table		C..
product_id	field	TEXT PRIMARY KEY	
parent_product_id	field	TEXT	
title	field	TEXT	
parent_title	field	TEXT	
author	field	TEXT	
narrator	field	TEXT	
publisher	field	TEXT	
copyright	field	TEXT	
duration	field	LONG	
pub_date	field	LONG	
purchased_date	field	LONG	
format_mask	field	LONG	
media_type	field	LONG	
type	field	LONG	
asin	field	TEXT	
parent_asin	field	TEXT	
item_delivery_type	field	TEXT	
sqlite_autoindex_library_books_1	index		

Fig. 9. com.audible.application.kindle/library.db - library_books table contains Audio book library

In addition to the discussed sources of evidence, Audible which is an amazon service for audio books that is integrated into Kindle Fire HD device may be relevant information to an investigation. Analyzing the image of the Amazon Kindle Fire HD identified that audio book library was stored in the "library.db" database file of the "com.audible.application.kindle" data directory in the table "library_books" see Fig. 9.

5 Conclusion and Future Work

The concept of mobility has transformed the computing technology market. With the introduction of devices such as the iPod, iPhone and later the iPad the tablet market continues to grow. Amazon Kindle Fire HD is a tablet with similar features to the iPad, and has been introduced to the market at a competitive price point, with an ecosystem for multimedia and ebook distribution provided by Amazon comparable to Apple's iTunes platform. The differences between the Amazon Kindle Fire HD and other Android-based tablets make it worthy of particular attention.

This research described the digital forensic acquisition and analysis of the Amazon Kindle Fire HD device. The paper presents two developed methods of acquisition, one requiring a special cable to reflash the boot partition of the device with a forensic acquisition environment, and the other exploiting a vulnerability in the device's Android operating system. After acquisition, the investigation of the system resulted in the identification of the system structure as well as the possible artifacts that could be used in a course of an investigation.

To the best of our knowledge, this is the first scientific paper discussing digital investigations of Amazon Kindle Fire HD devices. Our contributions are two techniques for physical acquisition (one of which, methodology A, we clearly prefer) of these devices, and a "road map" of storage locations on the device of key digital evidence items which may prove a useful starting point for digital forensic examiners.

This research targeted the acquisition and analysis of data on Amazon Kindle Fire HD, but still there is a lot of room for improvement and research. One of the possible areas is to explore third party applications and the artifacts left by them on the device. With devices such as Amazon Kindle Fire HD and iPads the door is open for research as they represent a move from the traditional computing era to the mobile computing era. There are many other areas of future work within the broader field of Android device forensics, such as live memory acquisition without the need for rooting the device, which will also have direct applicability to the Amazon Kindle Fire HD device.

References

1. Marturana, F., Me, G., Berte, R., Tacconi, S.: A quantitative approach to triaging in mobile forensics. In: 2011 IEEE 10th International Conference on Trust, Security and Privacy in Computing and Communications (TrustCom), pp. 582–588, 16–18 November 2011
2. Mobile Security And Forensics. NIST, 23 February 2009, Cited: 1, 19, 2013. http://csrc.nist.gov/groups/SNS/mobile_security/index.html
3. Zdziarski, J.: iPhone Forensics: Recovering Evidence. Personal Data and Corporate Assets, s.l. O'Reilly (2008)
4. Bader, M., Baggili, I.: iPhone 3GS forensics: Logical analysis using apple iTunes backup utility. Small Scale Digital Device Forensics J. 4(1) (2010)
5. Husain, M.I., Baggili, I., Sridhar, R.: A Simple Cost-Effective Framework for iPhone Forensic Analysis. In: Baggili, I. (ed.) ICDF2C 2010. LNICST, vol. 53, pp. 27–37. Springer, Heidelberg (2011)
6. Iqbal, B., Iqbal, A., Al Obaidli, H.: A novel method of iDevice(iPhone,iPad,iPod) forensics without jailbreaking. In: International Conference on Innovations in Information Technology (IIT), pp. 238–243, Abu Dhabi, Al Ain. IEEE (2012). doi:10.1109/INNOVATIONS.2012.6207740
7. Hoog, A.: Android forensics: investigation, analysis and mobile security for Google Android. Syngress (2011)
8. Vidas, T., Zhang, C., Christin, N.: Toward a general collection methodology for Android devices. Digital Invest. 8, S14–S24 (2011). doi:10.1016/j.diin.2011.05.003
9. Allyn S.: Amazon kindle forensics. A Safe Blog, 9 June 2011, Cited: 1, 19, 2013. www.blog.asafewebsite.com/2011/06/amazon-kindle-forensics.html
10. Thompson, M.: Introduction to kindle forensics. Practical Digital Forensics. 5 September 2011, Cited: 1, 19, 2013. http://practicaldigitalforensics.blogspot.com/2011/09/introduction-to-kindle-forensics.html
11. Eric H.: A cursory look at kindle forensics. In: A Fistful of Dongles. 13 April 2010, Cited: 1, 19, 2013. www.ericjhuber.com/2010/04/cursory-look-at-kindle-forensics.html
12. Kindle 3G Wireless Reading Device - forensically speaking. Computer Forensics and IR - what's new? 3 October 2010, Cited: 1, 19, 2013. newinforensics.blogspot.com/2010/10/kindle-3g-wireless-reading-device.html

13. Forensic Imaging of the Amazon Kindle. MacForensicsLab, Cited: 1, 19, 2013. http://www. macforensicslab.com/ProductsAndServices/index.php?main_page=document_general_info& cPath=5_18&products_id=338&zeni%ED%AF%80%ED%B2%AB

14. Hannay, P., Kindle forensics: Acquisition and analysis. In: Proceedings of the ADFSL 2011 Conference on Digital Forensics, Security and Law (2011)

15. Iqbal, B., Iqbal, A., Guimaraes, M., Khan, K., Al Obaidli, H.: Amazon kindle fire from a digital forensics perspective. In: 2012 International Conference on Cyber-Enabled Distributed Computing and Knowledge Discovery (CyberC), pp. 323–329, 10–12 October 2012. doi:10.1109/CyberC.2012.61

16. Oxygen Forensic Suite 2012 Adds Support for Amazon Kindle Fire HD, PRweb, 23 October 2012, Cited: 1, 19, 2013. http://www.prweb.com/releases/kindle-fire-hd/forensic-tools/ prweb10040657.htm50442462&pf_rd_i=B005890

17. qemu automated root, exploit, Cited: 14, 5, 2013. http://forum.xda-developers.com/ showthread.php?t=1893838

18. Android Debug Bridge, Developer Android. Cited: 14, 5, 2013. http://developer.android. com/tools/help/adb.html

19. Sylve, J., Case, A., Marziale, L., Richard, G.G.: Acquisition and analysis of volatile memory from android devices. Digital Invest. 8(3–4), 175–184 (2012). doi:10.1016/j.diin.2011.10. 003

20. Lessard, J., Kessler, G.C.: Android forensics: simplifying cell phone examinations. In: Small Scale Digital Device Forensics J. 4(1) September 2010

Resurrection: A Carver for Fragmented Files

Martin Lambertz$^{(\boxtimes)}$, Rafael Uetz, and Elmar Gerhards-Padilla

Fraunhofer FKIE, Friedrich-Ebert-Allee 144, 53113 Bonn, Germany
{martin.lambertz,rafael.uetz,elmar.gerhards-padilla}@fkie.fraunhofer.de

Abstract. The recovery of deleted files is an important task frequently carried out by professionals in digital forensics and data recovery. When carried out without information from the file system, this process is called file carving. The techniques implemented in today's file carvers are mostly sufficient for non-fragmented files. Fragmented files, on the contrary, are not well supported. In this paper we present a general process model for the recovery of fragmented files. This model is then applied to the JPEG file format which is the de facto standard for digital photographs. Moreover, we evaluate popular open source carvers and compare them with our proposed approach.

Keywords: File carving · Multimedia forensics · Fragmented files · JPEGs

1 Introduction

The discipline of digital forensics provides techniques to find evidence on digital devices. One task carried out to find digital evidence is the recovery of deleted data. When a file is deleted, the actual data making up this file is usually not removed from the storage device. Instead, only the corresponding entries in the file system metadata are removed or modified. This effectively marks the area that was occupied by the file as free. Therefore, deleted files are still present until overwritten by other data.

In most cases techniques used in traditional data recovery might suffice to restore the deleted files. These methods usually rely on information provided by the file system metadata. However, in cybercrime you often have a different situation. If no information from the file system is available, either because it is missing or corrupt, e.g. because a suspect tried to destroy evidence, those methods will most likely not be able to restore deleted files.

In such scenarios the files have to be restored by investigating their structure and contents rather than investigating the file system metadata. This process is called file carving or just carving. This gets even more difficult if the files are stored fragmented on a storage medium. Without file system information it is very hard to determine where the fragments of such a file begin and end. Thus, file carving can be a very time consuming process. Moreover, it possibly generates a large amount of data to be sifted by a forensic examiner. However, when dealing

© Institute for Computer Sciences, Social Informatics and Telecommunications Engineering 2014
P. Gladyshev et al. (Eds.): ICDF2C 2013, LNICST 132, pp. 51–66, 2014.
DOI: 10.1007/978-3-319-14289-0_5

with cybercrime, not all of this data is of interest during an investigation. For instance, files belonging to the operating system, when untampered with, are usually non-relevant. In most cases files generated by the user such as e-mails, text documents, pictures or videos are more important. On the one hand those files itself may prove or disprove a criminal act (e.g. when possession of a specific file is illicit). On the other hand the contents of a file may give important hints to the solution of a crime.

One type of user generated data are pictures in general and digital photographs in particular. Photographs can play central roles when investigating criminal acts. Consider cases of child pornography for example. Finding explicit photographs on the computer of a suspect may help the authorities to convict the suspect. Other crimes that possibly involve photographs are blackmailing, cyber-bullying, harassment, and falsification of documents.

The de facto standard algorithm for compressing digital photographs has been defined by the Joint Photographic Experts Group in [1] and is commonly known as the JPEG standard. Nowadays, most of the digital cameras produce JPEG-compressed images. This holds for low-end consumer cameras and cameras integrated into mobile phones as well as for high-end digital cameras.

Current file carvers are able to restore deleted files when they are stored contiguously on the storage medium. However, only very few carvers support the reconstruction of fragmented files and, if so, in a rudimentary manner only. To our knowledge the only product available with advanced support for fragmented images is Adroit Photo Forensics [2] developed by Digital Assembly. However, this product is proprietary and cannot be easily used by researchers for their own work.

Although modern file systems try to minimize fragmentation, it cannot always be avoided completely. In [3] Garfinkel presents detailed fragmentation statistics collected from more than 300 hard disks. An important conclusion that can be drawn from these statistics is that files of interest during a forensic investigation tend to fragment more likely than less interesting files. For instance, 16 % of the JPEG files were fragmented, 20 % of the AVI files, and 58 % of the PST files. These numbers may not sound very large, however, we think that they are too large for not considering fragmented files at all.

The rest of this paper is organized as follows: Sect. 2 presents related work and Sect. 3 formulates requirements for modern file carvers. In Sect. 4 we present our approach for carving fragmented JPEG files. Finally, in Sect. 5 we compare our carving approach with popular open source carvers and conclude this paper in Sect. 6.

A Note on Terminology. Throughout the rest of this paper we use the term *block* to denote the smallest unit of data that is processed by a file carver. This may be the smallest addressable unit of a storage medium such as a sector of a hard disk drive or a cluster of the file system.

2   Related Work

There exist various file carving approaches. In this section we introduce selected proposed techniques which our work is partially based on. Starting with approaches that do not consider fragmented files, we present fundamental works addressing fragmented files as well.

One of the most simple carving approaches is called header-to-footer carving. Using this technique a carver searches a given disk image for occurrences of certain byte sequences indicating the beginning (header) and end (footer) of a file. Afterwards the data between those signatures is restored. While being very fast, this approach is limited to contiguously stored files only. Nevertheless, it is one of the most widely used strategies in current file carvers such as Foremost [15] and Scalpel [16].

Motivated by his study on fragmented files, Garfinkel was one of the first to address the recovery of fragmented files. In [3] he introduces a technique called bifragment gap carving. This approach makes use of object validation, which means that a file candidate is validated before it is actually recovered. Depending on the file type a validation includes a verification of headers and footers, a verification of the file structure, and, if applicable, the decoding of the file. In case of a successful validation the file is recovered; otherwise, the file is deemed fragmented. Fragmented files are recovered by successively removing data between a found header and footer of a file and afterwards trying to validate the file. Starting with a gap size of one block, all possible positions of this gap are tested. If the file still does not validate, the gap size is increased by one block and again all possible positions of the gap are tested. This process is carried out for all gap sizes until the file is successfully validated or all combinations are exhausted. As the name implies this approach is limited to files split into two fragments; files split into more fragments are not recoverable.

In [4,5] a general process model for the reconstruction of fragmented files is proposed consisting of three steps: preprocessing, collation, and reassembly. In the preprocessing step encryption or compression possibly applied to the disk image is removed. The collation step is responsible for classifying the blocks of the disk image as belonging to one or more file types. Finally, in the reassembly step the files are reconstructed. Depending on the file type different reconstruction algorithms have to be applied in this step.

Moreover, the authors formulate the reassembly of fragmented files as a graph-theoretic problem where the blocks of a disk image form the set of nodes of a graph. The edges indicate the probability that two blocks are adjacent in the original file. The authors use different algorithms to approximate optimal paths within the resulting graph. This idea was subsequently refined in [6,7]. A problem with graph-theoretic carving is scalability. For large storage media the number of blocks to consider may exceed current computing and memory capabilities.

3   Requirements for File Carvers

The ever increasing capacities of today's storage media present a formidable challenge to file carving tools. Modern hard disk drives are capable of storing terabytes of data and even USB flash drives and mobile phones have capacities of several gigabytes. In order to be able to keep up with this trend a file carver should behave efficiently in terms of processing speed as well as in memory requirements.

Considering that a file carver is often part of a digital forensics investigation an even more important requirement is a correct and traceable functioning. If this cannot be granted, results produced by the file carver might not be usable as evidence in court.

Based on the aforementioned considerations we formulated three basic requirements for file carving tools. Moreover, we prioritized the requirements by their importance during a forensics investigation.

1. Correctness: A carver should be able to correctly recover as many files as possible. Moreover, it should not generate corrupted files that cannot be opened using a standard program for the corresponding file types.
2. Scalability: A carver should be able to handle today's and future high-capacity storage volumes.
3. Performance: A carver should be reasonably fast.

4   Fragmented JPEG Carving

Based on the general process model introduced in [4] and the requirements presented in the previous section we derived the file carving process model depicted in Fig. 1. We varied from the original process model because of the fragmentation statistics in [3] which imply that a large fraction of the files on a storage medium are stored contiguously. Such files can be restored comparatively easily and fast. Therefore, we restore the non-fragmented files first. On the one hand this approach can drastically reduce the amount of data to be considered in the more complex reconstruction of fragmented files. On the other hand there will already be a large number of recovered files for an examiner to sift.

4.1   Preprocessing Phase

As in [4], the preprocessing phase is responsible for converting the input into a format the file carver is able to process. This means that any encryption or compression has to be removed so that the following steps can operate on raw data. Moreover, if the storage medium under investigation contains a valid file system, the information stored in the file system metadata may be used to reduce the overall data the carver has to consider. This, however, requires the investigator to trust this information, which cannot always be assumed.

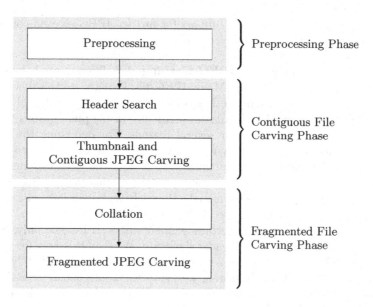

Fig. 1. Proposed carving model.

4.2 Contiguous File Carving Phase

As mentioned earlier, the first carving phase is used to restore non-fragmented files. Moreover, it is responsible for generating candidates for the reconstruction.

Header Search. In this step the storage medium is searched for occurrences of strings indicating the start of a JPEG file, thus generating candidates of files to be carved. Note that the results of this step will be used in all of the remaining carving steps, not only in this phase but also in the fragmented file carving phase. That is, only candidates generated in this step will be considered during the following carving processes.

Table 1. Byte sequences identifying JPEG headers. The question marks (?) represent wildcard characters representing one byte value each.

Header type	Byte sequence
JPEG/JFIF	0xFF 0xD8 0xFF 0xE0 ? ? 0x4A 0x46 0x49 0x46 0x00
JPEG/Exif	0xFF 0xD8 0xFF 0xE1 ? ? 0x45 0x78 0x69 0x66 0x00

Table 1 lists the byte sequences identifying the JPEG/JFIF and JPEG/Exif file formats. Whenever such a byte sequence is found, its starting position is stored in a sequence H which represents the candidates to be carved. We focus on these two formats here, as they are the predominant file formats for storing

JPEG-compressed files. However, support for further JPEG or even completely different file types may be added very easily.

Thumbnail and Contiguous JPEG Carving. We differentiate between regular JPEG files and thumbnails. Many JPEG file formats store a down-scaled version of the original image in the JPEG file. Moreover, a lot of digital cameras generate and store these thumbnails automatically in the photographs.

Thumbnails are interesting for several reasons. For one thing the forensic examiner can use them to get a rough overview of what images to expect. Depending on the contents of the thumbnail images the examiner may be in a better position to judge if more time-consuming techniques are worth being applied. For another thing the thumbnails themselves may already contain compromising material that can be used in the course of the investigation.

Thumbnails may appear in certain segments of a JPEG file only, located within a limited range after the header signature. We scan this area for possibly existent thumbnails and whenever a thumbnail is found, it is immediately carved.

After all thumbnails are restored, we carve the contiguously stored JPEG files. Based on Garfinkel's statistics provided in [3] these files will make up about 84 % of the JPEGs. Therefore, it is worthwhile to use appropriate carving strategies. That is, carving strategies that are simple and, more importantly, fast.

The obvious carving strategy would be header-to-footer carving. However, since correctness is our primary requirement, we have to make sure that only valid files are carved during this step. Header-to-footer carving alone provides no means to ensure the validity of the carved files. Hence, a second step to validate the files would be necessary.

In order to avoid having to first carve and afterward validate a file, we chose not to use the classical header-to-footer carving. Instead, we start decoding the JPEG from the header on until the JPEG is either completely decoded or until the decoder detects errors, such as an invalid file structure, invalid Huffman symbols or a premature end of the file for instance. Only files that are decodable without errors are finally carved and their headers are removed from the sequence H. Moreover, blocks that have been used to carve the non-fragmented files are marked as used and are not considered in the following carving phase anymore.

4.3 Fragmented File Carving Phase

In the second carving phase we try to restore the remaining JPEG files in set H, i.e. files that have not been restored in the first phase. At this point H contains candidates only that could not be carved using sequential decoding.

Collation. In the original process model the collation step is used to classify a given block as belonging to one or more file types. Especially for encoded data this multiclass classification problem is very hard and, in fact, not required at all. Since we focus on the recovery of JPEG files, we do not classify the blocks. Instead, in our case it is sufficient to determine if a data block belongs to a

JPEG file or not. This reformulation turns the multiclass classification problem into a binary classification problem, allowing the usage of more specialized methods, which are easier to compute and more accurate than general classification techniques most of the time.

Our preliminary assumption is that every block belongs to a JPEG file. Then, we subsequently perform tests on each block that may refute this assumption. As soon as one of these tests yields a negative result, we discard the block and do not consider it any further.

The first test exploits what is called byte stuffing in [1]. In a JPEG file a 0xFF byte introduces a marker. In order to distinguish markers from 0xFF bytes occurring in the encoded image data, each 0xFF that does not introduce a marker has to be masked with a 0x00 byte. Blocks without correct byte stuffing can easily be identified and do not have to be considered anymore.

In the next test we determine the frequency of printable ASCII characters contained in a block. We count the number of bytes from the interval [0x20,0x7E] as well as the bytes 0x09 (horizontal tab), 0x0A (line feed), and 0x0D (carriage return). If the percentage of these characters exceeds a certain threshold, then we assume the block to belong to some kind of text file rather than to a JPEG. We evaluated various thresholds and found 70 % to yield the best results which are presented in Table 3.

Finally, we check whether a block consists of 0x00 bytes only. If this applies, then we assume that the block has not been used to store any data yet or has been sanitized. Such blocks are discarded as well.

A block that passes all of the tests outlined above will be inserted into a set D. Along with the headers H, only these blocks are considered in the reassembly of fragmented JPEGs following the collation step. Therefore, it is important not to separate out blocks that actually belong to JPEG files.

Note that we considered implementing more tests in this step, for instance by using the information entropy or byte frequency distribution of a block. However, based on [8], where the authors assessed the probability of being able to distinguish a non-JPEG block from a JPEG block by checking the correctness of the byte stuffing, we know that with increasing block size this test alone is sufficient to eliminate more than 90 % of the non-JPEG blocks. For a block size of 4096 bytes, which is a common block size in many file systems, the probability to find an invalid byte sequence is even larger than 99 %. Therefore, we chose to omit further test, especially because tests based on entropy and byte frequency distribution are computationally more expensive.

Fragmented JPEG Carving. At this point we have completely classified every block of the disk image that has not yet been used to restore a JPEG. That is, each of the available blocks has either been included in H or D or has been determined not to belong to a JPEG file. Based on the blocks in the aforementioned sets the reassembly of fragmented JPEGs is performed in this step.

In order for the carving algorithm to be functioning, an essential assumption has to hold: the marker segments and the first few scanlines of the JPEG to be recovered have to be stored contiguously in the first fragment of the file. This is because our approach does not yet include mechanisms to reassemble fragmented marker segments and the first scanlines are required as a starting point for the following reassembly steps. Although this requirement may sound restricting, we believe that it is not in realistic scenarios. Since file systems try to avoid fragmentation, it is unlikely that fragmentation occurs that early in a file already.

The following pseudocode lists the basic steps of the recovery of a fragmented JPEG file:

```
FUNCTION carve-fragmented-jpeg(h)
    B, bₐ := initialize carving process
    WHILE JPEG is recoverable and JPEG is not complete DO
        b_safe := FastForwardStep(bₐ)
        b_z := FragmentationPointDetection(b_safe)
        B := (B, bₐ, b_{a+1},..., b_z)
        bₐ := FindNextFragment(b_z)
    END WHILE
END FUNCTION
```

Given a header $h \in H$, the carving process is initialized by reading the metadata (i.e. the marker segments) of the JPEG. This provides us with important information such as the number of pixels in vertical and horizontal direction and the number of color components. These values are essential for the further reconstruction steps. Moreover, the sequence of blocks B, which denotes the data blocks of a JPEG under reconstruction, is initialized with the blocks used to read the marker segments. The block b_a denotes the last block that has been used so far. This block serves as a starting point for the reassembly algorithm and is added to B not until later in the reassembly.

Decoding data not belonging to a JPEG typically causes corrupted image regions. These corruptions can visually be easily distinguished from valid image regions as they form sharp edges to the valid image regions in most cases. Thus, corrupted regions may be detected using edge detection algorithms known from the field of computer vision. In the *fast forward* step we try to find the maximum number of complete scanlines of an image that are not corrupted. We denote these scanlines as *safe scanlines*.

Given the first block of a fragment, b_a, we start to decode the image line by line. In order to detect image corruptions we use a simple edge detection technique similar to the one proposed by Cohen in [9]. This technique is based on Laplacian zero-crossings and is a well known approach in the field of computer vision. For every decoded scanline we compute an edge value according to Eq. 1:

$$e(y) = \frac{1}{X \cdot C} \cdot \sum_{x=0}^{X-1} \sum_{c=0}^{C-1} |I_c(x, y-1) - 2 \cdot I_c(x,y) + I_c(x, y+1)| . \qquad (1)$$

Here, X denotes the number of pixels in horizontal direction and C denotes the number of components per pixel. A grayscale image has only one component, an RGB image three. $I_c(x, y)$ denotes the cth component of pixel x in scanline y.

The edge value is subsequently compared to a dynamically computed threshold Θ. Such a threshold has to adapt to changing image characteristics without too much delay. Hence, we chose to compute the threshold based on a linear weighted average which on the one hand reacts faster to changing image characteristics than a median for example and on the other hand assigns higher weights to more currently processed scanlines.

A JPEG-compressed image is decoded in terms of blocks called minumum coded units (MCUs) of certain dimensions. Therefore, we do not have to check every image line for corruptions. Instead, we only examine the scanlines on the horizontal MCU block boundaries. Consider for example an MCU size of 8×8 pixels. Then we would check for image corruptions every 8 scanlines only.

The threshold Θ is computed by

$$
\begin{aligned}
\Theta_0 &= \alpha \\
\Theta_i &= 0.5 \cdot (\alpha + \mu) + \beta \cdot \Theta_{i-1}
\end{aligned}
\tag{2}
$$

with α and β being predefined constants. μ is the linear weighted average of the last n edge values values computed by

$$
\mu = \frac{2}{n \cdot (n+1)} \cdot \sum_{j=1}^{n} j \cdot s_j
\tag{3}
$$

where n denotes the number of edge values and s the ordered sequence of edge values computed in the current instance of the fast forward step. That means, $s = s_1, s_2, \ldots, s_n = e(y_1), e(y_2), \ldots, e(y_n)$, where y_1 is the first scanline read in this fast forward step and y_n the scanline just before the computation of μ.

Note that the weighted average and the threshold are computed only before the threshold is used in a comparison with an edge value. That is, the computations are carried out if the current scanline processed is at the boundary of two MCU blocks. Moreover, Θ and μ are only valid for one instance of the fast forward step. If the fast forward step is entered in the next round of the reconstruction algorithm, the computation of the two values starts over again.

Besides detecting image corruptions, the fast forward step serves another purpose. We do not only compute the linear weighted average, but also a long-term model of the image consisting of the arithmetic mean of the edge values and their standard deviation. This model is used in the following steps of the reassembly algorithm.

The fast forward step only determines the approximate region of the fragmentation point. The exact fragmentation point is identified in the *fragmentation point detection* step. Here, we try to find the last block belonging to the current file fragment.

The fragmentation point detection receives the last safe block, b_{safe}, as input which serves as a starting point for this step. In order to find the exact fragmentation point, we append the blocks following b_{safe} one by one and check whether an image corruption is detected. The detection of a corruption is again performed by using formula 1 and a threshold θ computed by

$$\theta = \kappa \cdot M + \lambda \cdot \sigma \ . \tag{4}$$

In formula 4, M is the arithmetic mean and σ the standard deviation of the long-term model computed during the fast forward step. κ and λ are two predefined constants.

If the edge value computed exceeds the threshold θ, an image corruption is assumed and the block causing this corruption will be considered as the first block not belonging to the current file fragment anymore.

Note that we only append blocks which are in D in this step. When a block following b_{safe} is not in D, we assume a fragmentation point to be detected. This is why we need a de facto perfect sensitivity of the block classifier used in the collation step.

After the last block of the current fragment, b_z, has been identified, we have to find the first block of the next fragment belonging to the file under reconstruction. This is accomplished in the *find next fragment* step.

Based on the fragmentation statistics provided in [3], we know that typically file fragments are not scattered randomly across the storage medium, but are stored relatively closely to each other. This suggests that most of the time the beginning of the next fragment can be found within a close range after the block b_z. In [3] Garfinkel lists the gap distribution for JPEG files split into two fragments with the largest common gap size observed being 636 KiB. However, we do not want to limit the search for the next fragment to a predefined range in order to be able to carve files in more complicated fragmentation scenarios, too. Therefore, this step is further subdivided. First, we check the blocks within a predefined range after b_z. If we already find a good candidate within this range, we stop here and return this block. If we do not find such a candidate, we exhaustively search the remaining blocks in D for a candidate.

To grade a candidate block, we append the block to the blocks already considered as belonging to the JPEG and decode a complete set of scanlines. Note that we might have to read further blocks in order to completely decode these scanlines. After the decoding, once again we use formula 1 to compute an edge value between the scanlines that have been determined to belong to the file earlier and the newly decoded ones. The grade of a block is then calculated by

$$\omega = \begin{cases} 1, & \text{if } e(y_{b_i}) = 0 \\ 1/e(y_{b_i}), & \text{else} \end{cases} \tag{5}$$

where y_{b_i} is the first of the newly decoded scanlines after block b_i has been appended.

We compute the value ω for all blocks within a predefined range of 2500 blocks. If the best weight is larger than a threshold ϕ, the candidate is considered as good and this block will be returned as the beginning of the new fragment. If no block yields a weight larger than the threshold, we exhaustively check all remaining blocks in D. We start right after the predefined range and proceed until the end of the disk image. Afterwards we start from the beginning of the disk image until we reach the header of the current file. Finally, we return the block with the best ω as the beginning of the next fragment and start another round of the algorithm until the JPEG is completely recovered or we detect that it is not recoverable at all.

5   Evaluation

To evaluate our proposed carving approach we implemented a prototypic carver and compared its capabilities with available open source carvers. The evaluation was performed on a machine with an Intel Core i7-3930K hexa-core CPU clocked at 3.2 GHz with 12 logical cores.

Table 2. Summary of the test sets.

Test set	Size in MiB	Non-fragmented JPEGs	Fragmented JPEGs	Thumbnails
Simple#1	≈50	2	0	3
Simple#2	≈50	1	1	3
Simple#3	≈50	0	2	3
Simple#1-notn	≈50	2	0	0
Simple#2-notn	≈50	1	1	0
Simple#3-notn	≈50	0	2	0
DFTT#8	≈10	6	0	0
DFTT#11	≈62	3	0	3
DFTT#12	≈124	1	2	1
DFRWS-2006	≈48	7	7	5
DFRWS-2007	≈331	1	13	13
nps-2009-canon2-gen6	≈32	30	6	38

Table 2 lists the test sets we used in our evaluation. The Simple#n test sets have been created by us to evaluate basic carving capabilities of the carvers. They consist of 50 MiB of random data and two JPEG files implementing fragmentation scenarios of different levels of difficulty. The Simple#n-notn test sets are the same as the Simple#n test sets but with the thumbnails removed from the JPEGs. The remaining test sets are publicly available standard test sets for file carvers frequently used in the literature. The DFTT test sets have been created by Carrier and Mikus specifically for the evaluation of file carvers. The test sets themselves and detailed descriptions are available at [10]. The DFRWS test sets were taken from the DFRWS challenges from the years 2006 and 2007 which were dedicated to file carving with a focus on fragmented files. Again, the test sets and detailed descriptions are publicly available [11,12]. Finally, we used the nps-2009-canon2-gen6 test set which is the image of a memory card used in a digital camera [13,14].

We used the test sets of the DFRWS challenges to evaluate our tests to differentiate between JPEG and non-JPEG blocks. Both test sets were processed with a block size of 512 bytes. The classification results with regard to sensitivity and specificity are presented in Table 3. Sensitivity and specificity are two standard metrics when measuring the quality of a classifier. In our case the former denotes the fraction of JPEG blocks which have been correctly classified as such and the latter denotes the fraction of non-JPEG blocks which have not been classified as JPEG blocks.

Table 3. Classification results for the DFRWS test sets.

		DFRWS'06	DFRWS'07
JPEG headers	Sensitivity	1.00	1.00
	Specificity	1.00	1.00
JPEG data blocks	Sensitivity	1.00	1.00
	Specificity	0.82	0.86

The first thing standing out is the perfect sensitivity of our classifier. For JPEG header blocks the specificity is perfect as well. For JPEG data blocks the specificity is notably lower. In the DFRWS-2006 test set the false positive rate is 18 %, in the DFRWS-2007 test set 14 %. These results correspond to the results of [8] mentioned in Sect. 4.3. Hence, we can expect the specificity of our classifier to become better with larger block sizes.

We evaluated various different combinations of the constant values α, β, κ, λ, and ϕ. We found that the carver achieved the best results with the values set to $\alpha = 1000$, $\beta = 0.32$, $\kappa = 1.9$, $\lambda = 4$, and $\phi = 0.001$. Therefore, we present the results for these values in our evaluation.

As already mentioned, we did not only evaluate our carver but also popular open source carvers. We included Foremost [15], Scalpel [16], and PhotoRec [17] in our evaluation each in at least two different configurations.

Figure 2 presents the results of the carvers with regard to the number of reconstructed files. The plot is tripartite: the top part shows the ratio of carved non-fragmented JPEGs, the part in the middle the ratio of carved fragmented JPEGs, and the bottom part the ratio of carved thumbnails. Each bar is divided into correctly carved files, partially carved files, and files not carved at all. In our evaluation a file is rated as correctly carved if it completely corresponds to the original file. A file is graded as partially carved if the file is not complete but the subject depicted is still identifiable. Finally, files are rated as not carved if the file is either missing completely or the subject is not identifiable.

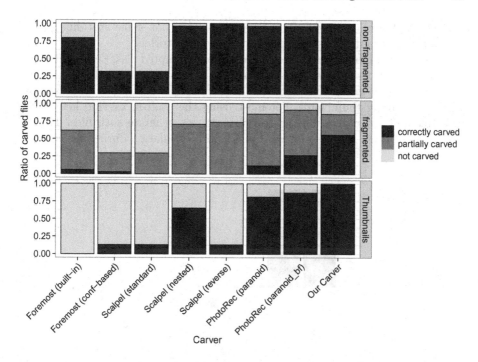

Fig. 2. Correctness of the file carvers.

Looking at the top part reveals that two configurations of Scalpel, PhotoRec, and our carver achieve very good reconstruction rates of more than 96 %, with our carver and one configuration of Scalpel being able to restore all files correctly.

When it comes to fragmented JPEGs, the number of correctly carved files significantly drops for all carvers evaluated. Especially Foremost and Scalpel, which have no dedicated support for carving fragmented files, are not able to completely recover a single fragmented JPEG. An exception is Foremost (built-in), which implements a heuristic to restore certain fragmented files from ext2/ext3 file systems [15].

PhotoRec implements basic mechanisms to carve fragmented files which is also reflected in our evaluation. Depending on the carving mode, PhotoRec is able to correctly restore about 12 % and 26 % respectively.

Finally, our carver is able to recover approximately 56 % of the fragmented JPEGs correctly which clearly outperforms the other carvers tested.

If we include the partially carved files, PhotoRec achieves slightly better results than our carver. The heuristic for carving fragmented files implemented by PhotoRec is comparatively simple and of minor computational complexity. Hence, it might be beneficial to adapt it to our carver as well.

Finally, the lower part shows that our carver is capable of restoring more thumbnails than every other carver tested. Only one thumbnail is not recovered because the header of the actual JPEG had already been overwritten. PhotoRec also differentiates between thumbnails and regular JPEGs and consequently achieves good results as well. The other carvers do not make this differentiation and do not perform as well as our carver or PhotoRec.

Moreover, thumbnails were often the cause for corrupted files. Figure 3 depicts the absolute number of corrupted files generated by the carvers. Scalpel and Foremost (conf-based) generate a large amount of corrupted files mainly caused by JPEGs containing thumbnails. Foremost using the built-in carving heuristics, PhotoRec and our carver, on the contrary, do not generate such files. This is because all of these carvers perform some kind of validation during the carving process.

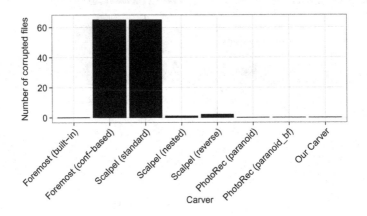

Fig. 3. Corrupted files generated by the file carvers.

Figure 4 illustrates the time the carvers took to process the individual test sets. The data points represent the arithmetic mean of 50 replications. The corresponding standard deviation is also plotted, but hardly visible due to virtually no variance in the results. In order to keep the plot clear, we only present a subset of the carvers, which generated the best results in terms of correctness.

The x-axis depicts the test sets sorted ascending by their size. The y-axis depicts the time the carvers took to process the test sets in seconds. Please note that this axis is scaled logarithmically in order to render all results visible.

The first thing to observe is that Foremost and Scalpel take less than two seconds for each of the test sets. Moreover, the time these two carver take seems to depend mainly on the size of the given input data.

PhotoRec exhibits a different behavior. Here, the input size is not the main factor influencing the runtime but rather the number of JPEGs and the complexity of the fragmentation scenarios contained in the test sets. In the paranoid mode, PhotoRec is nearly as fast as Foremost and Scalpel. All test sets have been processed in less than five seconds. The paranoid_bf mode is able to process half of the test sets in less than one second. The test sets DFRWS-2006 and nps-2009-canon2-gen6 took less than one minute. However, the time required for the test sets Simple#3 (>2.5 h), Simple#3-notn (12 min.), and DFRWS-2007 (25 min.) are significantly higher. Another thing to notice is the missing result

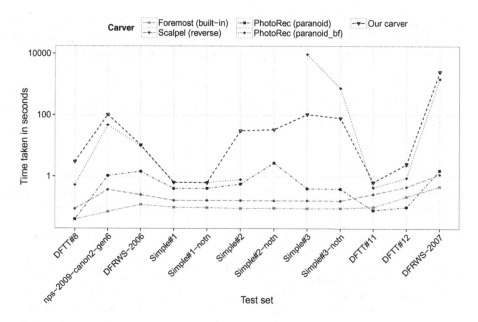

Fig. 4. Runtimes of the file carvers.

for PhotoRec (paranoid_bf) for the Simple#2-notn test set. Here, we stopped the execution after a time frame of more than 40 hours.

The trends of our carver is comparable to the execution times of PhotoRec. Again, the input size does not impact the runtime as much as the complexity of the fragmentation scenarios. Our carver is able to process all but the DFRWS-2007 test set in less than two minutes, some of them in less than one second. The DFRWS-2007 test set takes about 42 min to complete.

6 Summary and Future Work

In this paper we presented a carving approach for fragmented JPEG files. After formulating three key requirements for modern file carvers, we subsequently derived a process model for such a carver. Although we focused on fragmented JPEGs here, the general approach is suitable for different file types as well.

Afterwards we presented an algorithm to recover fragmented JPEG files following our process model. The evaluation revealed that our approach is capable of carving more files correctly than popular open source carvers, while still retaining good runtimes.

We are currently investigating techniques to further increase the correctness of our approach. For instance, exploiting features of the encoded image data might lead to better detection of corruptions and might as well increase the performance of our carver. Furthermore, a reconstruction of JPEG files which have no valid header anymore is on our agenda.

Moreover, we are evaluating the impact of parallelizing our carver. A parallelized prototype implementing our carving approach already yields promising results gaining a speedup of a factor greater than seven. In the course of this, we also consider modern graphics cards which allow massively parallel processing.

Finally, we are planning to extend our approach to further file types. Besides more image formats, the reconstruction of fragmented videos, PST files, and SQLite databases would be valuable for instance.

References

1. CCITT Recommendation T.81: Information technology - Digital compression and coding of continuous-tone still images - Requirements and guidelines. ISO/IEC 10918–1 (1992)
2. Digital Assembly - A smart choice for photo forensics. http://digital-assembly.com/products/adroit-photo-forensics/
3. Garfinkel, S.L.: Carving contiguous and fragmented files with fast object validation. Digital Inv. **4S**, 2–12 (2007)
4. Shanmugasundaram, K., Memon, N.: Automatic reassembly of document fragments via context based statistical models. In: 19th Annual Computer Security Applications Conference, pp. 152–159. IEEE Computer Society, Las Vegas (2003)
5. Pal, A., Memon, N.: The evolution of file carving. IEEE Signal Process. Mag. **26**(2), 59–71 (2009). IEEE
6. Memon, N., Pal, A.: Automated reassembly of file fragmented images using greedy algorithms. IEEE Trans. Image Process. **15**(2), 385–393 (2006)
7. Pal, A., Sencar, H.T., Memon, N.: Detecting file fragmentation point using sequential hypothesis testing. Digital Inv. **5**, 2–13 (2008)
8. Roussev, V., Garfinkel, S.L.: File classification fragment - the case for specialized approaches. In: Fourth International IEEE Workshop on Systematic Approaches to Digital Forensic Engineering, pp. 3–14. IEEE Computer Society (2009)
9. Cohen M.I.: Advanced JPEG carving. In: 1st International ICST Conference on Forensic Applications and Techniques in Telecommunications, Information and Multimedia (2008)
10. Digital Forensics Tool Testing Images. http://dftt.sourceforge.net
11. DFRWS 2006 Forensics Challenge. http://www.dfrws.org/2006/challenge/
12. DFRWS 2007 Forensics Challenge. http://www.dfrws.org/2007/challenge/
13. Digital Corpora: Disk Images. http://digitalcorpora.org/corpora/disk-images
14. Garfinkel, S.L., Farrell, P., Roussev, V., Dinolt, G.: Bringing science to digital forensics with standardized forensic corpora. Digital Inv. **6**, S2–S11 (2009)
15. Mikus, N.: An Analysis of Disc Carving Techniques. Master's thesis, Naval Postgraduate School, Monterey, California (2005)
16. Richard III, G.G., Roussev, V.: Scalpel: a frugal, high performance file carver. In: 2005 Digital Forensics Research Workshop (2005)
17. PhotoRec - CGSecurity. http://www.cgsecurity.org/wiki/PhotoRec

Taxonomy of Data Fragment Classification Techniques

Rainer Poisel[(⊠)], Marlies Rybnicek, and Simon Tjoa

St. Pölten University of Applied Sciences, St. Pölten, Austria
{rainer.poisel,marlies.rybnicek,simon.tjoa}@fhstp.ac.at
http://www.fhstp.ac.at

Abstract. Several fields of digital forensics (i.e. file carving, memory forensics, network forensics) require the reliable data type classification of digital fragments. Up to now, a multitude of research papers proposing new classification approaches have been published. Within this paper we comprehensively review existing classification approaches and classify them into categories. For each category, approaches are grouped based on shared commonalities. The major contribution of this paper is a novel taxonomy of existing data fragment classification approaches. We highlight progress made by previous work facilitating the identification of future research directions. Furthermore, the taxonomy can provide the foundation for future knowledge-based classification approaches.

Keywords: Digital forensics · Computer forensics · Data fragment · Classification · Taxonomy · File carving · Recovery · Collating

1 Introduction

The sources of digital fragments are manifold. Remnants of digital data can be found on all types of storage devices such as hard disks or USB sticks, in memory dumps, or in kind of packets in the case of computer networks [1]. Digital forensics deals with making sense of unstructured data in order to obtain evidence that can be used in court. Typical fields of application for data fragment classification are therefore general file recovery applications such as file carving, the analysis of memory or network dumps (e.g. detection of malware [2]).

The vast amount of data and the proliferation of file formats pose one of the major challenges which have to be solved by current and future developments in the field of digital forensics [3]. Garfinkel [3] concludes that these challenges will remain for the next 10 years. In order to overcome these issues, several strategies have been developed. In their work, Roussev et al. [4] propose to conduct partial analysis, so called "triage", in order to identify material that is relevant to an examination as quickly as possible. In that case, the analysis process takes place outside the actual forensics lab. Young et al. [5] follow a different approach to achieve the same objective. By using "sector hashing", investigators can automatically provide evidence about the existence of remnants from well-known

© Institute for Computer Sciences, Social Informatics and Telecommunications Engineering 2014
P. Gladyshev et al. (Eds.): ICDF2C 2013, LNICST 132, pp. 67–85, 2014.
DOI: 10.1007/978-3-319-14289-0_6

files on various types of digital storage media. In contrast to identifying fragments from known files, the topic of file fragment classification deals with the identification of the file type of known and unknown data fragments.

Up to now many research papers have been published in this field. They all aim at improving the accuracy and/or the performance of the data fragment classification process. Especially determining the file type of complex container formats such as multimedia file formats (e.g. AVI or MP4) or the Adobe PDF file format has proven difficult. Recent analysis has shown that it might be necessary to combine different approaches (e.g. determining the information entropy [6], the existence of signatures, and the fragmentation behavior) to achieve the goal of correct file type classification of digital fragments [7]. In course of this research paper we summarize our findings in the field of fragment type classification in a taxonomy.

The **main contribution** of this paper is the introduction of a novel taxonomy for approaches which can be used to classify data fragments. For each category we surveyed existing literature to clarify the structure and to facilitate the usage of the taxonomy.

In course of this paper we start with related work in Sect. 2. Section 3 describes existing approaches and classifies them into our taxonomy. Furthermore, we give a visual representation of our taxonomy. In Sect. 4 we summarize our findings and give an outlook for future developments in this field.

2 Prior and Related Work

In her publication, Beebe [8] points out that future research should address the volume and scalability issues digital forensics analysts see themselves confronted with. Only subsets of data should be selected strategically for image and further processing. This goal could be achieved by applying "Intelligent Analytical Approaches" which, exemplarily classify data feature-based without analyzing file signatures or file meta data. Furthermore, Beebe [8] mentions to apply artificial intelligence techniques to different applications (e.g. email attribution, data classification) in the field of digital forensics.

As shown later in this paper, numerous approaches that categorize input data of digital fragments into selected data type categories have been proposed. Most publications mention available solutions to perform this task in their related work section [7,9–12]. Other research papers elucidate different available data fragment type classification approaches in case, techniques are applied in order to achieve the actual research goal, e.g. recovering files from their fragments by applying the file carving approach [13,14].

Garfinkel [3] argues that some work has been conducted by the digital forensics community in order to create common schemas, file formats, and ontologies. However, to the best of our knowledge, no current research publication categorizes available fragment type classification solutions in kind of an extensible taxonomy. Several taxonomies have been published in recent digital forensics research publications. Raghavan [15] presented the current state of the art in digital forensics research in a taxonomy. The ultimate goal of his taxonomy was to summarize research directions for the future. In order to create the taxonomy, Raghavan reviewed research literature since the year 2000 and categorized developments since then into four major categories: digital forensics modelling, acquisition and modelling, examination and discovery, and digital forensics analysis. According to his findings, developments conducted in the field of fragment type classification can be found in the "examination and discovery" category. In their paper, Garfinkel et al. [16] present a taxonomy describing different types of corpora available to the digital forensics research community. By using the taxonomy the usage of available test data could e.g. be restricted to specific purposes or tailored to involved people.

3   Taxonomy of Classification Approaches

In this section, we introduce our taxonomy on data fragment classifiers. Our taxonomy aims at supporting experts from academia and industry by creating a common understanding on fragment classification within the discipline of data carving. For the development of our taxonomy we surveyed more than 100 research papers reflecting the state-of-the-art in this research area. In the following, we briefly outline the structure of our taxonomy before we present representatives of the individual classes.

In the course of our studies we identified several categories of data fragment classifiers. For our taxonomy we divided them into the following main-classes: signature-based approaches, statistical approaches, computational intelligence based approaches, approaches considering the context, and other approaches. Figure 1 schematically outlines our proposed taxonomy. The succeeding paragraphs contain more information on the structure and content of the abovementioned main-classes.

Signature-based approaches use byte-sequences for the identification of unknown file fragments by matching typical and well known byte sequences. A wide-spread application area in the context of digital forensics is to determine header and footer fragments by file signatures (e.g. File Signature Table [17]) which are often referred to as magic number. Another common field of application, where signatures are extensively used, is the identification of known files by hash values. Inspired by file hashes, recent approaches in research (referred to as "sector hashing") identify known data fragments by their hash-value. Because of the characteristics of hash functions, these approaches cannot interpret analyzed data and therefore are only valid for a fixed block size. To overcome this weakness, "similarity hashing" approaches can be applied. More details on signature-based approaches are presented in Sect. 3.1.

Statistical approaches use quantitative analysis techniques to identify fragments of given file types. Statistical properties such as the mean value, variance, binary frequency distribution (BFD), or the rate of change (ROC) are determined from fragments contained in reference data sets to obtain a model for each data type. The actual classification is then carried out by comparing (e.g. by calculating the Mahalanobis distance [18]) the fragments in question to the precalculated model.

The goal of *computational intelligence approaches* is to transform data into information after learning from a collection of given data. For data fragment and type classification, strong classifiers have to be trained. We further refine this class into supervised (if the training set consists of labeled data) and unsupervised (if patterns and structures are derived from unlabeled data) approaches. Both supervised and unsupervised machine learning algorithms are used to meet the goal of correct classification of data fragments and file type classification.

Context-considering approaches use information gained from meta-data extracted from other fragments or the transport medium. Such approaches can provide additional information necessary for the correct classification.

The category *other approaches* contains techniques which cannot be assigned to one of the other categories. A special sub-class of class are *combining approaches*.

Based on the characterization of classification approaches, the following subsections describe available data fragment classification approaches. For each classification approach we describe its properties such as availability, fields of use, its strengths and its weaknesses.

3.1   Signature-Based Approaches

Signature-based approaches are suitable to identify data fragments or their types by matching predefined byte-sequences and are applied widespreadly by different programs such as the "file" command [19] or by signature-based file carvers such as "scalpel" [20], "foremost" [21], "ReviveIT" [22], or "Photorec" [23] to determine the file type of files or file fragments e.g. by matching header/footer byte-sequences. Pal et al. [13,24] referred to this approach as "syntactical tests" because file types are identified by searching for signatures that are typical for specific file types (e.g. HTML tags in the case of HTML files). This approach has also been implemented for binary files by Al-Dahir et al. [25]. In order to determine whether subsequent blocks belong to a MP3 file, their contents have been searched for signatures of MP3 frame headers. Garfinkel et al. [26] extended the before mentioned approach by searching for additional signatures to be found in MP3 data fragments.

For the identification of known file content (and thus their type) and to reduce the amount of files that have to be processed in case of a digital forensics investigation, a library of hash-values from well-known files (e.g. files belonging to an operating system or device drivers) has been made publicly available on the Internet [27] by the National Institute of Standards and Technology (NIST). Using the National Software Reference Library (NSRL), well-known files can be excluded from the analysis process. Furthermore, using the NSRL investigators may find out which software applications are present on analyzed systems. In their work, Mead [28] examined whether file signatures contained in the NSRL produce unique results. The uniqueness of file identification has been analyzed both empirically as well as by conducting research in the field

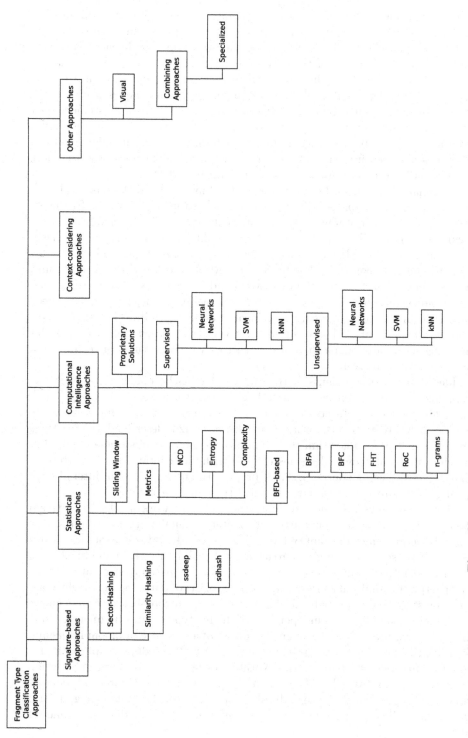

Fig. 1. Visual representation of our data fragment classification taxonomy

of attacks on hash algorithms used to generate the file signatures contained in the library. Garfinkel [29] mentions that the NSRL is part of his digital evidence research corpus. The NSRL Reference Data Set (RDS) has been extended by Kim et al. [30] to support for the exclusion of Korean software from the analysis process. Ruback [31] took this approach further by implementing data mining techniques in order to create hashsets that only contain samples from a given country or geographical region. Chawathe [32] proposes an improvement that allows for deciding on which files to consider for further analysis in the digital forensics process. His approach is based on hashing composite file signatures using a locality-sensitive hashing scheme. The more similar items are, the more it is likely that they are put into the same hash bucket [33].

A similar approach has been followed by Garfinkel [34] and Dandass et al. [35]. Instead of matching parts of data fragments hash-values of whole fragments (e.g. the sector of a storage medium) are calculated. The hash-value of data fragments' content is unique with high-probability. In case a fragment's hash-value matches a pre-calculated hash-value, its content is known and thus its file type. In [35] they conclude that both, the CRC32 and the CRC64 algorithms, produce shorter hash-values than the MD5 and the SHA1 algorithm while having a comparably low false positive rate. Collange et al. [36] proposed to speed up hash computations by using Graphical Processing Units (GPUs). Furthermore, Collange et al. [36] introduced the term "Hash-based Data Carving" for matching hash-based signatures of disk sectors with signatures of sectors from known contraband files.

Identifying data fragments by their hash-value has become a well-established technique in digital forensics research. It is referred to as "sector hashing" [5,37]. The main challenge of "sector hashing" is to store the vast amount of hashes in a suitable database. In their work, Garfinkel et al. [26] describe data structures (map-based) and an algorithm that minimize the amount of storage required to match contents of known files (master files) with files contained on an arbitrary image (image files). Experts [5,26,38] propose the usage of bloom filters before storing the hash-values in a database (a B-tree back end).

Hash algorithms are one-way functions and they work at the byte-stream level. As these functions do not attempt to interpret analyzed data, commonality can only be proven of the binary representations of digital fragments [39]. Hash values of the "sector hashing" approach are only valid for a given and fixed block size. In order to overcome this issue, Roussev [40] proposed to generate similarity fingerprints (similarity preserving hashing, SPH) of data fragments which are based on statistical improbable features. A generic, entropy-based scheme allows for the selection of features independent of the file type of data fragments. Using this approach, similarity digests finally consist of a sequence of bloom filters and their length is about 2–3 % of the input-length [39]. The "sdhash" approach proposed by Roussev [40] outperforms Kornblum's [41] "ssdeep" both in precision (94 % vs 68 %) and recall (95 % vs 55 %) [39]. Roussev and Quates [42] demonstrate the applicability of the "sdhash" approach to a large case (e.g. 1.5 TB of raw data). The purpose of using "sdhash" was to narrow down the amount of data that had to be processed from different types of media (disk images, RAM snapshots, network traces). Based on their findings on triage, the requirements for conducting real-time digital forensics and triage are discussed by Roussev et al. [4]. In order to process at a rate of approximately 120 MB/s Roussev et al. [4] state that about 120–200 computing cores are necessary. Breitinger et al. [43–47] propose advancements in the field of similarity preserving hashing (SPH). Bloom filters are used to represent fingerprints and the idea of majority voting as well as run length coding for compressing input data are applied to achieve improvements over existing approaches. As a result their new algorithm "mvHash-B" shows faster processing (20 times faster than "sdhash"), reduced hash value length (0.5 % of input length), and improvements regarding the rebustness against active manipulation of hashed contents.

3.2 Statistical Approaches

These approaches evaluate different characteristics, such as their information entropy or the binary frequency distribution (BFD) of data fragments, in order to determine their file type.

McDaniel and Heydari [48,49] introduced the concept of "fingerprints" for the file type identification of data fragments. These fingerprints contain characteristic features that are specific to each different file type. In their work [49] they propose three different algorithms: the Byte Frequency Analysis (BFA) algorithm, the Byte Frequency Cross-Correlation (BFC) algorithm and the File Header/Trailer (FHT) algorithm. The BFA algorithm determines the number of occurrences of possible byte values (0–255 inclusive) in a given sample which is referred to as the Binary Frequency Distribution (BFD). Different file formats show different characteristic patterns of BFDs which can be used to distinguish them from other file formats. For the given set of samples [49] the accuracy (true positive rate or TP-rate) of the BFA approach turned out to be 27.50 %. The BFC algorithm extends the BFA algorithm by considering differences of byte frequencies of different byte values. That way, the accuracy could be improved to 45.83 %. The FHT algorithm additionally considers signatures found in the beginning and in the end of analyzed files. That way, the accuracy could be improved to over 95 %. However, Roussev and Garfinkel [7] argue, that this approach is unsuitable for file type identification of data fragments, as usually no such signatures exist in digital artifacts. In their work, Dhanalakshmi and Chellappan [50] give an overview of various statistical measures that could be used for data fragment classification. However, the authors neither give detailed information on how to interpret these values nor do they provide the achieved classification accuracy.

Based on [48,49], Li et al. [18] propose the usage of so called "fileprints" which are based on n-grams which in turn have been derived from the BFD of block contents. Full 1-gram distributions (so called "fileprints") consist of two 256-element vectors at most: these two vectors represent the average byte frequency and their variance. The approach proposed by Li et al. [18] achieved remarkable results (nearly 100 % success rate for 20 byte fragments) for the classification of whole files. It was not intended to be used for fragments that originated from the middle of files and thus does not evaluate the classification rate of such fragments. In his thesis, Karresand [51] propose to calculate the centroid of contained 2-grams to identify the type of data fragments with high information entropy. In order to achieve good results, the centroid values are calculated for data blocks of 1 MiB and then scaled down to match fragment sizes of 4 KiB. The results for these approaches are presented in kind of "Receiver Operating Characteristic" (ROC) and in a confusion matrix. In the ROC charts, the true positive rates are lotted against the false positive rates (FP-rates) while varying the detection threshold. Different detection thresholds have been achieved by varying the centroid used. According to the confusion matrix for the 2-gram algorithm the detection rate for detecting fragments from JPEG files with no restart markers (RST) was close to perfection (99.94 % TP, 0.0573 % FP). Fragments from JPEG files containing restart markers were classified as fragments containing no restart markers with a probability of 42.668 %. In their later paper, Karresand and Shahmehri [52] build upon findings of their earlier work to reassemble fragments from JPEG files. Mayer [53] proposes approaches dealing with n-grams longer than 2 bytes. The algorithm is based on an approach to extract and summarize features as proposed by Collins [54]. In order to overcome the vast performance requirements of traditional n-gram based approaches, similar common n-grams have been collapsed into summarized n-grams where a summarized n-gram represents common features of a file type. Using this approach an overall accuracy of 66 % could be achieved for 14 file types out of 25. In order to detect executable code in network packets, Ahmed and Lhee [2] use the n-gram approach. They [2] conclude, that the order of used n-grams influences the achievable accuracy of the classification process. In their tests, 3-grams were accurate enough to identify executable contents (FP-rate: 4.69 %, false-negative or FN-rate: 2.53 %). Cao et al. [10] analyzed the influence of the number of grams evaluated on the classification accuracy. Experiments showed that best results could be achieved when selecting 300 grams per fragment classified.

Karresand and Shahmehri [55, 56] propose the "Oscar" method for file fragment classification. In contrast to [18], their approach additionally considered the Rate of Change (RoC). Karresand and Shahmehri's approach [56] is therefore well suited for the identification of JPEG fragments because they contain a large number of 0xFF 0x00 byte-pairs which have the highest RoC of almost any file type. For other file types, the approach is less suitable, due to the high false positive rate (e.g. 70 % for Windows executables).

Hall and Davis [57] proposed an algorithm based on a sliding window. The entropy and compressibility measurements were averaged and standard deviation values were calculated of each sliding window from reference files of the file types in question resulting in a profile plot. During the actual file type classification, each point of files in question sliding window values were subtracted from available profile plots ("goodness of fit"). The profile plot with the smallest difference determined the according file type. Besides subtracting sliding window values from profile plots, Hall and Davis also applied Pearson's Rank Order

Correlation in order to determine how well two data sets correlate. Results of their approaches ranged between 0 to 100 % accuracy with 20 out of 25 results having an accuracy greater than 80 % for the first approach. The second approach achieved accuracy values between 12 to 100 % with the most values having an accuracy between 50 to 75 %. The test data set consisted of 73,000 files from 454 different file types.

Approaches using several different statistical measurements are categorized as "metrics based" approaches by Roussev and Garfinkel [7]. Erbacher and Mulholland [58] differentiate between file formats by observing distributions, averages, and statistical measurements of higher momentum. In their later paper, Moody and Erbacher [59] propose a classification system that is based on their previous work [58]. It is suitable for determining the overall data type (text-based data, executable data, compressed data). Their so called "SÁDI" approach, as they call it, produces mixed results in a secondary analysis to distinguish between sub-classes of the overall data types (e.g. text, csv, or html in case of text-based data fragments).

Veenman [60] proposed to evaluate three different cluster content features in order to determine the file type of data fragments: the histogram of byte values (BFD), the information entropy of the content, and the algorithmic (or Kolmogorov) complexity. Veenman worked on a dataset of notable size (training set of 35.000 clusters and test set of 70.000 clusters) with a block size (4096 bytes) typically found when analyzing established file systems such as NTFS. Results are presented in kind of a confusion matrix. Best results could be achieved for fragments from JPEG or HTML files (true positive rate higher than 97 % for both). However, the classification results for most file types with higher information entropy were rather modest (e.g. 18 % true positive rate for ZIP files or 35 % for GIF files).

Calhoun and Coles [61] focused on the classification of data fragments without the presence of meta data. In their work, they extended the work of Veenman [60] by considering additional statistical measurements (i.e. Fisher linear discriminant, longest common subsequence). Roussev and Garfinkel [7] emphasize that Calhoun [61], with exception of the sample size, provide one of the first realistic evaluations. Results ranged between a 50 % and 95 % true positive rate for distinguishing JPEG fragments from PDF fragments (512 byte size) and between 54 % and 85 % for distinguishing JPEG fragments from GIF fragments.

Axelsson proposed to calculate the Normalized Compression Distance (NCD) [62,63] between reference blocks (blocks of known file type) and blocks in question. As a classification algorithm Axelsson implemented the k-nearest-neighbor algorithm. The class (file type) of an analyzed fragment is thus assigned based on a majority vote of the k-nearest feature vectors.

Depending on the k-value, the hit rate averaged from 36.43 % for the first nearest neighbor to 32.86 % for the 10-nearest neighbors. The hit rate of the k-nearest neighbor approach was compared to the hit rate of perfect randomness which calculates to approximately 3.5 % ($= 1/28$) as the reference corpus consisted of data fragments from 28 different file types. In their work, Poisel et al. [14] used the NCD approach for distinguishing data fragments from files with information entropy from those with low information entropy.

Savoldi et al. [64] presented an approach to discriminate between wiped and standard data fragments. Their findings are useful to detect the usage of anti-forensics measures [65] which do not leave traces on the system level (e.g. entries in the Registry, file systems, metadata, etc.). In order to determine whether byte sequences from data fragments have been produced by either hard- or software cryptographic random or pseudorandom number generators, Savoldi et al. drew on a test suite developed by the NIST [66]. In a case study with a chunk size of 4 KiB and a corpus of 104192 fragments, 97.6 % could be classified correctly in 142 min. With a chunk size of 4 MiB, the same amount of data could be processed in 15 min with an accuracy of 94.14 %.

3.3   Artificial Intelligence Approaches

Computational intelligence approaches explicitly operate in two phases: training and test. This group of file type identifiers utilize different types of classifiers from the field of computational intelligence [67] such as k-nearest neighbor (kNN), k-means, Support Vector Machines (SVM), Neural Networks (NN), or Bayesian Networks (BN).

TrID is a closed-source tool that identifies the type of files or data fragments based on their content [68]. Training of this product is accomplished by the "TrIDScan" tool [68] which creates databases that contain relevant file type definitions. However, as the TrID developer does not mention the accuracy (e.g. true-/false-positive rate, confusion matrix) or the methodology in detail it cannot be considered a forensic tool [59].

Ahmed et al. [69,70] analyzed the accuracy of popular classifiers (e.g. neural networks, kNN, SVMs, etc.) with high-frequency byte patterns (1-gram features). Byte patterns (features) were extracted from different samples of the same file type. Empirical tests showed, that using the union operation for extracted features of files from the same file type performed best when used together with the kNN classifier. In their tests, Ahmed et al. [70] identified the file type of segments of different size. With a test set consisting of 5,000 files from 10 different file types, the achieved classification accuracy for 4 kB fragments was 0 %, less than 20 %, and 85 % for JPEG, MP3, and EXE fragments respectively. In their later paper, Ahmed et al. [71] focus on the reduction of computational time necessary to identify the file type of digital fragments. They conclude that by randomly sampling file blocks and by only using a subset of features the computational time necessary could be reduced fifteen-fold.

Li et al. [72] elaborate on file type identification using SVMs. Selected features are similar to those selected by Ahmed et al. [70]. Instead of using only high frequency byte-patterns, Li et al. [72] used all 256 possible 1-grams as input to the SVM classifier. The accuracy achieved by this approach was highest ($>89\%$) when using the linear kernel for distinguishing between fragments from test sets consisting of only two different file types (JPEG from DLL, PDF, or MP3 fragments). Li et al. [72] do not address the problem of identifying fragments from one file type in a test set consisting of fragments from an arbitrary (or high) number of different file types as given in typical file type identification scenarios (e.g. file carving). Similar to Li et al. [72], Gopal et al. [73,74] utilize SVMs-classifiers (additionally to kNN-classifiers) for identifying the file type of data fragments. As features they selected 1- and 2-grams of classified fragments. They compare the accuracy of their classifiers to commercial of the shelf (COTS) applications such as libmagic [19] and TrID [68]. When applied on whole files, which had the first 512 bytes removed, both the kNN (1-gram) and the SVM (2-gram) classifiers (TP-rate >85 %) outperform COTS applications by a factor greater than 7.

In order to improve the classification accuracy of the SVM approach in dependence on searched file types, in their work, Sportiello and Zanero [75] focus on the feature selection part. Besides the BFD they identified comprehensive list of other features suitable for determining the file type of data fragments: BFD of all possible values or only part of it (e.g. ASCII range), the RoC, entropy, complexity, mean byte value, etc. Best reported results presented in a confusion matrix vary between a TP-rate of 71.1 % with a FP-rate of 21.9 % for doc files (using Entropy, and BFD and/or Complexity as features) and a 98.1 % TP-rate with a FP-rate of 3.6 % for bmp files (using the RoC as feature). Fitzgerald et al. [11] extended selected features by using additional features from the field of natural language processing (NLP): they computed the average contiguity between bytes of sequences and the longest contiguous streak of repeating bytes. Experiments conducted with a test set consisting of 512-byte long file fragments from 24 different file types showed, that a prediction accuracy of more than 40 % could be achieved (in contrast to random chance of $\frac{1}{24} \approx 4.17\%$). It is remarkable that file types from the same file type family (csv, html, java, txt, ... are all text-based) could be predicted with varying accuracy, thus making the approach especially suitable for specific file types (e.g. csv, ps, gif, sql, html, java).

Beebe et al. [76] identify several other features such as the Hamming weight, standardized kurtosis, standardized skewness, average contiguity, maximum byte streak, etc. which can be used as features by utilized SVMs. According to their evaluation, their DFRWS 2012 Forensics challenge winning open-source prototype "Sceadan" [77] achieved high classification accuracy (>80 %) for text-based and multimedia file formats (e.g. MP3, M4A, JPG, MP4).

As single file fragments may contain multiple types, Garfinkel et al. [26] refer to the process of determining the file type of data fragments as "fragment discrimination" rather than "fragment type identification". Container files may consist of unaltered files from other file types (e.g. JPEG files which are embedded in PDF files). However, Sportiello and Zanero [78] did not adopt this term. In their work they propose a "context-based classification architecture" [78] which takes into account that file blocks belonging to the same file are typically stored contiguously on various types of storage media. Sportiello and Zanero [78] improve the training set of their SVM approach. The training set for primitive file types (e.g. jpg, gif, bmp, mp3) was unchanged to their former paper [75], but the training sets of compound file types (doc, odt, exe, and pdf) consisted only of empty files, not containing any embedded files. Furthermore, they consider the context around currently classified fragments. By conducting experiments with varying context-sizes and by applying different context evaluation functions, they proved that the FP- and FN-rates were approximately 3–5 % lower than without considering the context. However, Sportiello and Zanero [78] only considered the file type of neighbor fragments rather than considering the actual fragmentation-behavior of involved storage-mechanisms (e.g. file-system characteristics) which could have improved the accuracy further.

In contrast to previous approaches presented in this chapter, Amirani et al. [79] followed the concept of unsupervised learning algorithms. With their approach, during the training phase, the Principal Component Analysis (PCA) projection matrix is calculated from the BFDs of the training set. After that an auto-associative neural network is trained with the output features obtained from the PCA using a back-propagation algorithm so that outputs are the same as inputs. Even though any classifier could have been used in the testing phase, the authors decided to use three layer Multi Layer Perceptron (MLP) [79] and SVM classifiers [80]. Experiments conducted with a small test set consisting of 200 files of each tested file type (doc, exe, gif, htm, jpg, pdf) showed that the approach gives promising results. The average total accuracy for 100 examined data fragments per file type calculated to 99.16 %, 85.5 %, and 82 % (TP-rate; running times all (<0.05 s) when applied to whole file contents, random file fragments with a size of 1500 bytes, and random file fragments with a size of 1000 bytes. However, Amirani et al. [79,80] do not mention details about the test set, which would have been of special interest for the chosen compound file formats (doc, exe, pdf).

Carter [12] identifies and locates fragments containing executable code using a KNN classifier which analyzes n-gram and semantics-based features of to-be classified fragments. Semantic features are derived from byte-streams by using a disassembler and n-grams are used in case the disassembler cannot extract semantic information from raw byte-streams. Carter's approach [12] is unsupervised as necessary features as well as the labels of the training material are determined in the first phase of the algorithm. Results showed, that the approach is resilient to certain obfuscation methods: in conducted experiments, 89 % of classified fragments could be associated with their original source.

Kattan et al. [81] propose a system that is based on Genetic Programming (GP). Intended fields of application for their classifier are spam filters and anti-virus software. It performs three major functions: segmentation, creation of fileprints, classification. Byte-series are segmented based on statistical features so that each segment consists of statistically uniform data. Fileprints are used to identify unique signatures that are characteristic for each file type. As fileprints consist of vectors that contain a series of abstracted numbers which describe the contents of files, they are referred to as GP-fingerprints. GP is then used to cluster the file fingerprints in a two-dimensional Euclidean space so that all fingerprints in the same cluster belong to the same file type. Classification of unseen data occurs then by applying the k-nearest neighbor approach. As a disadvantage the authors [81] mention, that their approach entails a long-lasting learning process and as an advantage they point out the high accuracy of their classifier (88.90 % for three file types, 70.77 % for five file types). However, training and test sets chosen by the authors are considerably small (less than 20 MiB per file type). Therefore it is hard to estimate the overall performance achievable with their approach.

3.4 Approaches Considering the Context

Approaches considering the context involve information from other fragments or information related to the transport medium (e.g. the fragmentation behavior in case of storage media). Sportiello and Zanero [78] extended the approach of using SVM classifiers with features extracted from the binary representation of data fragments by considering the file type of surrounding fragments when identifying the file type of data fragments.

Garcia and Holleboom [82,83] elaborated on an analytical model that describes the probability for the existence of micro-fragments in slack space in case the original containing blocks have been overwritten. Blacher [84] applied the generic analytical model of Garcia and Holleboom [82,83] to the NTFS. While the work of previously mentioned authors does not improve the accuracy or performance of data fragment classifiers directly, their analytical model could be of use for future applications such as sector hashing [5] or for determining filesystem related parameters in the recovery of classification [78] process. Xu et al. [85] proposed "...an adaptive method to identify the disk cluster size based on the content of sectors" [85]. Xu et al. [85] differentiate non-cluster boundaries from cluster boundaries by comparing entropy difference distributions. Unavailable or corrupted filesystem meta data complicates the recovery process of fragmented files [86]. As bigger fragments results in a better classification accuracy, this approach could be especially useful in the situation of missing filesystem meta data. Furthermore, this approach would support classification algorithms to consider correct block boundaries, thus making it easier to localize remaining signatures in analyzed data fragments.

3.5 Other Approaches

Conti et al. [87] proposed to visually represent binary structures in order to determine their file type. As part of their publication they developed a visual taxonomy that can be used by applying image processing operations. Conti et al. [88] applied their visualization approach to large binary fragments in order to speed up analysis activities of storage devices.

As there are many file formats with similar characteristics Roussev and Garfinkel [7] proposed to combine approaches from the fields of signature-based and statistical approaches. In their paper [7], they explain that their specialized approaches are suitable for identifying zlib, jpeg, and mp3 fragments with high accuracy (>98 % for fragments of 1500 bytes or more).

4   Conclusion and Outlook

Digital investigations are usually carried out to analyze traces left behind on information systems. Thus, the reconstruction of criminal activities often requires analysis of deleted, hidden or unallocated data. For this reason, the demand for reconstitute evidence from data fragments steadily increases.

Through the variety of different fragment type classification approaches it is difficult to maintain an overview. This paper addresses this issue by introducing a novel taxonomy which aggregates state-of-the-art fragment type classification approaches into the following five dimensions: (1) signature-based approaches, (2) statistical approaches, (3) trainable approaches, (4) content-aware approaches, and (5) other approaches. We further refined the individual categories into sub-categories, where appropriate. For each sub-category we performed a review of existing research and highlighted important representatives in order to provide insights how the taxonomy can be used and to facilitate new researchers to get an overview on the topic.

In the future we plan to further extend the taxonomy with new approaches. Ontologies go one step further than taxonomies by allowing to define (logical) restrictions between relations of elements [89]. Hoss and Carver [90] proposed to support digital forensics analysis by creating ontologies. Therefore, we are currently evaluating how the information of our taxonomy can be enriched to capture more detailed knowledge about fragment classification approaches. Our future research will focus on the development of an ontology which is capable of describing classification approaches in more detail. As the ontology-based representation can processed by information systems, new opportunities regarding the automated combination of classification approaches could arise.

References

1. Beverly, R., Garfinkel, S., Cardwell, G.: Forensic carving of network packet and associated data structures. Digtial Invest. **8**, 78–89 (2011)
2. Ahmed, I., Lhee, K.-S.: Classification of packet contents for malware detection. J. Comput. Virol. **7**(4), 279–295 (2011)
3. Garfinkel, S.L.: Digital forensics research: the next 10 years. Digital Invest. **7**(1), S64–S73 (2010). Proceedings of the Tenth Annual DFRWS Conference
4. Roussev, V., Quates, C., Martell, R.: Real-time digital forensics and triage. Digital Invest. **10**, 20–30 (2013)
5. Young, J., Foster, K., Garfinkel, S., Fairbanks, K.: Distinct sector hashes for target file detection. Computer **45**(12), 28–35 (2012)
6. Shannon, M.M.: Forensic relative strength scoring: ASCII and entropy scoring. Int. J. Digital Evid. **2**(4), 1–19 (2004)
7. Roussev, V., Garfinkel, S.L.: File fragment classification-the case for specialized approaches. In: Proceedings of the: Fourth International IEEE Workshop on Systematic Approaches to Digital Forensic Engineering (SADFE2009), Berkeley, CA, USA, IEEE, pp. 3–14 (2009)
8. Beebe, N.: Digital forensic research: the good, the bad and the unaddressed. In: Peterson, G., Shenoi, S. (eds.) Advances in Digital Forensics V. IFIP AICT, vol. 306, pp. 17–36. Springer, Heidelberg (2009). doi:10.1007/978-3-642-04155-6_2

9. Speirs, W.R., Cole, E.B.: Methods for categorizing input data. U.S. Patent 20 070 116 267, 05 24 (2007)
10. Cao, D., Luo, J., Yin, M., Yang, H.: Feature selection based file type identification algorithm. In: IEEE International Conference on Intelligent Computing and Intelligent Systems (ICIS'10), vol. 3, pp. 58–62. IEEE (2010)
11. Fitzgerald, S., Mathews, G., Morris, C., Zhulyn, O.: Using NLP techniques for file fragment classification. Digital Invest. **9**, S44–S49 (2012)
12. Carter, J.M.: Locating executable fragments with concordia, a scalable, semantics-based architecture. In: Proceedings of the Eighth Annual Cyber Security and Information Intelligence Research Workshop, Series of CSIIRW '13, pp. 24:1–24:4. ACM, New York (2013)
13. Pal, A., Memon, N.D.: The evolution of file carving. IEEE Sign. Process. Mag. **26**(2), 59–71 (2009)
14. Poisel, R., Tjoa, S., Tavolato, P.: Advanced file carving approaches for multimedia files. J. Wirel. Mob. Netw. Ubiquitous Comput. Dependable Appl. (JoWUA) **2**(4), 42–58 (2011)
15. Raghavan, S.: Digital forensic research: current state of the art. CSI Trans. ICT **1**(1), 91–114 (2013)
16. Garfinkel, S.L., Farrell, P., Roussev, V., Dinolt, G.: Bringing science to digital forensics with standardized forensic corpora. Digital Invest. **6**(1), S2–S11 (2009). Proceedings of the Ninth Annual DFRWS Conference
17. Kessler, G.: File signature table, May 2013. http://www.garykessler.net/library/file_sigs.html. Accessed 17 May 2013
18. Li, W., Wang, K., Stolfo, S.J., Herzog, B.: Fileprints: identifying file types by n-gram analysis. In: Proceedings of the Sixth Systems, Man and Cybernetics: Information Assurance Workshop (IAW'05), pp. 64–71. IEEE, New York (2005)
19. file(1). ftp://ftp.astron.com/pub/file/. Accessed 15 April 2013
20. Richard, G.G., Roussev, V.: Scalpel: a frugal, high performance file carver. In: Proceedings of the Fifth Annual DFRWS Conference, New Orleans, LA, pp. 1–10, August 2005. http://www.dfrws.org/2005/proceedings/richard_scalpel.pdf
21. Foremost. http://foremost.sourceforge.net/. Accessed 21 May 2013
22. ReviveIT. https://code.google.com/p/reviveit/. Accessed 21 May 2013
23. PhotoRec. http://www.cgsecurity.org/wiki/PhotoRec. Accessed 15 April 2013
24. Pal, A., Sencar, H.T., Memon, N.D.: Detecting file fragmentation point using sequential hypothesis testing. Digital Invest. **5**(Supplement 1), S2–S13 (2008)
25. Al-Dahir, O., Hua, J., Marziale, L., Nino, J., Richard III, G.G., Roussev, V.: Mp3 scalpel. Technical report, University of New Orleans (2007). http://sandbox.dfrws.org/2007/UNO/uno-submission.doc
26. Garfinkel, S.L., Nelson, A., White, D., Roussev, V.: Using purpose-built functions and block hashes to enable small block and sub-file forensics. Digital Invest. **7**(1), S13–S23 (2010). Proceedings of the Tenth Annual DFRWS Conference
27. National Institute of Standards and Technology, National Software Reference Library (NSRL). http://www.nsrl.nist.gov/. Accessed 15 April 2013
28. Mead, S.: Unique file identification in the national software reference library. Digital Invest. **3**(3), 138–150 (2006)
29. Garfinkel, S.: Lessons learned writing digital forensics tools and managing a 30TB digital evidence corpus. Digital Invest. **9**, S80–S89 (2012)
30. Kim, K., Park, S., Chang, T., Lee, C., Baek, S.: Lessons learned from the construction of a korean software reference data set for digital forensics. Digital Invest. **6**, S108–S113 (2009)

31. Ruback, M., Hoelz, B., Ralha, C.: A new approach for creating forensic hashsets. In: Peterson, G., Shenoi, S. (eds.) Advances in Digital Forensics VIII. IFIP AICT, vol. 383, pp. 83–97. Springer, Heidelberg (2012)

32. Chawathe, S.: Effective whitelisting for filesystem forensics. In: Proceedings of International Conference on Intelligence and Security Informatics (ISI 2009), IEEE, pp. 131–136 (2009)

33. Gionis, A., Indyk, P., Motwani, R.: Similarity search in high dimensions via hashing. In: Proceedings of the International Conference on Very Large Data Bases, pp. 518–529 (1999)

34. Garfinkel, S.L.: Forensic feature extraction and cross-drive analysis. Digital Invest. 3, 71–81 (2006)

35. Dandass, Y.S., Necaise, N.J., Thomas, S.R.: An empirical analysis of disk sector hashes for data carving. J. Digital Forensic Pract. 2, 95–106 (2008). http://www.informaworld.com/10.1080/15567280802050436

36. Collange, S., Dandass, Y.S., Daumas, M., Defour, D.: Using graphics processors for parallelizing hash-based data carving. In: Proceedings of the 42nd Hawaii International Conference on System Sciences, HICSS'09. IEEE, Los Alamitos, pp. 1–10 (2009)

37. Foster, K.: Using distinct sectors in media sampling and full media analysis to detect presence of documents from a corpus. Master's thesis, Naval Postgraduate School, Monterey, California, September 2012

38. Farrell, P., Garfinkel, S., White, D.: Practical applications of bloom filters to the nist rds and hard drive triage. In: 2008 Proceedings of Annual Computer Security Applications Conference, (ACSAC 2008), pp. 13–22 (2008)

39. Roussev, V.: An evaluation of forensic similarity hashes. Digital Investl. 8, S34–S41 (2011)

40. Roussev, V.: Data fingerprinting with similarity digests. In: Chow, K.P., Shenoi, S. (eds.) Advances in Digital Forensics VI. IFIP AICT, vol. 337, pp. 207–226. Springer, Heidelberg (2010)

41. Kornblum, J.: Identifying almost identical files using context triggered piecewise hashing. Digital Invest. 3, 91–97 (2006)

42. Roussev, V., Quates, C.: Content triage with similarity digests: the M57 case study. Digital Invest. 9, S60–S68 (2012)

43. Breitinger, F., Baier, H.: A Fuzzy Hashing Approach based on Random Sequences and Hamming Distance, May 2012, forthcoming issue

44. Baier, H., Breitinger, F.: Security aspects of piecewise hashing in computer forensics. In: 2011 Sixth International Conference on IT Security Incident Management and IT Forensics (IMF), pp. 21–36 (2011)

45. Breitinger, F., Stivaktakis, G., Baier, H.: FRASH: a framework to test algorithms of similarity hashing, August 2013, forthcoming issue

46. Breitinger, F., Astebøl, K.P., Baier, H., Busch, C.: mvHash-B - a new approach for similarity preserving hashing. In: 7th International Conference on IT Security Incident Management & IT Forensics (IMF), Nürnberg, March 2013

47. Breitinger, F., Petrov, K.: Reducing time cost in hashing operations. In: Proceedings of the 9th Annual IFIP WG 11.9 International Conference on Digital Forensics, Orlando, FL, USA, January 2013

48. McDaniel, M.B.: An algorithm for content-based automated file type recognition. Master's thesis, James Madison University (2001)

49. McDaniel, M., Heydari, M.H.: Content based file type detection algorithms. In: Proceedings of the 36th Annual Hawaii International Conference on System Sciences (HICSS'03) - Track 9, Washington, DC, USA, IEEE CS, p. 332.1 (2003)

50. Dhanalakshmi, R., Chellappan, C.: File format identification and information extraction. In: World Congress on Nature Biologically Inspired Computing, NaBIC, pp. 1497–1501 (2009)

51. Karresand, M.: Completing the picture: fragments and back again. Master's thesis, Linkoepings universitet (2008). http://urn.kb.se/resolve?urn=urn:nbn:se:liu: diva-11752. Accessed 22 January 2013

52. Karresand, M., Shahmehri, N.: Reassembly of fragmented JPEG images containing restart markers. In: Proceedings of the European Conference on Computer Network Defense (EC2ND), Dublin, Ireland, IEEE CS, pp. 25–32 (2008)

53. Mayer, R.C.: Filetype identification using long, summarized n-grams. Master's thesis, Naval Postgraduate School, Monterey, California, March 2011

54. Collins, M.: Ranking algorithms for named-entity extraction: boosting and the voted perceptron. In: Proceedings of the 40th Annual Meeting on Association for Computational Linguistics, Series of ACL '02. Association for Computational Linguistics, Stroudsburg, pp. 489–496 (2002)

55. Karresand, M., Shahmehri, N.: Oscar - file type identification of binary data in disk clusters and RAM pages. In: Fischer-Hübner, S., Rannenberg, K., Yngström, L., Lindskog, S. (eds.) Security and Privacy in Dynamic Environments. IFIP, vol. 201, pp. 413–424. Springer, Heidelberg (2006)

56. Karresand, M., Shahmehri, N.: File type identification of data fragments by their binary structure. In: Proceedings of the IEEE Information Assurance Workshop, pp. 140–147. IEEE, New York (2006)

57. Hall, G., Davis, W.: Sliding window measurement for file type identification. Technical report, Mantech Security and Mission Assurance (2006)

58. Erbacher, R.F., Mulholland, J.: Identification and localization of data types within large-scale file systems. In: Systematic Approaches to Digital Forensic Engineering (SADFE), pp. 55–70 (2007)

59. Moody, S.J., Erbacher, R.F.: Sádi - statistical analysis for data type identification. In: Systematic Approaches to Digital Forensic Engineering (SADFE), pp. 41–54 (2008)

60. Veenman, C.J.: Statistical disk cluster classification for file carving. In: Proceedings of the International Symposium on Information Assurance and Security (IAS'07), Manchester, UK, IEEE CS, pp. 393–398 (2007)

61. Calhoun, W.C., Coles, D.: Predicting the types of file fragments. Digital Invest. **5**, 14–20 (2008)

62. Axelsson, S.: Using normalized compression distance for classifying file fragments. In: Proceedings of the International Conference on Availability, Reliability and Security (ARES 2010), Krakow, Poland, IEEE CS, pp. 641–646 (2010)

63. Axelsson, S.: The normalised compression distance as a file fragment classifier. Digital Investl. **7**, S24–S31 (2010)

64. Savoldi, A., Piccinelli, M., Gubian, P.: A statistical method for detecting on-disk wiped areas. Digital Invest. **8**(3–4), 194–214 (2012)

65. Harris, R.: Arriving at an anti-forensics consensus: examining how to define and control the anti-forensics problem. Digital Invest. **3**, 44–49 (2006)

66. Rukhin, A., Soto, J., Nechvatal, J., Smid, M., Barker, E.: A statistical test suite for random and pseudorandom number generators for cryptographic applications. Information for the Defense Community, Technical report, May 2001. http://www.dtic.mil/cgi-bin/GetTRDoc?Location=U2&doc=GetTRDoc.pdf& AD=ADA393366

67. Ariu, D., Giacinto, G., Roli, F.: Machine learning in computer forensics (and the lessons learned from machine learning in computer security). In: Proceedings of the 4th ACM Workshop on Security and Artificial Intelligence, Series of AISec '11, pp. 99–104. ACM, New York (2011)

68. Pontello, M.: TrID - File Identifier. http://mark0.net/soft-trid-e.html. Accessed 21 April 2013

69. Ahmed, I., Lhee, K.-S., Shin, H., Hong, M.: Fast file-type identification. In: 2010 Proceedings of the ACM Symposium on Applied Computing, pp. 1601–1602. ACM, New York (2010)

70. Ahmed, I., suk Lhee, K., Shin, H., Hong, M.: Content-based file-type identification using cosine similarity and a divide-and-conquer approach. IETE Tech. Rev. **27**, 465–477 (2010). http://tr.ietejournals.org/text.asp?2010/27/6/465/67149

71. Ahmed, I., Lhee, K.-S., Shin, H.-J., Hong, M.-P.: Fast content-based file type identification. In: Peterson, G.L., Shenoi, S. (eds.) Advances in Digital Forensics VII. IFIP AICT, vol. 361, pp. 65–75. Springer, Heidelberg (2011)

72. Li, Q., Ong, A., Suganthan, P., Thing, V.: A novel support vector machine approach to high entropy data fragment classification. In: Proceedings of the South African Information Security Multi-Conference (SAISMC 2010) (2010)

73. Gopal, S., Yang, Y., Salomatin, K., Carbonell, J.: File-type identification with incomplete information. In: Proceedings of the Tenth Conference on Machine Learning and Applications, Honolulu, Hawaii, IEEE, December 2011

74. Gopal, S., Yang, Y., Salomatin, K., Carbonell, J.: Statistical learning for file-type identification. In: Proceedings of the 10th International Conference on Machine Learning and Applications and Workshops (ICMLA), vol. 1, pp. 68–73 (2011)

75. Sportiello, L., Zanero, S.: File block classification by support vector machines. In: Proceedings of the 6th International Conference on Availability, Reliability and Security (ARES 2011), pp. 307–312 (2011)

76. Beebe, N.L., Maddox, L.A., Liu, L., Sun, M.: Sceadan: using concatentated n-gram vectors for improved data/file type classification (2013, forthcoming issue)

77. Digital Forensics Research Conference (DFRWS), DFRWS 2012 Forensics Challenge (2012). http://www.dfrws.org/2012/challenge/. Accessed 5 April 2013

78. Sportiello, L., Zanero, S.: Context-based file block classification. In: Peterson, G.L., Shenoi, S. (eds.) Advances in Digital Forensics VIII. IFIP AICT, vol. 383, pp. 67–82. Springer, Heidelberg (2012)

79. Amirani, M.C., Toorani, M., Beheshti, A.A.: A new approach to content-based file type detection. In: Proceedings of the 13th IEEE Symposium on Computers and Communications (ISCC'08), pp. 1103–1108 (2008)

80. Amirani, M.C., Toorani, M., Mihandoost, S.: Feature-based type identification of file fragments. Secur. Commun. Netw. **6**(1), 115–128 (2013)

81. Kattan, A., Galván-López, E., Poli, R., O'Neill, M.: GP-fileprints: file types detection using genetic programming. In: Esparcia-Alcázar, A.I., Ekárt, A., Silva, S., Dignum, S., Uyar, A.Ş. (eds.) EuroGP 2010. LNCS, vol. 6021, pp. 134–145. Springer, Heidelberg (2010)

82. Garcia, J., Holleboom, T.: Retention of micro-fragments in cluster slack - a first model. In: First IEEE International Workshop on Information Forensics and Security, WIFS 2009, December 2009, pp. 31–35 (2009)

83. Holleboom, T., Garcia, J.: Fragment retention characteristics in slack space - analysis and measurements. In: Proceedings of the 2nd International Workshop on Security and Communication Networks (IWSCN), pp. 1–6, May 2010

84. Blacher, Z.: Cluster-slack retention characteristics: a study of the NTFS filesystem. Master's thesis, Karlstad University, Faculty of Economic Sciences, Communication and IT (2010)
85. Xu, M., Yang, H.-R., Xu, J., Xu, Y., Zheng, N.: An adaptive method to identify disk cluster size based on block content. Digital Invest. **7**(1–2), 48–55 (2010)
86. Li, Q.: Searching and extracting digital image evidence. In: Sencar, H.T., Memon, N. (eds.) Digital Image Forensics, pp. 123–153. Springer, New York (2013)
87. Conti, G., Bratus, S., Shubina, A., Lichtenberg, A., Ragsdale, R., Perez-Alemany, R., Sangster, B., Supan, M.: A visual study of primitive binary fragment types. White Paper, Black Hat USA 2010, Technical report, United States Military Academy, July 2010
88. Conti, G., Bratus, S., Shubina, A., Sangster, B., Ragsdale, R., Supan, M., Lichtenberg, A., Perez-Alemany, R.: Automated mapping of large binary objects using primitive fragment type classification. Digital Invest. **7**, S3–S12 (2010)
89. Noy, N.F., McGuinness, D.L.: Ontology development 101: a guide to creating your first ontology (2001). http://protege.stanford.edu/publications/ontology_development/ontology101-noy-mcguinness.html. Accessed 22 January 2013
90. Hoss, A., Carver, D.: Weaving ontologies to support digital forensic analysis. In: IEEE International Conference on Intelligence and Security Informatics, ISI '09, pp. 203–205, June 2009

Identifying Forensically Uninteresting Files Using a Large Corpus

Neil C. Rowe[(⊠)]

U.S. Naval Postgraduate School, CS/Rp, GE-328, 1411 Cunningham Road,
Monterey, CA 93943, USA
ncrowe@nps.edu

Abstract. For digital forensics, eliminating the uninteresting is often more critical than finding the interesting. We define "uninteresting" as containing no useful information about users of a drive, a definition which applies to most criminal investigations. Matching file hash values to those in published hash sets is the standard method, but these sets have limited coverage. This work compared nine automated methods of finding additional uninteresting files: (1) frequent hash values, (2) frequent paths, (3) frequent filename-directory pairs, (4) unusually busy times for a drive, (5) unusually busy weeks for a corpus, (6) unusually frequent file sizes, (7) membership in directories containing mostly-known files, (8) known uninteresting directories, and (9) uninteresting extensions. Tests were run on an international corpus of 83.8 million files, and after removing the 25.1 % of files with hash values in the National Software Reference Library, an additional 54.7 % were eliminated that matched two of our nine criteria, few of whose hash values were in two commercial hash sets. False negatives were estimated at 0.1 % and false positives at 19.0 %. We confirmed the generality of our methods by showing a good correlation between results obtained separately on two halves of our corpus. This work provides two kinds of results: 8.4 million hash values of uninteresting files in our own corpus, and programs for finding uninteresting files on new corpora.

Keywords: Digital forensics · Metadata · Files · Corpus · Data reduction · Hashes · Triage · Whitelists · Classification

1 Introduction

As digital forensics has grown, larger and larger corpora of drive data are available. To speed subsequent processing, it is essential in the triage process for a drive to first eliminate from consideration those files that are clearly unrelated to an investigation [8]. This can be done either by directly eliminating files to create a smaller corpus or by removing their indexing. We define as "uninteresting" those files whose contents do not provide forensically useful information about users of a drive. These are operating-system and applications-software files that do not contain user-created information, and also include common Internet-document downloads that do not provide user-discriminating information. (Metadata on uninteresting files may still be interesting, however, as in indicating time usage patterns.) This definition applies to most criminal investigations and data mining tasks but not to malware investigations. We can confirm that files are uninteresting

© Institute for Computer Sciences, Social Informatics and Telecommunications Engineering 2014
P. Gladyshev et al. (Eds.): ICDF2C 2013, LNICST 132, pp. 86–101, 2014.
DOI: 10.1007/978-3-319-14289-0_7

by opening them and inspecting them for user-created and user-discriminating data. Additional files may also be uninteresting depending on the type of investigation, such as presentation files in an investigation of accounting fraud. Uninteresting files usually comprise most of a drive, so eliminating them significantly reduces the size of the investigation. Unfortunately, uninteresting files occur in many places on a drive, and some software directories do contain interesting user files, so finding the uninteresting is not always straightforward.

Most decisions about interestingness can be made from file-directory metadata without examining the file contents. That is important because directory metadata requires roughly 0.1 % of the storage of file contents. Directory metadata can provide the name of a file, its path, its times, and its size, and this can give us a good idea of the nature of a file [1]. One additional type of data is also very useful, a hash value computed on the contents of the file, which enables recognition of identical content under different file names. Forensic tools like SleuthKit routinely extract directory metadata from drive images.

We can eliminate files whose hash values match those in published sets [5]. This has the side benefit of detecting modified files since their hash values are different [9]. However, published hash values miss many kinds of software files [11], especially files created dynamically. This paper will discuss methods for improving on this performance, in particular by correlating files on drives and across drives on a corpus. This provides both a new set of hash values and new methods for finding them.

2 Previous Work

A standard approach is to eliminate files whose hash values match those in the National Software Reference Library (NSRL) from the U.S. National Institute of Standards and Technology (NIST). The quality of the data provided in the NSRL is high [6]. However, our tests [11] found that it did not provide much coverage. Around one file of four in our international corpus appeared in the NSRL, and there were surprising gaps in coverage of well-known software. In part this is due to NIST's usual approach of purchasing software, installing it, and finding hash values for the files left on a drive. This will not find files created only during software execution, most Internet downloads, and user-specific uninteresting files like software configuration files. Furthermore, the fraction of files recognized by NSRL on a typical drive is decreasing as storage capacity increases. To fill the gap, commercial vendors like bit9.com and hashsets.com sell additional hash values beyond NSRL.

Chawathe [2] investigates the problem of recognizing uninteresting files (which they call "whitelisting") and suggests that pieces of files need to be hashed separately, a technique that considerably increases the workload. Tomazic et al. [14] details efficient methods for indexing and matching hash values found on files. Many of the issues are similar to the important problem of file deduplication for which file hashes are useful [7].

Ruback et al. [13] is the closest work to ours. They investigated methods for improving a hash set of uninteresting files by using locality and time of origin to rule out portions of the hash values in the NSRL, and their experiments showed they could reduce the size of the hash set by 51.8 % without significantly impacting performance.

They also identified as uninteresting those files occurring on multiple drives, similarly to [11]. Their experiments were based on less than one million files, a weakness since files in cyberspace are highly varied. A more serious weakness is that they used human expertise to provide guidance in indicating uninteresting files, and then trained a model. This seems risky because it may miss forensic evidence that is atypical or unanticipated. Legal requirements also often dictate that forensic evidence be complete, in which case elimination of forensic evidence must be done by better-justified methods than corpus-specific heuristic ones.

3   Experimental Setup

The experiments reported here were done with the Real Drive Corpus [3], which at the time had 3471 drives purchased as used equipment in 28 non-U.S. countries, supplemented with additional drives from our previous research. There were 83,787,499 files on these drives with 21,021,187 distinct hash values. We extracted directory metadata with SleuthKit and the Fiwalk tool. As these drives were obtained from ordinary users, we saw very little concealment or camouflage on them. Thus the hash values we derived from them should accurately represent file contents, an issue important in some forensic applications [4].

We also obtained the December 2012 version of the National Software Reference Library Reference Data Set (NSRL-RDS, www.nsrl.nist.gov), the June 2012 version of the database of hashsets.com, and an April 2013 download of the database of the Bit9 Cyber Forensics Service (www.bit9.com). Because hash values in Bit9 are encoded, we were only able to test hashes in our corpus that were also in Bit9. Basic data is given in Table 1.

Table 1. Hash set sources used in our experiments.

	NSRL RDS (NSRL), December 2012	hashsets.com (HSDC), June 2012	Subset of RDC in Bit9 cyber forensics service (BIT9), April 2013	Real drive corpus (RDC), March 2013
Number of entries	95,909,483	17,774,612	321,847	83,787,499
Number of distinct hash values	29,311,204	6,464,209	321,847	21,021,187
Fraction distinct	0.306	0.364	1.0	0.251

This work used SHA-1 hash values. They are widely available and serve as the primary key for the NSRL. MD5 hash values are also widely available, but 128 bits as opposed to 160 does not provide a sufficiently low probability, in our view, of hash collisions.

4 Methods for Finding Uninteresting Files

As explained earlier, "uninteresting" files will be defined as those that do not contain user-created or user-discriminating data. Nine methods to identify them and then their hash values were investigated as summarized in Table 2. Thresholds used by these methods were set by the experiments reported in Sect. 6.

Table 2. Summary of our methods for finding uninteresting files.

Method	Scope	Primary data focus	Secondary data focus	Considers deleted files?
HA	Corpus-wide	Hash values		Yes
PA	Corpus-wide	Full paths		Yes
BD	Corpus-wide	File name and containing directory		No
TM	Single-drive	Creation times within the minute		No
WK	Corpus-wide	Creation times within the week	Paths minus file name	No
SZ	Corpus-wide	File sizes	Full paths	No
CD	Single-drive	Full paths in a directory	File extensions	No
TD	Single-drive	Front and inside of paths		No
EX	Single-drive	File extension		No

The methods were:

- HA, frequent hashes: Files on different drives with the same hash value on their contents. Hash values that occur on 2–3 drives in a corpus suggest possibly interesting sharing of information between investigative targets. But hash values occurring often are likely to be distributions from a central source and are unlikely to be forensically interesting. An example was C2A3FCD0224B14AD6-B6A562992C3802CC711E6A2 in our corpus but not in NSRL, which occurred on five drives as Documents and Settings/Administrator/Local Settings/Temporary Internet Files/Content.IE5/ZBX73TSW/tabs[1].js, Documents and Settings/Friend/Local Settings/Temporary Internet Files/Content.IE5/0P2NOXY3/tabcontent[1].js, deleted file Documents and Settings/user/Local Settings/Temporary Internet Files/Content.IE5/KLM7E1U9/tabcontent[1].js, deleted file tabcontent[1].js with lost directory information, and deleted file E5/322B0d01. These represent information displayed with tabs in a Web browser. We set a threshold of occurrences on at least five drives for such "frequent hash values" based on our experiments. The threshold must be on number of drives, not occurrences, since copies of files on the same drive are common.
- PA, frequent paths: Files with the same full path (file name plus directories) on different drives. Frequently occurring paths are unlikely to be forensically

interesting since they are likely due to mass distribution. Such paths include different versions of the same file such as configuration files for different users or successive versions of an updated executable. An example from our corpus was restore/WINDOWS/inf/fltmgr.PNF which occurred on six drives, and none of its hash values were in NSRL. We set a threshold of at least 20 occurrences, including deleted files, for hash values based on our experiments.

- BD, frequent bottom-level directory-filename pairs: Files whose pair of the file name and the immediate directory above it occurred especially frequently. This will catch versions of the same file in different directories under different versions of an operating system or software. Examples from our corpus were WINDOWS/$NtUninstallWIC$ with 60 occurrences in our corpus and Config.Msi/4a621.rbf with 20 occurrences; neither of them had any hash values in NSRL. This will also catch many hidden files in common directories like the defaults "." and "..". We set a threshold of at least five undeleted occurrences based on our experiments.

- TM, clustered creation times: Files with the same creation time within a short period as that of many other files on the same drive. Such time clusters suggest automated copying from an external source, particularly if the rate of creation exceeded human limits. An example from our corpus were seven files created on one drive within one second under directory Program Files/Adobe/Adobe Flash CS3/adobe_epic/personalization: pl_PL, pl_PL/., pl_PL/.., pt_BR, pt_BR/., pt_BR/.., and pt_PT. All were 56 bytes, and two hash values were not in NSRL. Creation times are more useful than access and modification times because they indicate installation. We set a threshold of at least 50 files created within the same minute based on our experiments.

- WK, busy weeks: Files created unusually frequently in particular weeks across drives, which suggest software updates. A period of a week is appropriate since it takes several days for most users to connect to a site and get an update. Figure 1 shows a typical distribution of times by week in our corpus, showing some sharp peaks. We count file creations per week and find "busy" weeks having at least five times the average amount of creations, of which there were 116 in our corpus. Then we find "busy" directories (full path minus the file name) in the busy weeks, those whose frequency of creation was at least 100 times greater than their average creation time per week. Again, thresholds were set by experiments; the 100 was necessary to discriminate against user copying of file directories. We then collect the hash values for those busy directories on those busy days as proposed uninteresting file content.

- SZ, frequent sizes: Files with the same size and extension. This enables recognizing fixed-size formats with different contents, as certain kinds of log records. However, to reduce false matches we apply the additional criterion that the extension must occur unusually often in all files of that size. Examples from our corpus were all 31 files of size 512 in directory System/Mail/00100000_S, and 8 files of size 2585 in directory Program Files/Sun/JavaDB/docs/html/tools/ctoolsijcomref with extension html, none of which had hash values in published hash sets. Based on experiments, we set a threshold of occurrences of at least five drives where the occurrence rate of the file extension in everything with that size was at least ten standard deviations above the average rate in the corpus.

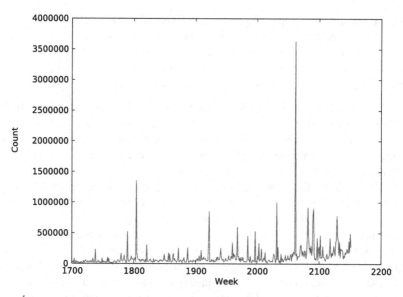

Fig. 1. Histogram of a sample range of creation times in our corpus.

- Small files (included in SZ): Files less than a minimum size are unlikely to contain forensically useful information. For example, there were 4,223,667 files of zero length in the corpus. We set a minimum of 5 bytes from experiments.
- CD, contextually uninteresting files: Directories in which more than a certain fraction of files were already identified as uninteresting by other methods suggest that the rest are also uninteresting by "contagion". An example from our corpus is directory Program Files/Yahoo!/Messenger/skins/Purple/images and previously unclassified files ".", "..", bg_hover.png, _GLH0307.TMP, and bg_selected.png. We set a threshold of 50 % known hash values in directories based on experiments. This method can be used to bootstrap better performance on each run on a corpus.
- TD, files in known uninteresting top-level or mid-level directories: We manually compiled lists from study of the files remaining after filtering on the other criteria mentioned here, and obtained 5749 top-level and 337 mid-level directories. Example top-level directories were APPS/Symantec AntiVirus, Documents and Settings/Admin/Templates, FOUND.029, Program Files (x86)/AutoCAD 2008, WINDOWS, and system/install; example mid-level directories were /Help/ and /Default User/. It is important not to exclude all applications directories (Program Files, Applications, etc.) because some software keeps user files there.
- DR, directory records: Default directory records such as "WINNT/Cursors/." as a path. These were excluded only in the final phase of processing (Sect. 7) since they can help establish directory and time trends.
- EX, files with known uninteresting extensions: Some extensions are exclusively associated with operating systems and software, such as exe, mui, log, dat, bin, and config. We used a classification of 5802 file extensions that we are developing [11] that maps extensions to 45 categories. The categories we labeled as nonuser and

thus uninteresting were operating-system, graphics, database, help, executable, disk image, XML, geography, copies, dictionary, query, integer, index, configuration, installs and updates, security, known malicious, games, engineering, science, signals, and virtual machines. Some investigations may want to shorten this list. Files with no extensions and extensions with more than one category were excluded.

36.7 % of the files in our corpus were identified by SleuthKit as deleted (unallocated). We excluded these as sources of new hash values with two exceptions because [11] found that once files are marked for deletion, their metadata can become corrupted. Directories were often missing for deleted files, and we even saw inconsistencies in the sizes of reported by SleuthKit for files with the same hash value, which should be virtually impossible. However, the same hash value or the same path appearing repeatedly is unlikely to be a coincidence even if they were all deleted, so we ignored deletion status in collecting frequent hash values and frequent paths.

These methods can be deceived into marking interesting files as uninteresting when a user engages in deliberate camouflage. For instance, a user could put copies of an interesting file on multiple drives to qualify for the HA, PA, BD, WK, or SZ sets; copy sensitive files to innocuous directories to qualify for TD, CD, or BD sets; and change the file extension to qualify for EX. But such actions can be detected as anomalous usage and found by statistical tests as described in [12].

5 Coverage and Redundancy of the Hash Sets

We assessed the coverage, redundancy, and accuracy of the methods. To analyze redundancy we computed the sizes of the intersections of the hash sets. Table 3 provides a summary of intersection counts for the hash sets for the 78,240,703 nonempty hash values of the 83,787,499 files in our corpus. Here and in Table 4 the row and column codes are:

- NS (only in Table 3): hashes in the NSRL RDS
- HS (only in Table 4): hashes in hashsets.com
- B9 (only in Table 4): hashes in our corpus that were also in the Bit9 database
- HA (only in Table 3): frequent hashes in our corpus
- PA: hashes of frequent paths
- BD: hashes of frequent immediate-directory plus filename pairs
- TM: hashes of files with time-clustered creation times
- WK: hashes of files created in unusually busy weeks
- SZ: hashes of files with unusually frequent sizes, plus files under 6 bytes
- CD: hashes of files in directories with mostly known-uninteresting files
- TD: hashes of files with top-level or mid-level uninteresting directories
- EX: hashes of files with non-user extensions.

We inspected a sample of hash values returned for each method and concluded that the NS hashes (NSRL RDS) and HA hashes (occurring on at least five drives in our corpus) were highly reliable since, in samples of size 200, we saw no interesting files incorrectly included. This makes sense for the NSRL hashes because the collection technique of NSRL (buying the software and inspecting its files) is a highly reliable at identifying uninteresting files. Similarly, the diversity of our corpus means that any file that occurs on at least five drives is highly likely to be a distributed sharable resource and thus uninteresting. So we recalculated our counts excluding NS and HA as shown in Table 4. Excluding NSRL hashes reduced the number of distinct hashes from the corpus from 21,021,187 to 19,735,599 (a reduction of 6.1 %) and the number of files from 78,240,703 to 62,774,546 (a reduction of 19.8 %). Excluding hash values occurring on at least five different drives in the corpus reduced the number of distinct hashes further to 19,343,552 (a further reduction of 1.6 %) and the number of files to 43,909,093 (a significant further reduction of 30.1 %). The remaining hash sets had significant amounts of overlap, supporting their validity for file exclusion.

Table 3. Number of files in the RDC corpus in March 2013 (in millions) that have hashes in each of two hash sets.

	NS	HA	PA	BD	TM	WK	SZ	CD	TD	EX
NS	21.0	18.9	18.4	17.8	20.2	15.4	3.8	20.7	20.0	17.2
HA	18.9	33.1	30.0	29.0	31.5	25.1	5.6	31.9	31.4	26.8
PA	18.4	30.0	35.4	33.1	33.5	26.5	6.6	33.8	34.2	26.8
BD	17.8	29.0	33.1	35.8	33.5	25.3	7.0	33.2	34.1	26.4
TM	20.2	31.5	33.5	33.5	47.3	27.5	9.2	38.3	41.0	32.4
WK	15.4	25.1	26.5	25.3	27.5	27.9	5.1	27.0	27.2	21.8
SZ	3.8	5.6	6.6	7.0	9.2	5.1	10.5	7.7	8.9	6.2
CD	20.7	31.9	33.8	33.2	38.3	27.0	7.7	40.9	38.1	30.2
TD	20.0	31.4	34.2	34.1	41.0	27.2	8.9	38.1	45.6	32.2
EX	17.2	26.8	26.8	26.4	32.4	21.8	6.2	30.2	32.2	35.7

Table 4. Number of files in the RDC corpus in March 2013 (in millions) that have hashes in each of two hash sets, after excluding NS (the National Software Reference Library) and HA (hashes occurring on at least five drives).

	HS	B9	PA	BD	TM	WK	SZ	CD	TD	EX
HS	0.9	0.0	0.3	0.0	0.7	0.2	0.1	0.9	0.9	0.1
B9	0.0	0.5	0.0	0.0	0.3	0.0	0.0	0.2	0.3	0.0
PA	0.3	0.0	5.0	4.3	4.0	1.5	1.6	4.7	5.0	1.5
BD	0.0	0.0	4.3	6.2	4.8	1.3	2.2	5.8	6.1	1.7
TM	0.7	0.3	4.0	4.8	14.0	2.3	3.5	12.1	12.1	5.1
WK	0.2	0.0	1.5	1.3	2.3	2.5	0.8	2.3	2.4	0.5
SZ	0.1	0.0	1.6	2.2	3.5	0.8	4.5	3.9	4.0	1.2
CD	0.9	0.2	4.7	5.8	12.1	2.3	3.9	15.5	14.7	6.2
TD	0.9	0.3	5.0	6.1	12.1	2.4	4.0	14.7	16.6	6.2
EX	0.1	0.0	1.5	1.7	5.1	0.5	1.2	6.2	6.2	7.1

To compare the coverage of the published hash sets and our corpus, we classified the file extensions of their associated files using our aforementioned taxonomy (Table 5). We did this for the four primary sources we used; the last column will be explained in Sect. 7. We used a sample of 30 million records of the Bit9 Cyber Forensics Service, not just those matching our corpus. These counts are on files and not hashes, so the same hash was weighted by how often it occurred. "None" means files with no extension and "miscellaneous" includes ten lesser categories as well as extensions occurring less than 200 times in our corpus. The statistics confirm that all these hash sets had broad coverage of a variety of file types, not just executables. That suggests that their coverage gaps are due to difficulties in covering all software rather than in covering all file types.

Table 5. Distribution of files by extension type for five hash sets.

Type of extension	NSRL RDS	Hashsets. com	Bit9 sample	Real data corpus	Final RDC filtering
None	10.56 %	13.78 %	9.62 %	21.85 %	10.21 %
Oper. system	3.74 %	4.55 %	1.53 %	6.89 %	0.00 %
Graphics	16.23 %	13.64 %	13.86 %	13.03 %	13.14 %
Camera images	3.14 %	0.80 %	2.36 %	6.13 %	22.11 %
Temporaries	0.08 %	0.02 %	0.06 %	2.20 %	4.25 %
Web	8.25 %	8.83 %	17.56 %	4.45 %	6.82 %
Misc. documents	1.71 %	1.74 %	1.46 %	2.00 %	4.69 %
MS Word	0.17 %	0.03 %	0.16 %	0.71 %	2.98 %
Presentations	0.26 %	0.02 %	0.07 %	0.13 %	0.51 %
Database	0.29 %	0.18 %	0.21 %	0.73 %	1.04 %
Other MS Office	0.09 %	0.11 %	0.05 %	0.21 %	0.15 %
Spreadsheets	0.43 %	0.38 %	0.14 %	0.46 %	1.60 %
Email	0.11 %	0.03 %	0.09 %	0.12 %	0.33 %
Links	0.01 %	0.04 %	0.05 %	1.08 %	2.00 %
Compressed	1.33 %	7.05 %	2.22 %	0.65 %	1.23 %
Help	0.94 %	0.28 %	0.51 %	1.01 %	0.00 %
Audio	1.47 %	0.38 %	0.71 %	3.21 %	4.42 %
Video	0.20 %	0.04 %	0.16 %	0.35 %	0.79 %
Program source	7.16 %	11.44 %	8.98 %	2.20 %	4.11 %
Executables	18.70 %	14.51 %	18.59 %	12.90 %	0.00 %
Disk images	0.78 %	1.87 %	1.40 %	1.15 %	0.52 %
XML	0.94 %	2.17 %	1.24 %	1.00 %	0.61 %
Logs	0.04 %	0.05 %	0.06 %	0.76 %	2.29 %
Geographic	0.25 %	0.05 %	0.09 %	0.18 %	0.20 %

(Continued)

Table 5. (*Continued*)

Type of extension	NSRL RDS	Hashsets. com	Bit9 sample	Real data corpus	Final RDC filtering
Copies	0.09 %	0.04 %	0.28 %	0.40 %	0.33 %
Integers	1.03 %	1.80 %	0.83 %	2.17 %	4.59 %
Configuration	5.32 %	5.10 %	3.66 %	5.14 %	2.35 %
Update	0.06 %	0.01 %	0.07 %	0.16 %	0.00 %
Security	0.22 %	0.20 %	0.13 %	0.33 %	0.26 %
Malicious	0.01 %	0.01 %	0.00 %	0.02 %	0.00 %
Games	2.44 %	1.70 %	1.64 %	3.24 %	0.00 %
Sci. and eng.	0.85 %	0.03 %	0.51 %	0.21 %	0.35 %
Virtual machine	0.12 %	0.04 %	0.09 %	0.08 %	0.08 %
Multipurpose	2.79 %	3.76 %	3.48 %	2.46 %	5.64 %
Miscellaneous	9.89 %	5.32 %	7.55 %	2.41 %	2.21 %

6 Accuracy of the New Methods of Finding Uninteresting Hash Values

These methods can err in identifying interesting hash values as uninteresting for several reasons:

- PA, frequent paths: Some configuration files can give clues about a user although they appear frequently in the corpus.
- BD, frequent bottom-level directories: A directory-filename pair may occur frequently if its words are common, such as pics/portrait.jpg, yet still be interesting.
- TM, clustered creation times: During an automated software download, the user may be working on their own files so that creation times are interspersed.
- WK, busy weeks: Users may also be working during busy weeks for software updates.
- SZ, frequent sizes: A user file may accidentally be the same size as a standard size used by an application. Also, the standard size may reflect a format imposed on a user, as with camera formats.
- CD, contextually uninteresting files: Users may put files in a directory that is mostly created by software.
- TD, files with known uninteresting top-level or mid-level directories: Users may copy executables to their own directories for backup.
- EX, files with known uninteresting extensions: Users may assign their own extensions to files.

To investigate how often these conditions occurred, we took random samples of 200 files produced by each method, 1600 in all. We then inspected the full paths, and did Web research as necessary, to determine which files were user-related or otherwise potentially interesting in an investigation (Table 6). A few files were unclear in function so we counted them at half weight.

Table 6. Testing the new hash sets for uninteresting files.

New hash set	Number of hash values not in any other set	Fraction of files in the set that were actually interesting
PA, frequent paths	4,050	.010
BD, frequent bottom-level directories	57,739	.005
TM, clustered creation times	1,739,083	.020
WK, busy weeks	1,316,465	.000
SZ, frequent sizes	159,229	.070
CD, contextually uninteresting	23,527	.025
TD, known uninteresting top-level or mid-level directories	434,840	.005
EX, known uninteresting extensions	457,558	.015

Example files judged as interesting were system/apps/NaturalRecorder/Message14678.amr (user data), WINDOWS/Recent/p-0.dwg (72).lnk (user link), BILDER/Freunde Mohaa/Engelsfeuer/PIC_0512.JPG (user picture), and Documents and Settings/hariom/Local Settings/Temporary Internet Files/Content.IE5/STIVWXYZ/actors [1].jpg (user download). Examples judged as uninteresting were WINDOWS/system32/localsec.dll (operating system), WINDOWS/Fonts/CONSOLAZ.TTF (font file), System Volume Information/_restore{8907E5C6-24EC-4C3A-BC96-8740D90875 EC}/RP22/A0320774.exe (system backup), Program Files/Condition Zero/valve/gfx/env/blackbk.tga (game graphics), Shortcut to GlobeSpan Dial-Up PPP Connection.lnk (frequent link), program files/Timbuktu Pro/Help/art/icon_exchange.gif (help graphics), and Temp/crt4349.tmp (display temporary).

The second column of Table 6 indicates the uniqueness of the method and the third column indicates the accuracy. The calculations for the third column were used to set thresholds for the methods, aiming at better than a 2 % error rate; unfortunately, the SZ (size) rate cannot be easily adjusted. Such error rates could be acceptable in preliminary investigation of a corpus, but might be unacceptable in legal proceedings because of the possibility of incorrectly excluding key evidence in a case. That suggests that we use only hashes that appear in results of at least K methods for some integer K (Table 7). K = 2 will give an estimated maximum error rate of 0.00175 when combining SZ and CD since the methods are relatively independent (and confirmed by experiments to be described in Sect. 7). So eliminating files with hash values appearing in at least two of our remaining eight methods, we obtained 11,181,072 hash values and 34,190,203 remaining files, 40.8 % of the original set of files, without any recourse to commercial hash sets.

Ruback et al. [13] suggested another criterion for interesting files, whether their "libmagic" or header analysis is inconsistent with their file extension, because then they may be camouflaged. SleuthKit/Fiwalk can provide libmagic strings for the files it analyzes. We manually defined a mapping on the 2304 distinct libmagic strings

Table 7. Number of files and hashes remaining after filtering out files having a given number of matches to our eight new hash sets.

Number of matches to hash sets required	0	1	2	3	4	5	6	7	8
Logarithm of number of files matched	18.1	17.5	17.0	16.8	16.5	16.3	16.0	15.5	13.5
Logarithm of number of distinct hash values matched	16.8	16.1	15.9	15.5	15.0	14.6	14.0	12.2	9.5

generated for our corpus to our set of 45 file-extension groups, so for instance "GIF Image Data" was mapped to "graphics extension". We compared the extension groups for the files in our corpus with the assigned libmagic extension groups. Of the 17,814,041 file records having libmagic values (since it was only added to Fiwalk recently), only 27.8 % groups matched between extensions and libmagic. A significant number of files do not have extensions, libmagic strings are insufficiently detailed about configuration files, and some records indicated outright errors in either extensions or libmagic. We conclude that libmagic classifications are insufficiently reliable as a way to detect camouflage. However, this subject needs further investigation.

7 Final Hash and File Eliminations

Files for which SleuthKit did not find hash values, 16.2 % of our remaining files, can also be eliminated if they match some of our criteria. Missing hash values occur for deleted files with incomplete metadata. For these we applied the BD (bottom-directory), TD (top-directory), and EX (extension) criteria to individual file records, and eliminated files matching at least two criteria. 2.5 million files matched BD, 10.0 million matched TD, 1109 matched EX, and 5.9 million matched two of the three criteria. For deleted files having just a file name, we inferred a path when it was unambiguous in 0.28 million cases, correcting underscores for missing characters if necessary. For instance, file name REXXUTIL.DL_ was inferred to have path OS2/DLL/REXXUTIL.DLL since only one path in our corpus had that file name after correcting the underscore.

We also eliminated in the final processing 2.9 million records of default directory files (the DR criterion), 4.1 million files smaller than 6 bytes, and executables, and files with extensions strongly suggesting uninterestingness: executables, support for the operating system, installations, updates, help, hardware-related files, and games.

This reduced the number of potentially interesting files to 16,923,937, 20.2 % of the original set of files. (If we allow matching to only one of the three criteria and not just to files without hash values, we reduce the number of files to 11.1 % of the original set, but increase the error rate as estimated in the last section.) 83.9 % of the remaining files were deleted (they are ignored by most methods) and many could also be eliminated in investigations. To assess correctness, we took a random sample of 1000 files excluded in all the phases and found that only one file was possibly incorrectly excluded, a flowchart that had been downloaded with a cluster of other files. Thus we estimate the false negative rate at 0.1 %. We also took a random sample of 1000 of the files identified as interesting and found that 19.0 % of them were uninteresting false positives, not too large a number.

The last column of Table 5 gives the distribution of extension types for the remaining "interesting" files. Filtering increased the fraction of camera images, temporaries, Word documents, presentations, spreadsheets, and integer extensions as expected, but did not exclude all non-user files due to missing metadata.

As mentioned earlier, we also tested two commercial hashsets, the full database of Hashsets.com and a sample of the database of Bit9. Hashsets.com matched hashes on 5,906 of the remaining hashes, an unimpressive 0.06 %. We confirmed matches to the Bit9 database for 79,067 of the remaining hashes; we had difficulty identifying which actually matched, but we estimate Bit9 had hash codes for about 154,000 or 1.56 % of the remainder, 0.73 % of the original number of hash values. (Bit9 stores hashes in a proprietary encoding, so to guess which hashes it matched we used the file name and size returned by Bit9 and matched them to our own data, then extrapolated the number.) So Bit9 is also not much help in reducing files beyond our own methods, something important to know since it is costly.

8   Generality of the Hashes Found Over Corpora

A criticism made of some hash-value collections is that their values will rarely occur again. So an important test for our proposed new "uninteresting" hash values is to compare those acquired from different drives. For this we split the corpus into two pieces C1 and C2, roughly drives processed before 2012 and those processed in 2012. We extracted uninteresting hash values using our methods for both separately, and then compared them. Table 8 shows the results.

This table provides two kinds of indicators of the generality of a hash-obtaining method. One is the average of the second and third columns, which indicates the overlap between the hash sets. On this SZ is the weakest method and WK is second weakest, which makes sense because these methods seek clustered downloads and some clusters are forensically interesting. Another indicator is the ratios of column 7 to column 4 and column 6 to column 5, which indicate the degree to which the hash values found generalize from a training set to a test set. The average for the above data was 0.789 for the average of column 7 to column 4, and 0.938 for the average of column 6 to column 5, which indicates a good degree of generality. No methods were unusually poor on the second indicator.

Table 8. Statistical comparison of hashes derived from partition of our corpus into two halves, where HA = hashes, PA = paths, TM = time, SZ = size, BD = bottom-level directory, CD = directory context, TD = top-level directory, EX = extension.

Method of obtaining new hash values	Fraction of values found for C1 also found for C2	Fraction of values found for C2 also found for C1	Fraction of all hash values for C1 identified by method using C1	Fraction of all hash values for C2 identified by method using C2	Fraction of all hash values for C2 identified by method using C1	Fraction of all hash values for C1 identified by method using C2
HA	.717	.597	.438	.355	.344	.389
PA	.661	.458	.399	.291	.299	.312
TM	.529	.365	.668	.493	.430	.477
WK	.457	.234	.445	.303	.358	.323
SZ	.339	.246	.196	.187	.157	.145
BD	.583	.484	.474	.384	.350	.406
CD	.640	.486	.558	.447	.411	.467
TD	.553	.436	.627	.485	.419	.474
EX	.603	.439	.497	.373	.338	.397

9   Proposed File-Elimination Protocol

We suggest then the following protocol for eliminating uninteresting files from a corpus:

1. Run methods HA (hashes), PA (paths), WK (weeks), SZ (sizes), and BD (bottom-level directories) to generate hash sets of candidate uninteresting files on the full corpus to see trends.
2. Eliminate all files whose hash values are in NSRL, our list at digitalcorpora.org, and any other confirmed "uninteresting" lists available.
3. On the remaining files, run methods TM (times), CD (directory context), TD (top-level directories), and EX (extensions) to generate further hash sets of candidate uninteresting files.
4. Find hash values that occur in at least two candidate hash sets, and eliminate files from the corpus with those hash values.
5. Eliminate files without hash values in the remainder from the corpus that match on two of the three criteria BD, TD, and EX, are directories, are small files, and have strongly-uninteresting extensions.
6. Save the list of eliminated hash codes for bootstrapping with future drives in step 2.

For the final run on our own corpus with additional new data, eliminating NSRL hashes reduced the number of files by 25.1 %, eliminating hashes found by the nine methods of this paper reduced the number by an additional 37.1 %, and eliminating files by the remaining criteria reduced the number by an additional 21.6 %, resulting in

20.2 % of the original number of files. The disadvantage of this approach is that does require additional computation on a corpus before starting to investigate, not just matching to hash lists; the advantage is that if finds considerably more files to eliminate.

10 Conclusions

Although uninterestingness of a file is a subjective concept, most forensic investigators have a precise definition that is usually based whether a file contains user-created or user-discriminating information. It appears that relatively simple methods can be used to automate this intuition, and can eliminate considerable numbers of such uninteresting files beyond just looking them up in the NSRL hash library. It also appears that commercial hash sets are of limited additional value to most forensic investigations if the methods proposed here are used. Our methods can eliminate files unique to a drive, but also will provide hashes that should be useful for other corpora. Investigators can choose which methods to use based on their investigative targets, can set thresholds based on their tolerance for error, and can choose to eliminate further files based on time and locale as in [13]. We have already published some of our common-hash and common-path data for free download on digitalcorpora.org and will be publishing more soon based on this current work. Future work will extend this work to hashes on portions of files as in [10].

Acknowledgements. Riqui Schwamm assisted with the experiments, and Simson Garfinkel provided the corpus. The views expressed are those of the author and do not represent those of the U.S. Government.

References

1. Agrawal, N., Bolosky, W., Douceur, J., Lorch, J.: A five-year study of file-system metadata. ACM Trans. Storage **3**(3), 9:1–9:32 (2007)
2. Chawathe, S.: Fast fingerprinting for file-system forensics. In: Proceedings of the IEEE Conference on Technologies for Homeland Security, pp. 585–590 (2012)
3. Garfinkel, S., Farrell, P., Roussev, V., Dinolt, G.: Bringing science to digital forensics with standardized forensic corpora. Digit. Invest. **6**, S2–S11 (2009)
4. Ke, H.-J., Wang, S.-J., Liu, J., Goyal, D.: Hash-algorithms output for digital evidence in computer forensics. In: Proceedings of the International Conference on Broadband and Wireless Computing, Communication and Applications (2011)
5. Kornblum, J.: Auditing hash sets: lessons learned from jurassic park. J. Digit. Forensic Pract. **2**(3), 108–112 (2008)
6. Mead, S.: Unique file identification in the national software reference library. Digit. Invest. **3**(3), 138–150 (2006)
7. Panse, F., Van Keulen, M., Ritter, N.: Indeterministic handling of uncertain decision in deduplication. ACM J. Data Inf. Qual. **4**(2), 9 (2013)
8. Pearson, S.: Digital Triage Forensics: Processing the Digital Crime Scene. Syngress, New York (2010)

9. Pennington, A., Linwood, J., Bucy, J., Strunk, J., Ganger, G.: Storage-based intrusion detection. ACM Trans. Inf. Syst. Secur. **13**(4), 30 (2010)
10. Roussev, V.: Managing terabyte-scale investigations with similarity digests. In: Advances in Digital Forensics VIII, IFIP Advances in Information and Communication Technology vol. 383, pp. 19–34. Pretoria SA (2012)
11. Rowe, N.: Testing the national software reference library. Digit. Invest. **9S**, S131–S138 (2012). (Proc. Digital Forensics Research Workshop 2012, Washington, DC, August)
12. Rowe, N., Garfinkel, S.: Finding suspicious activity on computer systems. In: Proceedings of the 11th European Conference on Information Warfare and Security. Laval, France (2012)
13. Ruback, M., Hoelz, B., Ralha, C.: A new approach to creating forensic hashsets. In: Advances in Digital Forensics VIII, IFIP Advances in Information and Communication Technology vol. 383, pp. 83–97. Pretoria SA (2012)
14. Tomazic, S., Pavlovic, V., Milovanovic, J., Sodnik, J., Kos, A., Stancin, S., Milutinovic, V.: Fast file existence checking in archiving systems. ACM Trans. Storage **7**(1), 2 (2011)

FaceHash: Face Detection and Robust Hashing

Martin Steinebach[✉], Huajian Liu, and York Yannikos

Fraunhofer SIT, Rheinstrasse 75, 642955 Darmstadt, Germany
martin.steinebach@sit.fraunhofer.de

Abstract. In this paper, we introduce a concept to counter the current weakness of robust hashing with respect to cropping. We combine face detectors and robust hashing. By doing so, the detected faces become a subarea of the overall image which always can be found as long as cropping of the image does not remove the faces. As the face detection is prone to a drift effect altering size and position of the detected face, further mechanisms are needed for robust hashing. We show how face segmentation utilizing blob algorithms can be used to implement a face-based cropping robust hash algorithm.

Keywords: Robust image hash · Face detection · Blob detection

1 Motivation

Today we see a rapid increase of hard disk drive capacities, which allows storing a huge amount of data, including media files. This leads to sometimes massive collections of files, especially in the case of images. These can be private or third party images from the Internet. The content of the images goes from legal personal, natural to synthetic but also to illegal (e.g. child pornographic).

If an investigation of such a collection occurs, manual scanning and classification parts of these collections is very time consuming, ethically questionable and practically unfeasible. In digital forensics, searching in over one terabyte of images for evidence against an offender is common and needs to be very fast and accurate.

This problem is addressed by several methods in image forensics, such as content classification and image identification [1]. One common approach is the use of cryptographic or robust hashing. While robust hashing is resistant against many operations, many of the known methods only take the whole picture into account. To prevent evidence from being detected, offenders can crop out regions of interests of their illegal image and save them, removing unwanted environmental parts of the image. Then, the above methods cannot recognize these saved parts, since the rest of the image is absent. The result is missing evidence against the offenders.

We introduce a new approach named FH (Face Hash), which aims at solving this problem. FH contains a combination of digital forensics and computer vision methods. The focus region of this approach is the face. Identifying and distinguishing faces is an ability every human possesses and masters with growing age over time [2]. By looking at a picture every human detects known people, recognizes and judges about their emotional reaction at that moment. Hence, if someone modifies an image by cropping, the region of interest not to be removed will contain the face.

© Institute for Computer Sciences, Social Informatics and Telecommunications Engineering 2014
P. Gladyshev et al. (Eds.): ICDF2C 2013, LNICST 132, pp. 102–115, 2014.
DOI: 10.1007/978-3-319-14289-0_8

Fig. 1. Face detection and robust hashing (© http://www.cheerleader-frankfurt.de/galacticdancers)

Also in child pornography face expressions are an important part, which the offender uses as proof of their entertainment to normalize the process of collecting [3]. An offender would therefore keep the face as part of his region of interest from the image. Therefore the FH approach uses a combination of face detection and image identification methods to quickly recognize illegal images. The result would be a manageable set of binary hash values (face hashes), which describe the victims or offenders within an illegal content in specific images. Comparing those face hashes against others from a police database, enables classifying them as legal or known illegal.

2 Robust Hashing

There are many approaches in the literature suggesting robust hash functions. They mainly compete with respect to robustness against various attacks like lossy compression, scaling, distortion, cropping or rotation. For our forensic application we analyzed their computational complexity and found most of them using complex transformations like DCT or wavelet. While these operations help to survive many attacks and increase the robustness, they slow down the hashing process.

Therefore a comparison of hash algorithms with respect to their robustness and complexity is important. In [5] the authors show that the robustness of the Block Mean Value algorithm featuring the lowest complexity compares well with those of higher complexity. An optimization of this algorithm based on block mean computation improves robustness, speed and error rates [6].

2.1 Block Mean Value Hash

In 2006, Yang et al. proposed a block mean value based perceptual image hash function in [4]. Four slightly different methods are proposed. The latter two additionally incorporate an image rotation operation to enhance robustness against rotation attacks. This increases the computational complexity of the latter two methods. Due to our low complexity requirement we focus on the simplest method.

This method is described as follows:

1. Convert the image to grey scale and normalize the original image into a preset size.
2. Let N denote the bit length (e.g. 256 bits) of the final hash value. Divide the pixels of the image I into non-overlapped blocks $I_1, I_2, \ldots, I_N$.
3. Encrypt the indices of the block sequence $\{I_1, I_2, \ldots, I_N\}$ using a secret key K to obtain a block sequence with a new scanning order. The authors specify no further details about what encryption algorithm to use. For our application encryption is not required, therefore this step is skipped.
4. Calculate the mean of the pixel values of each block. That is, calculate the mean value sequence $\{M_1, M_2, \ldots, M_N\}$ from the corresponding block sequence. Finally obtain the median value M_d of the mean value sequence.
5. Normalize the mean value sequence into a binary form and obtain the hash value h(i) as 0 if $M_i < M_d$ or 1 if $M_i \geq M_d$.

Yang's analysis against cropping attacks on the mean block perceptual hash showed that the original and cropped images differ after 10 % cropping up to 24 % and after 20 % cropping up to 33 %. So while it is robust against many common attacks, cropping remains a major challenge for this algorithm.

2.2 Optimization

In [6] the algorithm is improved by a number of additional features: To make it robust against mirroring, it automatically flips the image to be hashed in such a way that the brightest corner always lies in the upper left. It calculates the hash by dividing the 16×16 area into four 8×8 subareas and computes the median for each of these areas to achieve a higher difference of images featuring a similar structure. And it uses a weighted hash comparison to increase the rate of correct rejections. In the following, only the optimization steps one and two are utilized.

3 Face Detection

Face detection today is a common mechanism in security and entertainment. Photo software uses face detection for tagging and organizing image collections. Facebook and Google+ use face detection and recognition for tagging and searching. In this section we briefly describe the face detection we use in our face hash. Both are based on the work of Lienhart and Mayds [7], one is the OpenCV implementation, the other one the face detection of the Scilab Image and Video Processing Toolbox.

At this stage of our work we only consider frontal face detectors, due to the lack of open source implementation of multi view face detector.

3.1 Viola and Jones Rapid Face Detector

One of the fastest state of art algorithms with real time processing abilities is Viola and Jones Face Detector [8, 10]. It uses Haar-like features, which can be computed very fast. Afterwards classifiers are trained with a machine learning technique called AdaBoost. Detecting faces with only these two techniques is possible but still the computation costs are too high for real time face detection. The speed of the face detector is increased with a so-called "cascade" structure of classifiers. It is a degenerated tree with n stages. The Viola and Jones detector has five stages. At each stage negative examples are filtered out. The detection rate of the detector is around 95 % by 50 false positives on the MIT and CMU test set.

Lienhart and Maydt extended the feature set from the Viola and Jones face detector with 45° rotated Haar-like features. For calculating these features, a new rotated integral image version was created. This face detector implemented in OpenCV is used for FH. Also the face detector of the Scilab Image and Video Processing Toolbox implemented by Shiqi Yu and Jia Wu quotes the work of Lienhart and Maydt as its base.

4 Challenge

As introduced in Sect. 1, we combine a face detector with a robust hashing algorithm. One of the major challenges for robust hashing still is cropping. While in theory it is simple to deal with cropping by using sections and redundancy, this will lead to very complex and time consuming search strategies in the forensic analysis. Therefore we utilize the detection of face areas and calculate hashes of these areas. As robust hashes are robust against scaling and lossy compression, it can be assumed that as long as the face detector always provides the same area of the image to the hashing software, the detection will be successful.

But this is a challenge for the face detectors. As we show in Fig. 2, detected face areas differ from version to version of an image. For a face detector it is not important to provide exactly the same area in every time as long as it successfully identifies the area containing the face. Cropping the image leads to a drift of the area's size and position. Detailed test results are given in Sect. 6.1.

Fig. 2. Face detector inconsistency (© http://www.cheerleader-frankfurt.de/galacticdancers)

5   Face Blob Hashing

To counter the challenge of face drifting, we propose to utilize sub partitioning of the faces to be analyzed. As the faces are still rather similar even under the effect of drifting, our concept is to use individual objects within the face which can be detected and hashed. The position of these objects should move together with the detected face. Face detection and blob segmentation work well together as face detection is very robust except its drift against cropping and lossy compression. Without face detection, cropping would have a serious impact on the blob analysis. Only the relatively stable structure of a face can be utilized for blob analysis and robust hashing.

Our approach uses blob segmentation. For our test implementation, we apply the SearchBlobs and AnalyzeBlobs algorithms of IPT [12]. Blob thresholds are also calculated by IPT based on Otsu [11]. The Face Blob Hashing algorithm can be summarized as follows (see also Fig. 3):

1. Detect faces in an image using Viola and Jones Rapid Face Detector.
2. For each face, analyze its blobs.
3. For each blob, calculate its bounding box. A minimum of pixels (1 % of all face pixels) must be present in the bounding box, otherwise the blob is discarded.
4. For each bounding box, calculate its robust block hash.

In the training phase, all images to be recognized run through the four steps above. Each robust hash of each blob is stored in a database together with the name of the original image it is retrieved from.

As a result, a set of robust hashes for the individual blobs derived from all detected faces in the image is created. If more than one face is found in the image, the blob hashes of all face blobs are stored in the database as the goal of the algorithm is to identify images and not individual faces. It is not necessary to distinguish between the individual faces of an image.

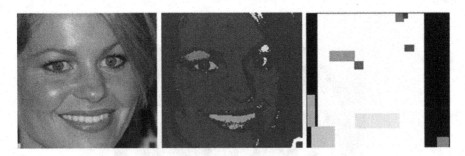

Fig. 3. Face (left), Blobs (middle) and Blob Areas (right)

In the detection phase, for an image to be analyzed also all four steps above are executed. Then the minimum hamming distance for each blob hash to all blob hashes in the database is calculated. For all blobs featuring a reference with a hamming distance equal to or smaller than a given threshold (usually 32) the reference to the image in the database and the hamming distance is stored in a result set. The blob hashes can be discarded at this point.

Now the image in the database with the most blobs similar to the analyzed image is derived from the result set. Only if at least two blobs in the result set point to the same image, the result is trusted and the image is tagged is identified. By this, false positives are reduced significantly. Random occurrences of small hamming distances between blobs and database entries happen in some cases, but as they are random, they do not share the same reference image and thereby can easily be filtered.

The average hamming distance of all result set entries pointing to that image is calculated to provide a quality rating for the detected match.

6   Test Results

In the following we provide our current state of test results, both for the motivating drift and for the blob hash detector. We also provide performance information comparing face detection and hash calculation.

6.1   Face Drift

To better understand the individual behavior of the face detection algorithm, we executed a deep analysis of the drift of the detected face area from version to version.

We used 10 images with one or more faces in it, and executed an automatic cropping starting in the upper left of the image. Both in the x and y axis between 0 and 20 pixels were cropped, resulting in 441 cropped versions per image. Images for this stage were taken from stock photo catalogues (Fig. 5) and model set cards (Fig. 7). Therefore a very high image quality was given for all 10 test images.

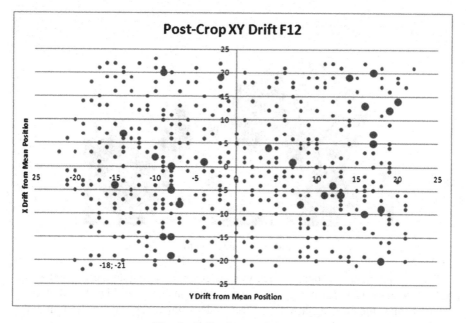

Fig. 4. Drift of example images

We determined the individual position of the identified face area and matched it to the original area of the image before cropping. After doing this for each of the 441 version of a face, we calculated the mean identified face position. Then we calculated the individual distance of all versions to this mean value. Figure 4 shows the result of this analysis. The positions of the detected face drift almost randomly in a range from ±22 in horizontal and vertical direction. A drift of this strength means that the detected face will not have robust hash equal or similar to the one retrieved from the original image.

Figure 6 shows examples of area drifts. Figure 5 was cropped several times and these three face areas have been among the ones detected by the face detector. While the face is equal for a human observer, for the robust hash algorithm they differ largely.

6.2   Face Blob Hamming Distance Results

To evaluate our face blob robust hash, we took 4600 images and tried to extract all faces within. These images are the same test set we already used in [13], so test results can be directly compared. The set consists of the online gallery of a cheerleader team, showing one or more person on almost any photo. We use these photos as the inter-photo similarity due to similar poses and dresses is very high, resulting in a challenge similar to distinguishing legal and illegal pornographic images. Figures 1 and 2 show examples of the set.

Due to the behavior of the face extractor, also false positives, meaning regions of the image wrongly identified as a face, have been extracted. Altogether, 6411 faces and false positives were detected. For each of these, the blob hash set as discussed in Sect. 5 was calculated and stored in a database.

Fig. 5. Original Photo

Then an automated cropping attack was executed, cropping an area of 300 × 300 pixels at position (20, 20) out of each of the 4600 images (see Fig. 7). From these cropped copies, the faces again were extracted. This time, 3237 faces were found, the rest was lost due to the cropping.

Fig. 6. Real world drift results

Now for each face the overall blob hamming distance was calculated to verify that the correct images have been found by the face blob robust hash. Figure 8 shows the result of our evaluation. The average hamming distance of all blobs for the correct faces ranges from 0 to 32 as could be expected. At the end, half of all faces could be correctly identified after cropping. False positives did not occur.

In Fig. 9 we can see that for most images, more than one face blob with a hamming distance below the threshold of 32 could be found. This is helpful when it comes to identifying false positives. For test images not stored in the database the average amount of blobs coming from a single image (a false positive) in the database is 1.03, while for known images it is 2.79. Therefore, combining a low hamming distance threshold for the individual blobs with a minimum requirement of two detected blobs is a reliable strategy for detecting images containing faces.

Fig. 7. Left: Original, Right: Cropped (http://models.com/newfaces/dailyduo/3624)

To verify that false positive rates can be expected to remain low, in Fig. 10 we provide the histogram of blob hamming distances of blobs derived from 100 faces not stored in the database. The average hamming distance is 52 in this case. This is the average hamming distance of a blob found in the database matching the unknown blob most closely.

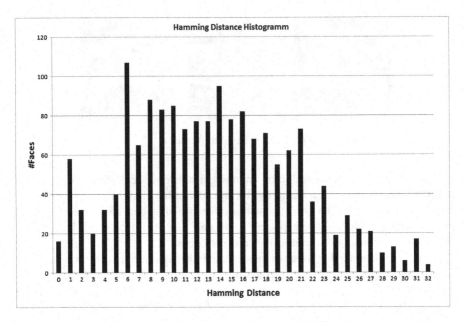

Fig. 8. Hamming Distance Histogram of 1658 faces

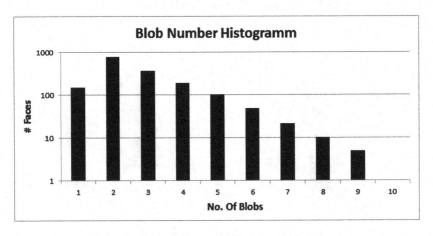

Fig. 9. Correct elements (Blobs) found per image

In Fig. 11 we provide an example of our decision strategy. Here in addition to cropping and JPEG compression also horizontal mirroring has been executed on the test image. For better visualization, we select 10 example images. The black rectangles show the average hamming distance calculated from all blob candidates. This means: Only if at least 2 blobs share the same face reference with a hamming distance below 33 they are taken into account. At face#6 one of the blobs pointing to the correct face has a hamming distance of 44 and therefore is ignored as the hamming distance

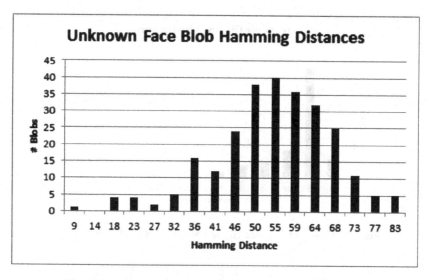

Fig. 10. Hamming Distance Histogram for 100 unknown faces

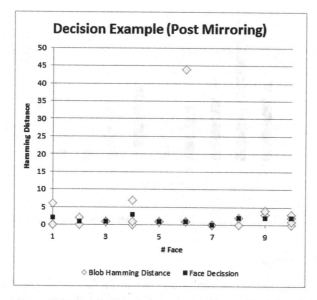

Fig. 11. Decision example for 10 faces

threshold is 32. As still 2 other blobs pointing to face#6 with a hamming distance of 1 were detected, the face is nevertheless identified correctly.

In Figs. 12 and 13 an example of the blob hash robustness against scaling, a common attack besides cropping is given. In this case, 100 images were either scaled down by 20 % or scaled up by 100 %. The histograms show that the hamming distance is below the threshold of 32 in most cases. Overall, similarly to only cropping the image, after adding scaling the images could be identified in half of the cases.

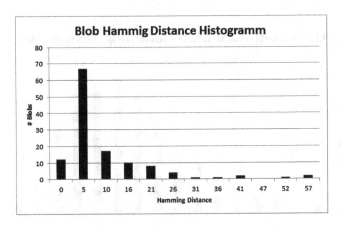

Fig. 12. Hamming Distance Histogram after downscaling by 20 %

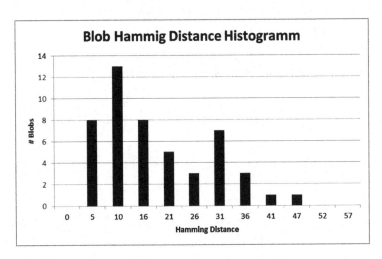

Fig. 13. Hamming Distance Histogram after upscaling by 100 %

6.3   Processing Speed

Using robust hashing in forensic application requires a processing speed high enough not to become a hindrance in examinations. Therefore in this section we provide a first impression of the performance of our approach. As stated above, a detailed view on its performance cannot be given as parts of the application have only been implemented in a prototypic manner.

We compare the speed of robust hash generation and face detection. As a test base, we use 198 images in which 340 faces are detected. The implementation of Lienhart's face detector in OpenCV is used for face extraction. The test is performed on a PC with Intel Core 2 Duo T9400 CPU (2.53 GHz) and 4 GB RAM.

The face detection takes 128.5 s. Hashing these faces only requires 0.57 s. Processing one image with face detection takes an average of 649 ms; hashing one face takes 1.6 ms. When applying the robust hash directly on an image, average hashing will take 4 ms. The speed-up in face hash calculations comes from smaller face areas compared to full images, resulting in lower costs for scaling and JPEG decoding (Figs. 14 and 15).

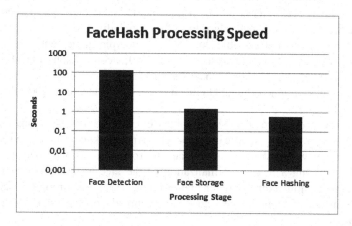

Fig. 14. FaceHash Processing Speed for 198 Images

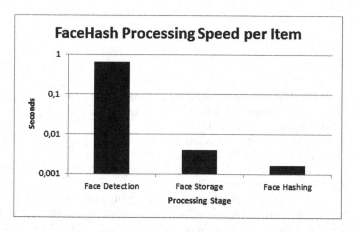

Fig. 15. Average Processing Speed for 198 images (Face Detection) and 340 faces (Face Storage, Face Hashing)

7 Conclusion and Future Work

In this work we present a novel approach to achieve robustness of robust image hashing against cropping. We show that a combination of face detector, blob segmentation and robust hashing provides promising test results and is able to re-identify images even after strong cropping combined with scaling and lossy compression. Our evaluation focuses on cropping, as most other image modifications like brightness and contrast changes or strong lossy compression have been successfully addressed by existing robust hash algorithms including the one we utilize as the robust hash base function.

The approach successfully detected half of all faces after a significant amount of cropping. Mirroring and scaling did not cause a serious reduction in detection quality. Utilizing the algorithm therefore provides a good chance to detect illegal images featuring human faces even after cropping. The computational complexity is kept as low as possible using only efficient algorithms for the individual steps. A real-world benchmark currently is not possible due to the prototypic implementation in Scilab. The resulting speed would be unrealistically low. Still, a comparison of our hash and a face detection mechanism shows that the difference between both mechanisms regarding computation time is huge. On the average, face detection is 200x slower than hashing.

Future work needs to evaluate how robust our approach is if a combination of cropping and other image modifications occurs. Another known challenge is image rotation. Here we will first need to evaluate the robustness of face detection. After successfully detecting a face, a normalization of the face angle should be possible, enabling image identification. Another line of future research is dropping the need of face detection and utilizing image segmentation directly on the images and not on extracted faces.

Acknowledgments. This work has been supported by the projects ForSicht and CASED, both funded by the State of Hessen.

References

1. Poisel, R., Tjoa, S.: Forensics investigations of multimedia data: a review of the state-of-the-art. In: 2011 Sixth International Conference on IT Security Incident Management and IT Forensics (IMF), pp. 48–61, May 2011
2. Schwarzer, G., Massaro, D.W.: Modeling face identification processing in children and adults. J. Exp. Child Psychol. **79**(2), 139–161 (2001)
3. Quayle, E., Taylor, M., Holland, G.: Child pornography: the internet and offending. Isuma Can. J. Policy Res. **2**(2), 94–100 (2001)
4. Yang, B., Gu, F., Niu, X.: Block mean value based image perceptual hashing. In: Proceedings of the International Conference on Intelligent Information Hiding and Multimedia Multimedia Signal Processing (IIH-MSP), pp. 167–172. IEEE (2006). (ISBN 0-7695-2745-0)
5. Zauner, C., Steinebach, M., Hermann, E.: Rihamark: perceptual image hash benchmarking. In: Proceeding of Electronic Imaging 2011 - Media Watermarking, Security, and Forensics XIII (2011)
6. Steinebach, M.: Robust hashing for efficient forensic analysis of image sets. In: Gladyshev, P., Rogers, M.K. (eds.) ICDF2C 2011. LNICST, vol. 88, pp. 180–187. Springer, Heidelberg (2012)
7. Lienhart, R., Maydt, J.: An extended set of haar-like features for rapid object detection. In: IEEE ICIP 2002, pp. 900–903 (2002)

8. Viola, P., Jones, M.: Rapid object detection using a boosted cascade of simple features. In: Proceedings of the 2001 IEEE Computer Society Conference on Computer Vision and Pattern Recognition 2001, CVPR 2001, vol. 1, pp. I–511. IEEE (2001)
9. Viola, P., Jones, M.: Robust real-time object detection. Int. J. Comput. Vis. **57**(2), 137–154 (2001)
10. Viola, P., Jones, M.J.: Robust real-time face detection. Int. J. Comput. Vis. **57**(2), 137–154 (2004)
11. Otsu, N.: A threshold selection method from grey level histograms. IEEE Trans. Syst. Man Cybern. **9**, 62–66 (1979). ISSN 1083-4419
12. Galda, H.: IPD - image processing design toolbox version 2.0, Scilab Toolbox (2009)
13. Steinebach, M., Liu, H., Yannikos, Y.: ForBild: Efficient robust image hashing. In: Media Watermarking, Security, and Forensics 2012, SPIE, Burlingame, California, United States (2012). ISBN,978-0-8194-8950-02012

Information Warfare, Cyber Terrorism, and Critical Infrastructure Protection

Regulating Social Network Services for Lawful Interception

Esti Peshin[(✉)]

Cyber Programs, ELTA Systems Ltd, Jerusalem, Israel
epeshin@elta.co.il

Abstract. Lawful interception has evolved over the past decades from the target based monitoring and interception of telecomm conversations, to the monitoring and interception of packet switched communications. The lawful monitoring and interception of both telecomm and packet switched communications is regulated by law enforcement agencies, with the cooperation, under the Lawful Interception regulation and legislation, of the service providers.

Social networks are also a means of communicating; but the nature of communication therein is extremely more complex, as it allows both for linear communication (one to one) and broadcasting of information (one to many/crowd) to selected groups and communities.

Social networks are a haven for criminals and insurgents. The open nature of the media provides criminals with ample access to potential victims and provides insurgents with a virtual Hyde Park, where they can openly voice their opinions, gain followers and instigate and organize disruptive activities.

The nature of the communication within social networks, the ease of establishing fake identities therein, the fact that the client-server communication can be encrypted, and the huge amount of data that passes through these networks on a daily basis - however, are far from law-enforcement friendly. Furthermore, the fact that social networks are operated by commercial, usually foreign based, companies, which do not necessarily adhere to the local Lawful Interception legislation and regulation, increases the challenge of monitoring of communication with social media.

The paper will discuss the technological challenges that law-enforcement agencies face when trying to monitor social networks, and the technological, regulatory and legislative provisions that can and should be put in place, by the operators of the Social Network Services and local law enforcement agencies, in order to prevent social network services from continuing to foster criminals and insurgents.

This paper is based on public domain information.

Keywords: Lawful interception · Social networks · Regulation · Cyber intelligence · Cyber crime · Cyber security · Law enforcement

© Institute for Computer Sciences, Social Informatics and Telecommunications Engineering 2014
P. Gladyshev et al. (Eds.): ICDF2C 2013, LNICST 132, pp. 119–129, 2014.
DOI: 10.1007/978-3-319-14289-0_9

1   Introduction: Social Networks - An Unregulated Communication Medium

Lawful interception (LI) is defined [1] as obtaining telecommunication data for the purposes of analysis or evidence. The obtained data may consist of signalling information, network management information and the content of the communications themselves.

Lawful interception is regulated by law enforcement agencies (LEAs), with the cooperation, under global lawful interception regulation and legislation, of the telecomm, Internet and network service providers.

The principal global legal instrument relating to LI is the Convention on Cybercrime treaty, also known as the Budapest Convention, which entered into force on July 1st, 2004, and sought to address computer and Internet crimes by harmonizing national laws, improving legislative techniques and increasing international cooperation [2]. As of October 2010, 30 countries signed, ratified and acceded to the convention, whereas 16 additional countries have signed the convention, but have not ratified it [3].

Individual countries have different legal requirements relating to lawful interception. The European Telecommunications Standard Institute (ETSI) [4] standardized the manner in which information should be transferred from the Telecomm and Internet service providers to the law enforcement agencies. This standard was adopted by European and other countries. The US passed the Communication Assistance for Law Enforcement Act (CALEA), also known as the US "wiretapping" law, in 1994 [5]. The European Council (EC) resolved in 1995 to mandate similar, though not identical, measures to CALEA within Europe [6].

Lawful Interception (LI) has evolved over the past decades from monitoring and interception of telephone (voice) conversations, to the monitoring and interception of packet-switched (IP) communications (such as emails, instant messages, web browsing activities, etc.).

However, throughout the evolution, the nature of the communication remained linear, where the initiator communicates with one, or a number of, recipients. In telephone communications, generally, all of the participants in the call were online, i.e. active participants during the call. After the introduction of packet-switched communications, some of the interaction between the participants became turn-based, where the recipients receive the information from the initiator, and may decide to respond or not, after an interval. Good examples of turn-based communication means are emails or instant messages (IM), where the sender, the initiator of the interaction, submits a message to one or several recipients, from whom he may or may not receive a response.

Social networks are, by nature, a means of interacting and communicating. However, unlike voice and IP interactions, the nature of communication in social networks can be linear, one to one; exponential - one to many; and viral, in case the recipients of the communication proceed to forward the communication to many more participants. The viral nature of social networks allows a sender to reach a huge number of recipients. However, the recipients of the communication do not, necessarily, actively participate in the communication; some do not even opt to receive it.

Users are able to conduct practically any type of interaction through social networks. They are able to broadcast information to their connections and/or to the general public, respond publicly or privately to information within the network, send email-like messages (AKA direct messages), chat with one of more users via instant messages, and even conduct voice conversations.

The use of social networks has soared over the past few years. Facebook reached 1 billion monthly active users on September 14th, 2012 [7], including 600 million mobile users, and an average of 584 million daily active users [8]. It is humbling to note that the number of Facebook users, as of September 2012, is more than three times the population of the United States, and in fact, exceeds the population of all the countries in the world, except for China and India.

However, the crux of the matter is that although social networks are an extremely prominent communication medium, social networks are, generally, not regulated by specific and adequate Lawful Interception (LI) legislation as a unique means of communication. Rather, the monitoring and interception of social network traffic is still regulated under the legislative provisions for the interception of packet- switched (IP) communications and data. The subsequent chapters will show why this is a highly undesirable situation.

2   Social Networks - A Haven for Insurgents and Criminals

Social networks are a haven for insurgents and criminals. Social networks, by nature, can provide anonymity and obscurity. Practically anyone can join a social network without any scrutiny, define a profile for themselves and start gaining followers and friends.

The open nature of social networks provides insurgents with a viral platform, where they can voice their opinions, gain followers and support, and instigate disruptive action.

The Guardian argues, in a February 2011 article [9], that social networks played several distinct and crucial roles in the Middle East and North Africa uprisings. Social networks provided the instigators and leaders of the uprisings with the means to gain followers and distribute ideas and information within their countries. Furthermore, social networks served a means to communicate openly with the outside world, and gain international public support. Social networks were used to smuggle sensitive footage and videos; material which was subsequently used by the mainstream media, in its coverage of the events, and which was instrumental in moulding the public opinion with regard to the events.

It is interesting to note that several social networks were prominently used and best suited to play a different role during the uprisings. Facebook was effective as a means of finding others with similar political views and planning street protests; YouTube was suited for citizen journalism by broadcasting videos, which were in turn picked by the mainstream global television channels and seen around the world; Twitter enabled on-the-move coordination and communication, and was also used for outreach to the international media and communities in the Diaspora [10].

The widespread and easy access to these online communication tools posed new and threatening challenges to the regimes. The simultaneous, coordinated and multi-dimensional utilization of all these different types of social networks created a very strong communication network which became difficult to disrupt.

Consequently, the uprisings triggered a surge of growth in the user base of Social Networks. The memeburn.com blog [11] quotes data according to which more than 200,000 Tunisians joined Facebook during the January 2011 uprising - a 11.4 % growth in the Tunisian Facebook users over the span of a month. Similarly, between January 20th and 25th, 217,600 Egyptians joined Facebook - a 4.2 % growth in the user base over the span of only 5 days.

The open nature of social networks provides criminals with access to potential victims, allowing them to leverage the users' personal details into financial gain.

The National White Collar Crime Center (NW3C) published in 2011 a study on criminal use of social networks [12]. NW3C cites various types of crimes enabled by or instigated on social networks: perpetrators may utilize social networks to look for potential victims in the vicinity who will not be at home at a certain time; perpetrators may utilize social engineering techniques within social networks in order to gain information from unsuspecting users or in order to manipulate them into an undesired action; and, finally, perpetrators may take advantage of the social network users' tendency to click on links, view files and respond to messages in order to infect their computer with malware.

A proof of concept conducted by Comsec Consulting in 2011 exhibited how simple it was to establish a fake identity of a corporate employee, and within one day, gain 74 friends from the same company [13]. A fake persona with so many friends from within the company would have inherent credibility, and could immediately proceed to engage in social engineering attacks, or, to utilize his fake, and now credible, identity to publish online content on behalf of or pertaining to the company.

FBI Assistant Director, Mr Gordon M. Snow, addressed the threats of crime on social networks in a testimony he gave before the House Judiciary Subcommittee on Crime, Terrorism and Homeland Security on July 28th, 2010 [14]. Mr Snow testified that "[...] the surge in use of social networking sites over the past two years has given cyber thieves and child predators new, highly effective avenues to take advantage of unsuspecting users".

Mr Snow, subsequently, outlined how the threat of social engineering attacks, where a user is fooled online by persons claiming to be somebody else, is accentuated in social networks. Mr Snow testified that "Unlike the physical world, individuals can misrepresent everything about themselves while they communicate online, ranging not only from their names and business affiliations (something that is fairly easy to do in-person as well), but extending as well to their gender, age, and location (identifiers that are far more difficult to fake in-person)".

The nature of the communication within social networks; the huge amounts of data that pass through these networks on a daily basis; and, the ease with which an identity can be set up and gain credibility, are far from being law-enforcement friendly. Furthermore, the fact that social networks are operated by commercial companies that do not necessarily adhere to local Lawful Interception legislation and regulation, increases the complexity of monitoring communications and interactions within social networks.

3   Lawful Interception of Social Networks

Lawful interception and monitoring of packet-switched data generally relies either on known identities and/or on the identification of content of interest.

By way of example, a law enforcement agency may obtain a court order for monitoring a certain individual, and may proceed to monitor their unique packet-switched IDs (IP address, MAC address, email address, Instant Messaging ID, etc.).

A malicious user may attempt to set up a completely anonymous framework for communication. A user can quite simply set up an anonymous email account (Hotmail, Yahoo, Gmail or other), communicate via emails, only from public hotspots, and never from their own computer; and, potentially, utilize TOR [15], a freeware platform of anonymous worldwide servers, enabling users to surf the web through an ever-changing network of proxies. A LEA would be hard pressed to intercept such a communication based on the user's distinct IDs; however, notwithstanding legislation and regulation, which may require in certain countries a warrant related to a distinct ID, a LEA may be able to intercept such an email based on its content, by identifying pre-defined keywords that were included within the email.

The European Parliament and Council adopted, in 2006, advanced and unique LI legislation, in the form of the Data Retention Directive, regulating how electronic data should be captured, retained and provided, upon request, to Law Enforcement Agencies [16]. The Data Retention Directive requires service providers to retain, for a predefined amount of time, information regarding calls, emails, websites visited, etc. Thus, if an email address, for example, is identified over time, as belonging to a suspect individual, the LEA would be able to obtain from the service provider data related to previous communications involving the same email address.

It should be noted that since its passage, the Data Retention Directive has faced intense criticism and has been opposed by legislators in the European Parliament who argue that it fosters a surveillance society and undermines fundamental human rights [16]. In April 2011, the European Commission published an evaluation report of the Directive that revealed inconsistencies with how EU members implement the legislation and which authorities can access the data [16]. In May 2011, the European Data Protection Supervisor (EDPS) published his evaluation of the EU report and expressed the view that the Directive does not meet the requirements imposed by the fundamental rights to privacy and data protection [17].

The interception and monitoring of an individual's traffic within social network services is compounded by three major factors: First and foremost, an individual can set up a completely anonymous and bogus profile within a few minutes in a large set of social networks. Furthermore, their activity will be masked within more than 2.5 billion content items, which according to Facebook statistics released in August 2012 [18], are shared by Facebook's users every day. Finally, and this is a crucial point, the corporations operating the social networks - the social network service providers or social network operators - are not regulated as of yet.

By way of example, let us consider criminal or insurgent activity conducted within a certain country through a social network. Even if the activity and/or instigators would eventually be identified by a LEA, would the affected country be able to obtain retroactive information from the foreign corporation that operates the social network? It is quite safe to assume that, more often than not, the answer would be negative. The social network operators are presently not required to do so by law, and quite naturally, would tend to favour the privacy of their user base - their raison d'être - over the security needs of a foreign country.

The social network operators' bias of favouring privacy over security was exemplified in the uprisings in Tunisia and Egypt in the beginning of 2011.

The uprisings demonstrated the importance of a viable and widespread communication means in promoting, facilitating, and, most importantly, accelerating insurgent activities.

The Atlantic published a fascinating article [19] on how Facebook openly aided the Tunisian insurgents during the uprisings. According to the Atlantic, quoting Facebook's Chief Security Officer, Joe Sullivan, the Facebook security team realized, early January 2011, that the Tunisian Internet service providers (ISPs) were running a malicious piece of code - allegedly, a keystroke logger - that was recording users' credentials and passwords when they accessed secure sites like Facebook. Facebook responded by routing all Tunisian requests for Facebook to an HTTPS server, which encrypts the information sent across, and thus renders the information insusceptible to monitoring, interception and the key-logging strategy that was utilized by the regime. Facebook further employed a "roadblock"[1], ensuring that users that were affected by the regime's hack, are indeed who they claim to be.

It is tempting to commend the role social networks can play when utilized by self-proclaimed forces of freedom, the good guys. However, we must not lose sight for an instant that the same means can be and are used also by insurgents and terrorists - the bad guys - aiming to destabilize, harm and potentially overthrow legitimate governments and regimes.

Facebook itself announced on January 26th, 2011 [20], that it is allowing users to choose full SSL/HTTPS encryption to secure all communications between the users' browsers and the Facebook Web servers. Twitter added, in March 2011, a

---

[1] A roadblock is a technique where a user is identified by a question or a series of questions, such as asking users to identify photos of their friends before allowing them to log into the network.

user setting that allows users to always use HTTPS when accessing the Twitter site [21]. At the onset, both social network operators left it up to their users to decide whether to encrypt their traffic or not. Users who chose to encrypt their traffic significantly impaired, knowingly or not, the local LEAs ability to intercept and monitor their traffic.

Facebook has taken another leap forward and announced [22] in its developer blog that it is starting, as of November 2012, to roll out default HTTPS encryption for all North America users, and will be soon rolling out default encryption to the rest of the world. *The immediate derivative is that once the change is rolled-out, coverage of all Facebook traffic - the traffic of 1 billion users worldwide - via legacy packet-switched (IP) Monitoring systems will be lost.* Needless to say, this development may have severe impact on security.

Granted, the increased security is important for legitimate users, assisting them in preventing identity theft. However, the fact that social networks use strong encryption further hampers the ability of LEAs to intercept and monitor the traffic without the cooperation of the social network service providers.

The immediate conclusion is that social networks must not remain unregulated!

4   Social Networks Must be Regulated!

The lawful interception regulation and legislation must undergo a paradigm shift in order to ensure the cooperation, under the proper legislation, of corporations operating widespread social networks with a significant user base.

This can and should be achieved, in the long run, through the international standardization and certification of social networks, to include the necessary provisions for local lawful interception. Similarly to the manner in which telecommunications and Internet service providers are required, by law, to facilitate the local LEAs interception of the communications thereof, widespread social network service providers should be required, prior to launching their services within a country or region, to undergo an international certification process and to ensure that the local LEA has access to the communications pertaining to and affecting the country and/or region.

Furthermore, the LI legislation and regulations must eventually be amended, where necessary, to ensure that the LEAs are legally allowed to scrutinize all the traffic within the social networks, and not be limited only to the traffic of identified targets. This would naturally require employing also data retention provisions, allowing LEAs retroactive access to the social networks' traffic. The timeframe for such access should be pre-defined and limited, in order to minimize the potential violation of privacy.

The wheels have already been set in motion. ETSI published in April 2012 a draft technical report addressing the Lawful Interception of Cloud/Virtual Services [23]. ETSI addresses one of the main regulatory/legal challenges pertaining to the lawful interception of social network traffic, or for that matter any cloud based traffic, pertaining to a nation state - the fact that *the imposition of LI requirements is largely oriented around national jurisdiction and geography.*

Hence, it is unlikely that LEAs can serve a warrant on a social network operator directly unless that operator has an "in country" presence.

ETSI states social network operators (or any cloud based service provider) should implement a Cloud Lawful Interception Function (CLIF), which will allow them to intercept traffic on behalf of LEAs.

Addressing the challenge of jurisdiction and geography, ETSI further states that in order for the social network operator (or any cloud based service provider) to be able to intercept traffic on behalf of a local LEA, the LEA must pass the following tests:

- The warrant must be legal in that country.
- The traffic must be routed or handled in the same country.
- The traffic must be distinguishable from others in order to prevent collateral interception.

Finally, ETSI mandates, that in case the traffic is encrypted, the entity responsible for key management must ensure it can be decrypted by the social network operator or by the LEA.

ETSI's technical draft makes a lot of sense. As each new form of communication was introduced and evolved, it presented the LI community with new challenges. Some examples are the evolution of public switched telephone networks (PSTNs) from fixed-line analog telephony systems to digital cores and mobile networks; the exponential growth of packet-switched networks, the introduction of Voice over IP (VoIP) communications, and so on. Faced with these challenges, and in order to maintain their monitoring capabilities, regulators, governments and LEAs have had to adjust their LI regulations and legislation, and industry was required to come up with the enabling technologies.

The adoption of new standards, regulations and technologies may take time. In the meantime, the charter of international law enforcement agencies, such as the Interpol, and international and regional cooperation bodies, should be extended to act as intermediaries for obtaining lawful interception information in foreign countries.

However, and until the international standardization and certification of social networks is achieved, governments and law enforcement agencies should ensure, through technological means, international cooperation and other means, that they have the capabilities to access, intercept, and monitor the social network traffic of suspect individuals pertaining to and affecting their own country.

4.1   The Snowden and PRISM Case-Study

An example of a controversial program aiming to gain access, intercept and monitor social network services and cloud based services is the PRISM program.

PRISM is a clandestine mass electronic surveillance data mining program operated by the United States National Security Agency. The PRISM program was publicly revealed when classified documents about the program were revealed to The Guardian [24] and The Washington Post [25] by Edward Snowden.

The leaked documents included PowerPoint slides, which were published in the news articles [26], and which identified several US based technology companies as participants in the PRISM program. The identified companies included Microsoft, Yahoo!, Google, Facebook, Paltalk, YouTube, AOL, Skype and Apple. The slides reveal that the PRISM program allows for collecting data and information directly from the companies' servers. In order to comply with the US laws, the specified targets should be a foreign national who is overseas at the time of collection. The collected data includes emails, chats, videos, photos, stored data, VoIP, File Transfers, video conferencing and notifications of targets activity (logins, etc.).

To conclude, PRISM, essentially, allows the US to bypass the Lawful Interception challenge illustrated in this article by enlisting the cooperation of the major commercial corporations running social network services and cloud bases services. Notwithstanding, *the controversy and adverse public sentiment following the disclosure of the program, illustrate that the path to regulating the access of LEAs to the data and information within social networks and cloud bases services is expected to be lengthy and rocky.*

5 Summary

To conclude, social networks have emerged as a prominent medium of communication, with unique viral, exponential and multi-dimensional characteristics. Social networks provide privacy and can ensure anonymity. However, social networks are yet to be regulated in terms of Lawful Interception, and, as such, can be a safe haven for insurgents and criminals. Governments, Law Enforcement Agencies, and international cooperation and standardization bodies, must proceed rapidly to ensure the proper Lawful Interception regulations, legislation, certification processes, international treaties and technologies are adjusted and adopted in order to provide LEAs with a similar level of access to the traffic within social networks, as their access to telecom and packet-switched traffic.

References

1. Wikipedia: Lawful Interception. http://en.wikipedia.org/wiki/Lawful_interception
2. Council of Europe: Convention on Cybercrime, 2001, ETS No. 185. http://conventions.coe.int/Treaty/EN/Treaties/Html/185.htm
3. Council of Europe: Convention on Cybercrime Treaty Signature Status (2010). http://conventions.coe.int/Treaty/Commun/ChercheSig.asp?NT=185&CM=8&DF=28/10/2010&CL=ENG
4. European Telecommunications Standards Institute: About ETSI. http://www.etsi.org/about
5. Electronic Frontier Foundation: CALEA F.A.Q. https://www.eff.org/pages/calea-faq
6. European Telecommunications Standards Institute: Lawful Interception (LI); Concepts of Interception in a Generic Network Architecture, Technical report, ETSI TR 101 943 v2.1.1 (2004–10)

7. Facebook: One billion - key metrics. http://newsroom.fb.com/download-media/ 4227

8. Facebook: Key Facts. http://newsroom.fb.com/Key-Facts

9. Beaumont, P.: The truth about Twitter, Facebook and the uprisings in the Arab world, The Guardian, 25 February 2011. http://www.theguardian.com/world/ 2011/feb/25/twitter-facebook-uprisings-arab-libya

10. Khamis, S., Gold, P.B., Vaughn, K.: Beyond Egypt's "Facebook Revolution" and Syria's "YouTube Uprising:" Comparing Political Contexts, Actors and Communication Strategies. Arab Media & Society, no. 15, Spring 2012

11. Daniel, J.: Surge in Facebook users coincides with North African uprisings, meme-burn.com, 28 January 2011. http://memeburn.com/2011/01/surge-in-facebook-users-coincides-with-north-african-uprisings/

12. National White Collar Crime Center: Criminal Use of Social Media (2011). http:// www.iacpsocialmedia.org/Portals/1/documents/External/NW3CArticle.pdf

13. Comsec Consulting: The Social Networking Corporate Threat, March 2011, http:// www.comsecglobal.com/FrameWork/Upload/The%20Social%20Networking%20 Corporate%20Threat%20-%20Comsec.pdf

14. Snow, G.M.: Statement before the House Judiciary Subcommittee on Crime, Terrorism and Homeland Security, 28 July 2010. http://www.fbi.gov/news/testimony/ the-fbi2019s-efforts-to-combat-cyber-crime-on-social-networking-sites

15. Tor Project. https://www.torproject.org/

16. Electronic Frontier Foundation: European Union Mandatory Data Retention Directive. https://www.eff.org/issues/mandatory-data-retention/eu

17. European Data Protection Supervisor: Evaluation shows that the Data Retention Directive does not meet privacy and data protection requirements, says EDPS, EDPS/11/6, 31 May 2011. http://europa.eu/rapid/press-release_EDPS-11-6_en. htm?locale=en

18. King, R.: How Facebook Wrangles Big Data, CIO Journal, 23 August 2012. http:// blogs.wsj.com/cio/2012/08/23/how-facebook-wrangles-big-data/

19. Madrigal, A.C.: The Inside Story on How Facebook Responded to Tunisian Hacks, The Atlantic, 24 January 2011. http://www.theatlantic.com/technology/archive/ 2011/01/the-inside-story-of-how-facebook-responded-to-tunisian-hacks/70044/

20. Rice, A.: A Continued Commitment to Security, Notes by Facebook, 26 January 2011. https://www.facebook.com/notes/facebook/a-continued-commitment-to-security/486790652130

21. Twitter: Making Twitter more secure: HTTPS, Twitter Blog, 15 March 2011. https://blog.twitter.com/2011/making-twitter-more-secure-https

22. Asthana, S.: Platform Updates: Operation Developer Love, Facebook Developers Blog, 15 November 2012. https://developers.facebook.com/blog/post/2012/ 11/14/platform-updates-operation-developer-love/

23. European Telecommunications Standards Institute: Lawful Interception (LI); Cloud/Virtual Services (CLI), Draft Technical Report, DTR 101 567 v0.05 (2012–04)

24. Greenwald, G., MacAskill, E.: NSA Prism program taps in to user data of Apple, Google and others, The Guardian, 7 June 2013. http://www.theguardian.com/ world/2013/jun/06/us-tech-giants-nsa-data

25. Gellman, B., Poitras, L.: U.S., British intelligence mining data from nine U.S. Internet companies in broad secret program, The Washington Post, 7 June 2013. http://www.washingtonpost.com/investigations/us-intelligence-mining-data-from-nine-us-internet-companies-in-broad-secret-program/2013/06/06/3a0c0da8-cebf-11 e2-8845-d970ccb04497_story.html
26. The Washington Post, NSA slides explain the PRISM data-collection program, 10 July 2013. http://www.washingtonpost.com/wp-srv/special/politics/prism-collection-documents/

Determining When Conduct in Cyberspace Constitutes Cyber Warfare in Terms of the International Law and *Tallinn Manual on the International Law Applicable to Cyber Warfare*: A Synopsis

Murdoch Watney[✉]

University of Johannesburg, Johannesburg, South Africa
mwatney@uj.ac.za

Abstract. Article 2(4) of the UN Charter provides that nation-states will refrain from the threat or use of force against the territorial integrity or political independence of any state. It is doubtful whether it will deter states from waging war in cyberspace. Cyber warfare is a perplexing and contentious issue within the ambit of international law. Discussions have focused on whether the existing rules and principles may be extended to cyberspace or whether new treaty law on cyber warfare must be drafted. Against this background the International Group of Experts drafted the Tallinn Manual on the International Law Applicable to Cyber Warfare at the invitation of the NATO Cooperative Cyber Defense Centre of Excellence. The Tallinn Manual provides rules in respect of cyber warfare. In the absence of a multilateral treaty it may be asked whether the Tallinn Manual will achieve acceptance on a global level as rules governing cyber warfare.

Keywords: Cyber warfare · Cyberspace · International law · Tallinn Manual · DDoS attacks on Estonia · Stuxnet attack on Iran · Armed attack

1 Introduction

On a national level nation-states are concerned about cyber threats and/or risks that may threaten their national cyber security and national critical information infrastructure. Not only on a national level, but also on an international level peace and security in cyberspace are an ongoing concern to ensure a safer and better cyber world for all.

There has been some debate on whether the existing rules and principles of the international law which were developed in a physical environment can be extended to the cyber environment or whether new treaty laws in respect of cyber warfare will have to be established.

This article is based on research supported in part by the National Research Foundation of South Africa (UID 85384). Opinions expressed are those of the author and not the NRF.

© Institute for Computer Sciences, Social Informatics and Telecommunications Engineering 2014
P. Gladyshev et al. (Eds.): ICDF2C 2013, LNICST 132, pp. 130–143, 2014.
DOI: 10.1007/978-3-319-14289-0_10

It is therefore not surprising that the release in March 2013 of the Tallinn Manual on the International Law Applicable to Cyber Warfare (hereafter referred to as the Tallinn Manual) [1] have evoked some discussion. The Tallinn Manual is based on the application of the existing rules and principles of international law to cyberspace. In this paper the debate in determining when conduct in cyberspace amounts to cyber warfare will be specifically explored.

It is important to note that the Tallinn Manual is not the first to codify the application of international law in cyberspace. In January 2011 the EastWest Institute released the first joint Russian-American bilateral report "Working towards Rules for Governing Cyber Conflict: Rendering the Geneva and Hague Conventions in Cyberspace" (hereafter referred to as the EWI Cyber Conflict Rules). [2] The EWI Cyber Conflict Rules is a Russia – US bilateral that focuses on the protection of critical infrastructure in cyberspace by means of international humanitarian law (IHL), also referred to as *jus in bello* (the law governing conduct in armed conflict and the treatment of combatants and civilians in time of armed conflict). The aim of the report was to explore how the humanitarian principles provided for in the Geneva and Hague Conventions on war may be extended to govern war in cyberspace [3].

For purposes of this discussion, the Tallinn Manual is applicable as its purpose is to identify the international law applicable to cyber warfare. It outlines for example the rules applicable to conduct that constitute cyber warfare.

The Tallinn Manual was drafted at the invitation of the North Atlantic Treaty Organisation Cooperative Cyber Defence Centre of Excellence (hereafter referred to as the NATO CCD CoE) under the directorship of Michael Schmitt, professor of international law at the United States Naval War College in Rhode Island. According to Schmitt: "We wrote it as an aid to legal advisers, to governments and militaries, almost a textbook. We wanted to create a product that would be useful to states to help them decide what their position is. We were not making recommendations, we did not define best practice, we did not want to get into policy" [3].

The main purpose of this paper is to investigate:

- When will conduct constitute cyber warfare in terms of the international law and the interpretation of the international law in accordance with the Tallinn Manual and other authors? The cyber attack in the form of a DDoS on Estonia and the attack by means of the Stuxnet worm on Iran will be evaluated in this regard.
  The following inter-related and overlapping aspects will also be referred to:
- As there are no treaty provisions that deal directly with 'cyber warfare', will the Tallinn Manuals' interpretation of international law in respect of cyber war be considered as a so-called textbook to all governments of not only western but also non-western nation states? This question is relevant as the author of this paper is from a non-western state and developing country, namely South Africa. Here cognizance should be taken of the controversy regarding the outcome of the World Conference on International Telecommunications (WCIT–12) held in 2012 by the International Telecommunications Union (ITU), which is a specialized agency of the United Nations.
- Although the Tallinn Manual [1] as well as the EWI Cyber Conflict Rules [2] make a valuable contribution to the better understanding of the application of international

law in cyberspace, would it not be better for the United Nations as a central body to conduct such a study involving the participation of all internet-connected nation-states?

2 Defining Concepts Relevant to the Discussion

There exists no universal definitions of the concepts relevant to the discussion but for purposes of this paper conceptualisation serves as a point of reference, despite the criticism that may be invariably leveled against the definitions.

It is proposed that the concept, 'cyber threat' or 'cyber risk' be used as an umbrella term which encompasses all threats to the interests of law enforcement and/or national security.

Cyber threats (risks) may be divided into cybercrime which will fall within the ambit of law enforcement investigations or so-called cyber-intelligence crimes such as cyber warfare, cyber terrorism or espionage which will fall within the ambit of national security. In the latter instance specific attention should be given to the protection of the critical infrastructure of a nation-state. The national critical information infrastructure includes all ICT systems and data bases, networks (including buildings, people, facilities and processes) that are fundamental to the effective operation of a nation-state [4]. The EWI Cyber Conflict Rules define critical infrastructure as those infrastructure whose continued operation is essential for sustaining life, economic stability and continuation of government that includes national security [2].

The Tallinn Manual paid particular attention to terminology [1]. It uses the term 'cyber operations' that is not derived from a legal term with a concrete meaning. 'Cyber operations' refers to the employment of cyber capabilities with the primary purpose of achieving objectives in or by the use of cyber space [1]. 'Cyber operations' includes cyber attacks as a specific category of cyber operations. 'Cyber attack' is defined in Rule 30 of the Tallinn Manual as 'a cyber operation whether offensive or defensive that is reasonably expected to cause injury or death to persons or damage or destruction to objects.' Non-violent attacks such as cyber espionage would in general not constitute a cyber attack.

The EWI Cyber Conflict Rules [2] states that there is no clear internationally agreed upon definition of what could constitutes 'cyber war'. For purposes of this paper 'cyber war' is defined as an action by a nation-state to penetrate another nation's computers and networks for purposes of causing damage or disruption. [5]. The Tallinn Manual state that there may be instances where the cyber operations by non-state actors will resort under 'cyber warfare.'

3 Cyber Warfare: Myth or Reality?

Prior to 2007 cyber attacks were nothing new. But 2007 saw the first reported cyber attack launched by means of distributed denial of service attacks (DDoS) against a nation-state namely Estonia. It was apparently the largest DDoS attacks ever seen [5]. The Estonian government estimates a million personal computers in a number of different countries, including the US, Canada, Vietnam and Brazil were used to conduct the attack. The damage was thought to amount to tens of millions of Euros [6].

The cyber attack was allegedly caused by the removal of a statue of a Russian soldier, who had fought during the Second World War, from the main square in the capital city, Tallinn to a military cemetery. The removal of the statue was perceived by ethnic Russians living in Estonia and Russia as an affront to Russia and their sacrifices during World War II [5].

The Estonian cyber attack served as a wake-up call to the international community of the growing security threat of cyber attacks launched against a nation-state as well as the vulnerability of a nation-state regarding the protection of its national security which includes its critical infrastructure [6].

NATO took the cyber attack on Estonia seriously enough to result in the establishment of a NATO Co-operative Cyber Defence Centre of Excellence (CCD CoE) based in Talinn, Estonia. In October 2008 NATO's Northern Atlantic Council granted the NATO Co-operative Cyber Defence Centre of Excellence (NATO CCD CoE) full NATO accreditation and the status of an international military organisation. The NATO CCD CoE is a partnership between 11 states and the sponsoring nations are Estonia, Germany, Hungary, Italy, Latvia, Lithuania, the Netherlands, Poland, Slovakia, Spain and the US. In January 2013 David Cameron announced that the UK would be joining the CCD CoE in 2013 [7].

Whether the attack on Estonia amounted to an armed conflict will be discussed hereafter at paragraph 5. The attack however confirmed that any nation-state may become the victim of a cyber attack against its critical infrastructure, affecting national security.

Nation-states are currently implementing national cyber security framework policies to ensure the existence of a central body to oversee a legal framework to ensure a coordinated and aligned approach to cyber security issues that may affect the national cyber security of a nation state. Although such a coordinated and aligned approach on a national level may assist in the protection of its critical infrastructure, it is not infallible. If a national intelligence crime is committed against a state's critical infrastructure, the victim nation-state is confronted on an international level with the following questions:

- When will the conduct committed in cyberspace be defined by international law as armed conflict; and
- Which recourse does the victim nation-state have against the state responsible for the attack within the ambit of the international law?

Returning to 2009 and 2010 and possibly also 2008 when the worm, Stuxnet was created to cripple Iran's nuclear program by sabotaging industrial equipment used in uranium purification. Stuxnet targeted systems controlling high-speed centrifuges used in the Iranian nuclear programme to enrich uranium, causing them to slow down and speed up repeatedly until they failed under the abnormal mechanical strain. [8] The penetration technique of this 'cyber weapon' had never been seen before and was therefore what hackers call a 'zero-day attack', the first time use of a specific application that takes advantage of a hitherto unknown glitch in a software program [5]. The EWI Cyber Conflict Rules [2] refers to examples of cyber weapons used in cyberspace such as worms, viruses, remote manual control and key loggers.

The question focuses again on whether the conduct constitutes an example of cyber warfare [1]. What recourse did Iran have? These questions will be discussed at paragraph 5 hereafter.

In the EWI Cyber Conflict Rules [2] the following was stated regarding cyber warfare: '... there is considerable confusion. Senior government leaders from the same country have incompatible opinions about the most basic aspects of cyber war – its existence now, its reality or likely impact in the future. The current ambiguity is impeding policy development and clouding the application of existing Convention requirements.'

Against above-given background, NATO CCD CoE is of the opinion that cyber warfare is a reality and more than a mere myth otherwise it would not have invited the international law experts as far back as 2009 to draft a manual on the international law applicable to cyber warfare.

In 2010 NATO acknowledged this threat in its 2010 *Strategic Concept* wherein it committed itself to 'develop further our ability to prevent, detect, defend against and recover from cyber attacks including by using the NATO planning process to enhance and coordinate national cyber defence capabilities, bringing all NATO bodies under centralized cyber protection, and better integrating NATO cyber awareness, warning and response with member nations.' [1, 9].

Other nation-states have also indicated that they consider cyber warfare as a serious threat to national security which includes the critical infrastructure. In 2010 the UK's national security strategy characterised cyber-attacks, including those by other states, as one of four "tier one" threats alongside terrorism, military crises between states and major accident [8]. The US 2010 National Security Strategy likewise cited cyber threats as 'one of the most serious national security, public safety, and economic challenges we face as a nation' and in 2011 the US Department of Defense issued its *Strategy for Operating in Cyberspace* which designates cyberspace as an operational domain. In response to the threat the US has now established the US Cyber Command to conduct cyber operations. During the same time Canada launched *Canada's Cyber Security Strategy,* the UK issued the *UK Cyber Security Strategy Protecting and Promoting the UK in a Digitized World* and Russia published its cyber concept for the armed forces in *Conceptual Views Regarding the Activities of the Armed Forces of the Russian Federation in Information Space* [1, 9].

4 Scope and Application of the Tallinn Manual

The Tallinn Manual is a comprehensive legal manual that was drafted over a period of 3 years by 20 researchers which consisted of legal scholars and senior military lawyers (referred to as the International Group of Experts) from NATO countries. NATO consists of 28 independent member countries, consisting mostly of EU member countries as well as the US and Canada.

The Tallinn Manual is not on 'cyber security', but it specifically focuses on the application of international law in respect of cyber warfare which is one of the challenges facing nation-states. The International Group of Experts that drafted the Tallinn Manual was unanimously of the opinion that the general principles of international law applies to cyberspace and that there is no need for new treaty law. The Tallinn Manual represents the International Group of Experts' interpretation of the international law in respect of cyber warfare.

The Tallinn Manual examines the international law governing

- *Jus ad bellum* (the law governing the right to the use of force by states as an instrument of their national policy) where it has to be determined in which circumstances cyber operations will amount to the use of force or armed attack justifying the use of necessary and proportionate force in self-defence or an act of aggression or threat to the international peace and security, subject to UN Security Council Intervention.
- *Jus in bello* (the international law regulating conduct in armed conflict; also referred to as the law of war or humanitarian law) with reference to armed conflict.

The Tallinn Manual's emphasis is on cyber-to-cyber operations such as the launch of a cyber operation against a states' critical infrastructure or a cyber attack targeting enemy command and control systems.

It is divided into 95 black-letter rules and accompanying commentary. The rules set forth the International Group of experts' conclusions as to the broad principles and specific norms that apply in cyberspace regarding cyber warfare. Each rule is the product of unanimity among the authors. The accompanying commentary indicates the legal basis, applicability in international and non-international armed conflicts and normative content of each rule. It also outlines differing or opposing positions among the experts as to the rules' scope or interpretation. The rules reflect the consensus among the International Group of Experts as to the applicable *lex lata*, the law that is currently governing cyber conflict. It does not set forth *lex forenda*, best practice or preferred policy.

Although the Tallinn Manual is not an official document that represents the views of the NATO CCD CoE or the Sponsoring Nations or NATO, Colonel Kirby Abbott (an assistant legal adviser at NATO) said at the launch of the Manual in March 2013 that the manual was now 'the most important document in the law of cyber warfare. It will be highly useful' [7].

It should be noted that NATO CCD CoE has launched a three year follow on project, 'Tallinn 2.0' that will expand the scope of the Tallinn Manual primarily in the law of State responsibility realm. 'Tallinn 2.0' will also be dealing with other bodies of so-called peacetime international law, as they relate to State responses, such as international telecommunications law, space law and human rights law [11].

5   Application of the International Law in Determining When Conduct Constitutes Cyber Warfare

5.1   International Law

International law does not apply the concept of 'act of war' in evaluating the legality of state violence, but international lawyers assess whether state actions constitute an 'illegal intervention', 'use of force', 'armed attack' or 'aggression.' This assessment involves

i. Interpreting these concepts in international law (doctrinal analysis); and
ii. Understanding how states react to events (evaluation of state practice).

International law as a matter of doctrine prohibits a state from intervening in the domestic affairs of other states, using force or the threat of force against another state or engaging in acts of aggression [12, 13].

Article 2(4) of the UN Charter states: 'All members shall refrain in their international relations from the threat or use of force against the territorial integrity or political independence of any state or in any other manner inconsistent with the Purposes of the United Nations.'

These rules establish thresholds that distinguish between

- Intervention from uses of force; and
- Uses of force from an armed attack.

Determining into which category state behaviour falls is not easily established. The International Court of Justice has ruled that not all types of force constitute armed attacks [10]. Only where the use of force is a serious use of force can the victim state react in self-defense and then the self-defense must comply with the proportionality requirement. Similarly some damaging covert actions are illegal intervention but not use of force.

A state can only legally use force if it is the victim of an armed attack or if the United Nations Security Council has authorized it.

Article 51 of the UN Charter states: 'Nothing in the present Charter shall impair the inherent right of individual or collective self-defense if an armed attack occurs against a Member of the United Nations, until the Security Council has taken measures necessary to maintain international peace and security. Measures taken by members in the exercise of this right of self-defense shall be immediately reported to the Security Council and shall not in any way affect the authority and responsibility of the Security Council under the present Charter to take at any time such action as it deems necessary in order to maintain or restore international peace and security.'

Determining which type of threshold an action crosses usually involves evaluating its effect or consequences on a case-by-case basis. The International Group of Experts also states that the effects and scale of the attacks are relevant in determining when the threshold of the attack will rise from unlawful intervention to illegal use of force to armed conflict. Fidler [12] refers to the following criteria to assess whether the incident constitutes an intervention, use of force or armed attack:

(a) Instrumentalities refer to the means or methods used;
(b) Effects refer to the damage to tangible objects or injury to humans;
(c) Gravity refers to the damage or injury's scale or extent;
(d) Duration refers to the incidents' length of time;
(e) Intent refers to the purpose behind the act(s) in question; and
(f) Context refers to the circumstances surrounding the incident.

Fidler [12] states that applying doctrinal analysis alone is insufficient to understand how international law applies to events. International lawyers must also consider how states respond to incidents because state practice helps reveal how states view such incidents politically and legally. States shape the meaning and interpretation of international legal rules through their behaviour, which is important in areas in which international agreements don't define concepts such as the use of force and armed attack [12].

5.2 Interpretation of International Law in Terms of the Tallinn Manual and Other Authors on When Conduct Constitutes Cyber Warfare

5.2.1 Tallinn Manual

Melzer [10] a participating expert to the Tallinn Manual gives a concise and clear summary of the application of international law to cyber warfare which makes for good reading.

Chapter II of the Tallinn Manual deals with use of force. The International Group of Experts discussed chapter II with reference to the International Court of Justice which stated that Article 2(4) of the UN Charter regarding the use of force (Rules 10–12 of the Tallinn Manual) and Article 51 of the UN Charter regarding the use of self-defense (Rules 13–17 of the Tallinn Manual) apply to 'any use of force regardless of the weapons employed.' The International Group of Experts unanimously agreed that cyber operations falls within the ambit of this statement and is an accurate reflection of the customary international law.

To determine whether cyber operations constitute use of force and armed attack, the Tallinn Manual refers to various rules. Since this discussion focuses on determining when conduct would constitute an act of war with specific reference to the attacks launched in 2007 on Estonia and 2010 on Iran, only those rules relevant to the discussion will be referred to.

A. *Ius ad bellum* (right to use force)

Regarding the use of force in terms of article 2(4) of the UN Charter:

Rule 11 provides that cyber actions will constitute use of force when its scale and effect are comparable to non-cyber operations rising to the level of a use of force. When it comes to use of force, the Tallinn Manual (Rule 13) refers to the following scenarios and whether it would amount to use of force:

- Non-destructive cyber psychological operations intended solely to undermine confidence in a government or economy will not qualify as a use of force.
- Funding a hacktivist group conducting cyber operations as part of an insurgency will not be use of force, but providing an organized group with malware and the training necessary to use it to carry out a cyber attack against another state will constitute use of force.
- Providing sanctuary (safe haven) to those mounting cyber operations of the requisite severity, will not be use of force but if the provision of sanctuary is coupled with other acts such as the substantial support or providing cyber defenses for the non-state group, it could in certain circumstances amount to use of force.

Rule 9 provides that a victim state may resort to proportionate countermeasures against the responsible state, for example if state B launches a cyber operation against state A's electricity generating facility at a dam in order to coerce state A to increase the flow of water into a river running through state B, state A may lawfully respond with proportionate countermeasures such as cyber operations against state B's irrigation system.

The International Group of Experts found that although the cyber operations against Estonia were persistent, the attack did not rise to the level of an armed conflict (Rule 20). The attack could also not be attributed to a specific nation-state as there was no confirmed evidence of attribution. As the attack brought down government websites, a major bank's online services and telephone networks it constituted a serious breach of the nation-state's security and its' critical information infrastructure. But within the ambit of the international law which recourse or remedy did Estonia have against the attack? The comment that the suspension by Estonia of some services to internet protocol (IP) addresses from Russia, is not considered as a countermeasure in terms of the Tallinn Manual, is interesting.

Although the International Group of Experts were unanimous that Stuxnet was illegal as an act of force in terms of article 2(4) of the UN Charter, they were divided on whether its effects were severe enough to constitute an 'armed attack.'

Regarding an armed attack in terms of article 51 of the UN Charter:

Had the use of the Stuxnet malware been an armed attack it would give rise to the right of unilateral self-defense on the part of Iran in accordance with article 51.

Rule 13 states that the scale and effects required for an act to be characterized as an armed attack necessarily exceeded those qualifying as use of force. Only in the event that the use of force reached the threshold of an armed attack is a state entitled to respond by using force in self-defense.

The International Group of Experts agreed that any use of force that injures or kills persons or damage or destroys property would satisfy the scale and effect requirement. They also agreed that acts of cyber intelligence gathering and cyber theft as well as cyber operations that involve brief or periodic interruption of non-essential cyber services do not qualify as an armed attack.

However, the International Group of Experts could not agree on whether or not actions that do not result in injury, death, damage, or destruction but would otherwise have extensive negative affect would constitute an armed attack. They were for example divided in respect of a cyber incident directed at the New York Stock Exchange that resulted in the market to crash: some felt that the mere financial loss did not constitute damage for purposes of an armed conflict whereas others were of the opinion that the catastrophic affect of such a crash, could constitute an armed attack. However, a cyber operation directed against major components (systems) of a state's critical infrastructure that caused severe, although not destructive effects, would qualify as an armed attack.

In respect of cyber espionage by state A against state B that unexpectedly results in significant damage to state B's critical infrastructure, the majority of the International Group of Experts agreed that intention is irrelevant in qualifying an operation as an armed attack and that only the scale and effects matter. Any response would however have to comply with the necessity and proportionality criteria (Rule 14) as well as imminence and immediacy (Rule 15). The majority of the International Group of Experts agreed that a devastating cyber operation undertaken by terrorists (non-state actors) from within state A against the critical infrastructure located in state B qualified as an armed attack by the terrorists.

The majority of the International Group of Experts agreed that although article 51 does not provide for defensive action in anticipation of an armed attack, a state does not have to wait 'idly as the enemy prepares to attack', but it may defend itself if the armed conflict is imminent (anticipatory self-defense).

The International Group of Experts agreed that although there has not yet been a reported armed conflict that can be publicly characterised as having solely been pre-cipitated in cyberspace, cyber operations alone have the potential to cross the threshold of international armed conflict.

B. *Ius in bello* (the law governing armed conflict)

A condition precedent to the application of the law of armed conflict is the existence of the armed conflict (Rule 20). The only example where the law of armed conflict was applicable to cyber operations was during the international armed conflict between Georgia and Russia in 2008 as the cyber operations were undertaken in the furtherance of that conflict. For instance if a hacker attack occurs after two countries become engaged in open conflict then the hackers behind the cyber attack have effectively joined hostilities as combatants and can be targeted with 'legal force' [8]. Although *ius in bello* is important, it is less relevant to the topic under discussion.

5.2.2   The Interpretation of International Law by Other Authors
In support of the interpretation given by the Tallinn Manual:

Joyner [14] agrees with the interpretation the Tallinn Manual gives to whether the use of the malware, Stuxnet constituted illegal intervention, illegal use of force and armed attack. He states that there has been a debate amongst international legal scholars over whether, and to what extent, the criteria for use of force under article 2(4) and the criteria for armed attack under article 51 differ. Joyner feels that there is a difference in intensity evidenced in the applicable legal sources. He is of the opinion that as the use of force was illegal in terms of article 2(4) it would allow Iran the right to engage in lawful countermeasures as defined in the law on state responsibility. Rule 9 of the Tallinn Manual suggests proportionate countermeasures are permitted against online attacks carried out by a state. Such measures cannot involve the use of force, however, unless the original cyber-attack resulted in death or significant damage to property. There must also be clear evidence that the target of the countermeasure is the state responsible for the illegal use of force. Evidence and attribution are some of the difficulties facing the legal regulation of cyber attacks. It should also be kept in mind that Iran did not know that its infrastructure was under attack or by whom until long after Stuxnet had done its damage [8].

Fidler [12] takes an interesting view of Stuxnet. As Stuxnet constituted a deliberate, hostile, highly sophisticated, state-created and critical infrastructure threatening offensive use of malware, he is of the opinion that by applying the criteria referred to at paragraph 5.1 to Stuxnet, a plausible argument can be made that its deployment constituted an illegal use of force, armed attack and an act of aggression. But he goes on to say that although doctrinal analysis is important, state practice must also be taken into account. Fidler remarks that nation-states have curiously been quiet about Stuxnet. He indicates that nation-states such as the victim state (Iran), emerging great powers not suspected of involvement (for example China, Russia and India) and developing countries have refrained from applying international law on the use of force, armed attack and aggression. Fidler therefore comes to the conclusion that the state practice of silence suggests that from a legal and technical perspective states may not have perceived that this situation triggered the international rules on the use of force, armed attack and aggression.

He comes to the following conclusion - and one that may necessitate some debate - namely that after Stuxnet there may have been a development of cyber-specific rules that increase the political and legal space in which states can use cyber technologies against one another. In the light of state practice in the wake of Stuxnet, he suggests that especially big cyber-powers such as China, Russian and the US are seeking to establish higher use-of-force and armed-attack thresholds for cyber-based actions to permit more room to explore and exploit cyber technologies as instruments of foreign policy and national security. For example, states engage in cyber espionage on a scale, intensity and intrusiveness that signals a tolerance for covert cyber operations. Cyber espionage imposes adverse political, economic and military pressure on governments which in a physical world would have been considered illegal threats or uses of force. Therefore he argues that in the light of state practice, Stuxnet did not cross the threshold into use of force.

After the DDoS attacks on Estonia, the Estonian government argued that it was the victim of an armed attack but NATO and Russia opposed this characterization. [12] It should be noted that although Iran may not have publicly denounced the states responsible for the attacks as Estonia did, it did not accept the attacks without reprisals. It was reported in August 2012 that a virus infected the information network of the Saudi Arabian oil major, Aramco, and erased data on three-quarters of its corporate computers. All the infected screens were left displaying an image of a burning American flag. Chaulia [15] states that it was a symbolic counter-attack by Iran against the 'economic lifeline of a U.S ally and a deadly rival in the Middle East.' In the same article [15] it is reported that in September 2012 Iran launched a series of sequential attacks against the US financial industry including JP Morgan and Wells Fargo which resulted in the slowing down of overwhelmed servers and denying customers access to the bank services.

It is clear from Clarke and Knake's comments in respect of the launch of the Stuxnet worm that they are of the opinion that the conduct of the US was not in its best interest. The comments are interesting taking into account that Clarke was a former cyber-security advisor to President Obama. They state that with Stuxnet the US had crossed a Rubicon in cyber space. It launched a cyber attack that not only caused another nation's sensitive equipment to be destroyed, but it also legitimized such behaviour in cyberspace. It is however debatable whether the US and Israel succeeded in their object: the process only delayed the Iranian nuclear program by months. The biggest problem is that Stuxnet fell into the hands of hackers throughout the world who now have a sophisticated tool to attack the kind of networks that turn electrical power grids, pipeline networks, railways, and manufacturing processes in refineries and chemical plants.

6 The Way Forward Regarding the Governance of Conduct that Constitutes Cyber War

Melzer [10] concludes that although cyber warfare is subjected to established rules and principles within the ambit of the international law, transporting the rules and principles of international law that were developed in a physical world to cyber space pose some difficulties. He states that some of these questions require unanimous policy decisions by the international legislator, the international community of states.

I am of the opinion that this 'international legislator' will have to convene under the auspices of the United Nations. My opinion [16] is based on the following:

- The Council of Europe Convention on Cybercrime of 2001 (referred to as the Cybercrime Convention) which came into operation in 2004 have not reached a global level of acceptance by nation-states. In 2013 approximately 34 nation-states have become members of the Cybercrime Convention. South Africa was interestingly enough one of four states that participated in the drafting of the Cybercrime Convention. Since its implementation, South Africa became a member state in 2010 of the economic organization, BRICS which consists of Brazil, Russia, India and China. It is doubtful whether South Africa will ratify the Cybercrime Convention.
- In 2011 Russia, China, Tajikistan and Uzebikistan sent a letter to the UN Secretary-General Ban Ki-moon calling for a UN resolution on a code of conduct relating to the use of information technology by countries. [17] The proposed UN resolution called on countries to co-operate in order to combat criminal and terrorist activities involving cyberspace. It also called on countries to give an undertaking that it would not use technology to carry out hostile acts of aggression. The code provides that a nation-state should be in the position to protect their information 'space' and critical information infrastructure from threats, disturbance, attack and sabotage. Many states have developed cyber warfare capabilities [15].
- The purpose of the ITU World Conference on International Telecommunications (WCIT – 12) was to agree on updates to the International Telecommunications Regulations (ITR) which had last been discussed in 1988. Unfortunately the WCIT – 12 highlighted the tension between so-called western and non-western states in respect of internet regulation. On the one hand there is the so-called western nation-states under the leadership of the US who opposes international regulation. The US favours bi- and multi-national agreements between nation-states to address across border concerns, such as cybercrime investigations. Opposing this group of nation-states, the so-called non-western nation-states under leadership of Russia and China, propose a central international body to regulate cybercrime and cyber warfare [18].

Although the WCIT-12 was not the ideal forum to air the differences in respect of the legal regulation of the internet, it is inevitable that in the absence of any forum, the conflict – long expected – would openly come to the fore. One can only speculate on the root causes for the tension. Not only did internet connectivity of nation-states result in many nation-states of different cultural, economic and political views joining the international cyber environment, but it may be that some nation-states are of the opinion that as the internet is not owned by a specific nation-state that all nation-states should participate as equal partners in the governance of cyberspace and this may have resulted in a power-struggle between nation-states for dominance of the internet.

7 Conclusion

The Tallinn Manual is a commendable document. It provides comprehensive rules pertaining to when conduct constitutes cyber warfare. It also shows that determining when and which conduct constitutes cyber warfare is complex and in some instances the position is far from certain. Similarly it is also not certain when a victim state may use countermeasures or act in private-defense against the state responsible for the attack.

Chaulia [15] states: 'Eventually, in the absence of any multilateral agreement at the level of the United Nations to moderate and set limits on cyber war, there could (be) a balance of power and a "balance of terror" that will set in to regulate the murky business of hacking and destroying the internet assets of adversaries.' This is apparent in the reprisals in respect of attacks that may not constitute cyber war in terms of the international law.

This discussion concludes with an extract of a speech by President Obama: 'But cyberspace has also been abused … Because cyber weapons are so easily activated and the identity of an attacker can sometimes be kept secret, because cyber weapons can strike thousands of targets and inflict extensive disruptions and damage in seconds, they are potentially a new source of instability in a crises, and could become a new threat to peace … And our goal as signers of the United Nations Charter is, as pledged in San Francisco well over half a century ago, to save succeeding generations from the scourge of war. I ask you to join me in taking a step back from the edge of what could be a new battle space and take steps not to fight in cyberspace but to fight against cyber war' [5].

These words are on the one hand quite ironic taking into account the US and Israel's co-operative launch of Stuxnet against Iran, but on the other hand the US now realizes its vulnerability with reference to Clarke and Knake who states: '… the US has launched also what is likely to be a cyber boomerang, a weapon that will someday be used to attack some of America's own defenceless networks' [5].

Unfortunately I am of the opinion that not all the internet-connected nations has heard the plea by the US or if they have, it is debatable whether there exists sufficient trust, confidence and transparency between nation-states to believe, in the absence of a multilateral treaty on cyber warfare, that a nation-state will uphold its' pledge not to use cyber warfare.

References

1. Schmitt, M.N.: Tallinn Manual on the International Law Applicable to Cyber Warfare. Cambridge University Press, Cambridge (2013)
2. Rauscher, K.F., Korotkov, A.: Russia-U.S. Bilateral on Critical Infrastructure Protection: Working towards Rules for Governing Cyber Conflict Rendering the Geneva and Hague Conventions in Cyberspace, p. 8, 11, 14, 18. EastWest Institute, New York (2011)

3. Zetter, K.: Legal experts: Stuxnet attack on Iran was illegal 'act of force' (2013). http://www. wired.com/threatlevel/2013/03/stuxnet-act-for
4. National Cybersecurity Policy Framework for South Africa (2013). http://www.cyanre.co. za/national-cybersecurity-policy.pdf
5. Clarke, R.A., Knake, R.K.: Cyber War, p. 6, 11–14, 278–279, 290–296. HarperCollins Publishers, New York (2012)
6. Kirchner, S.: Distributed Denial-of-Service Attacks Under Public International Law: State Responsibility in Cyberwar. In: The Icfai University Journal of Cyber law, p. 13. Icfai University Press, Hyderabad (2009)
7. Bowcott, V.: Rules of cyberwar: don't target nuclear plants or hospitals says NATO manual (2013). http://www.guardian.co.uk/world/2013/mar/18/rules-cyberw
8. Leyden, J.: Cyberwarfare playbook says Stuxnet may have been 'armed' attack (2013). http://www.theregister.co.uk/2013/03/27/stuxnet_cyverwar_r
9. Into the Intro: The Tallinn Manual on the International Law Applicable to Cyber Warfare (2013). http://www.cambridgeblog.org/2013/04/into-the-intro-the-tal
10. Melzer, N.: Cyberwarfare and International Law (2011). http://www.unidir.org/files/ publications/pdfs/cyberwarfare-and-international-law-382.pdf
11. Vihul, L.: The Tallinn Manual on the International Law applicable to cyber Warfare. http:// www.ejiltalk.org/the-tallinn-manual-on-the-internation
12. Fidler, D.P.: Was Stuxnet an act of war? decoding a cyberattack. In: IEEE Computer and Reliability Societies, pp. 56–59 (July/August 2001)
13. Dugard, J.: International Law: A South African Perspective. Juta, Cape Town (2011). Chapter 24 (pp. 495–513) and chapter 25 (pp. 519–525)
14. Dan Joyner, D.: Stuxnet an "Act of Force" Against Iran". http://armscontrollaw.com/2013/ 03/25stuxnet-an-act-of-force-agains
15. Chaulie, S.: Cyber Warfare is the new threat to the global order (2013). http://www. nationmultimedia.com/opinion/Cyber-warfare-is
16. Watney, M.M.: The way forward in addressing cybercrime regulation on a global level. J. Internet Technol. Secur. Trans. 1(1/2) (2012)
17. United Nations General Assembly, '66th session developments in the field of information and telecommunications in the context of international security'. http://www.chinadaily. com.cn/cndy/201109/14/content_13680896.htm. Accessed Feb 2012
18. Watney, M.M.: A South African legal perspective on State Governance of Cybersecurity within an African and global context. In: Lex Informatica, South Africa (2013)

Digital Forensics - Standards, Certification and Accreditation

Measuring Accuracy of Automated Parsing and Categorization Tools and Processes in Digital Investigations

Joshua I. James[1]([⊠]), Alejandra Lopez-Fernandez[2], and Pavel Gladyhsev[3]

[1] Digital Forensic Investigation Research Laboratory, SoonChunHyang University,
Shinchang-myeon, Asan-si, South Korea
joshua@cybercrimetech.com
[2] Computer Science and Informatics, University College Dublin,
Belfield, Dublin 4, Ireland
[3] Digital Forensic Investigation Research Laboratory, University College Dublin,
Belfield, Dublin 4, Ireland

Abstract. This work presents a method for the measurement of the accuracy of evidential artifact extraction and categorization tasks in digital forensic investigations. Instead of focusing on the measurement of accuracy and errors in the functions of digital forensic tools, this work proposes the application of information retrieval measurement techniques that allow the incorporation of errors introduced by tools and analysis processes. This method uses a 'gold standard' that is the collection of evidential objects determined by a digital investigator from suspect data with an unknown ground truth. This work proposes that the accuracy of tools and investigation processes can be evaluated compared to the derived gold standard using common precision and recall values. Two example case studies are presented showing the measurement of the accuracy of automated analysis tools as compared to an in-depth analysis by an expert. It is shown that such measurement can allow investigators to determine changes in accuracy of their processes over time, and determine if such a change is caused by their tools or knowledge.

Keywords: Digital forensic investigation · Investigation accuracy · Information retrieval · Precision and recall · Digital investigation measurement · Digital investigation verification

1 Introduction

In digital forensics, the verification and error rates of forensic processes are a common topic. This is mostly due to the evidence admissibility considerations brought on as a result of Daubert v. Merrell Dow Pharmaceuticals, 509 US 579 [25]. "The Daubert process identifies four general categories that are used as guidelines when assessing a procedure" [4]. These are procedure Testing, Error Rate, Publication and Acceptance.

© Institute for Computer Sciences, Social Informatics and Telecommunications Engineering 2014
P. Gladyshev et al. (Eds.): ICDF2C 2013, LNICST 132, pp. 147–169, 2014.
DOI: 10.1007/978-3-319-14289-0_11

Tools are commonly tested and organizations such as the National Institute of Standards and Technology (NIST) have created test methodologies for various types of tools which are outlined in their Computer Forensic Tool Testing (CFTT) project [20]. But beyond testing, error rates for tools are not often calculated [2,11,18]. The argument has been made that a tested tool with a high number of users must have a low error rate because if there was a high rate of error, users would not use the tool [9]. So far this argument appears to be widely accepted, however Carrier [4] submits that "At a minimum this may be true, but a more scientific approach should be taken as the field matures". Furthermore, Lyle [18] states that "[a] general error rate [for digital forensic tools] may not be meaningful", claiming that an error rate should be defined for each function. Because of this, and the lack of Law Enforcement's (LE) time and resources [7], verification of a tool rarely passes beyond the testing phase of the Daubert process. The same can also be said for the investigator's overall examination process. Some groups claim that a Standard Operating Procedure (SOP) should dictate the overall examination process [14,23]. Validation of this process is commonly done by peer review, but according to James and Gladyshev [11] peer review does not always take place. They found that none of the survey respondents mentioned any form of objective measurement of accuracy for the examination process. Further, there has been little research in the area of overall examination accuracy measurement.

Forensic examinations are a procedure for which performance measurement, specifically the measurement of accuracy, is not being conducted, for reasons such as concerns about the subjectivity, practicality and even abuse of such measures [13]. Error rates are created for procedures, tools and functions to determine their probability of failure, and also as a measure for which other methods can be compared against. "... [E]rror rates in analysis are facts. They should not be feared, but they must be measured" [22]. This work is a brief introduction to the problem of accuracy measurement in subjective areas such as digital forensic analysis, why it is needed, and how it may allow investigators to identify when their tools or training is becoming outdated.

1.1 Contribution

Previous work has shown that current digital forensic investigations do not normally attempt to quantify the accuracy of examinations beyond the percentage error of investigation tools [11]. This work proposes the application of previously known information retrieval accuracy measurement methods to measure the accuracy of digital investigation tools and processes. This work demonstrates that application of the proposed method allows investigators to determine accuracy and error rates of automated or manual processes over time. Further, the proposed method allows investigators to determine where error is being introduced: either at the artifact detection or categorization level. Finally, accuracy measurements can be used to compare the accuracy of highly automated tools – such as those used in 'intelligent' triage – against a human-created 'gold standard' to determine how effective such next-generation digital investigation tools are.

2 Related Work

Many fields attempt to measure the accuracy of their processes. In Crawford v. Commonwealth, 33 Va. App. 431 [26] – in regards to DNA evidence – the jury was instructed that they "...may consider any evidence offered bearing upon the accuracy and reliability of the procedures employed in the collection and analysis..." and that "DNA testing is deemed to be a reliable scientific technique...". Although the technique may be reliable "occasional errors arising from accidental switching and mislabeling of samples or misinterpretation of results have come to light..." [27]. Furthermore, the relatively recent "Phantom of Heilbronn" incident has led to questions of not just internal, but also the external processes that may ultimately effect evidence [21,28]. While the DNA testing technique itself has been deemed to be reliable, erroneous results are still possible due to human error. Digital examinations are not much different in this regard. While a tool may be able to accurately display data, that data is not evidence until an investigator, or a human, interprets it as such. No amount of tool testing can ensure that a human interprets the meaning of the returned results correctly. The law in a region being measured may be used to attempt to objectively define the correctness of an investigation; however, correctness in an investigation is somewhat vulnerable to the subjective conclusions of the investigator and their biases.

Information Retrieval (IR) is one area where accuracy measurement is paramount. Much work has been done in the area of IR, and IR accuracy measurement techniques have previously been applied to forensic text sting searching [3], document classification [6], and even fragmented document analysis in digital forensics [17]. The focus, however, has been on the accuracy measurement of particular techniques or tools within the digital examination process, and not for the examination process itself.

3 Objective Measures of Analysis Performance

At present, the efficacy of digital forensic analysis is, in effect, a function of the duration of an examination and of the evidence it produces. These factors force investigators to increase their use of automated tools, and explore autonomous systems for analysis [15]. Many automated digital forensic tools focus on inculpatory evidence, such as the presence of images, leaving the search for exculpatory evidence to the investigator. Also, many investigators are not comparing their automated tools to a baseline performance measure, such as other similar tools or the results of a manual investigation, which could lead to missed evidence and incomplete investigations. Tools are also not the only component in a digital forensic analysis. Even if all data is displayed correctly, the investigator must then interpret the data correctly. As such, a system of accuracy measurement capable of considering both tools and analysis is needed.

Two simple but informative metrics used in Information Retrieval systems are precision and recall [24]. This work submits that precision and recall measures can be applied to tools and categorization (analysis) processes in digital investigations. An overall performance measure relative to both the precision and recall, called an F-measure, may be used as the score for overall accuracy of the process. This measurement can help to identify fluctuations in overall process accuracy over time. Precision and recall may then be specifically analyzed to determine if there are problems with artifact identification or categorization. Such metrics may lead to more focused training, smarter budgeting, better tool or technique selection and ultimately higher-quality investigations.

The use of precision and recall is suggested rather than current percentage error methods normally employed in digital forensic tool testing. Percentage error is commonly used to determine the error of a particular function of a tool. While percentage error could be used to evaluate the overall error of artifact categorization in an investigation process with various tools, there is no clear indication where error is being introduced. By using precision and recall, precision can be thought of as the investigator's (or automated tool's) ability to properly classify a retrieved artifact. Recall can be thought of as the investigator's (or automated tool's) ability to discover and retrieve relevant artifacts. These scores can then be used to calculate overall accuracy, which can allow not only identification of weaknesses over time but also whether problems are arising from classification or recall challenges.

3.1 Digital Analysis

Evidence, as defined by Anderson and Twinning [1], is "any fact considered by the tribunal as data to persuade them to reach a reasoned belief [of a theory]". Digital forensic analysis attempts to identify evidence that supports a theory, contradicts a theory, as well as evidence of tampering [4]. If an investigator focuses only on inculpatory evidence, it is possible that they could miss a piece of evidence that may prove the innocence of the suspect, and vice versa. Current digital forensic tools help an investigator to view objects that may have possible evidential value, but what that value is – inculpatory, exculpatory, tampering, or nothing – is determined manually by the investigator. The investigator must take the type of case, context of the object and any other evidence into account. This means that the identification of evidential artifacts strongly relates to the knowledge of the investigator. For example, in a survey, 67 % of investigators claimed only a basic familiarity with the Microsoft Windows Registry [10]. If an investigator has little or no knowledge of the Microsoft Windows Registry, he or she may not consider it as a source of evidence. In this case the accuracy of the tool may not be in question, but instead the accuracy of the process or investigator. By using precision and recall compared to a gold standard, the accuracy of both the tool and investigator can be measured, allowing an investigator to determine where error is being introduced.

3.2 Precision and Recall

The area of Computer Science known as information retrieval, among others, uses methods to measure the accuracy of the information that is retrieved.

Two commonly used metrics are precision and recall. As defined by Russell and Norvig [24], "precision measures the proportion of documents in the result set that are actually relevant... [and] recall measures the proportion of all the relevant documents in the collection that are in the result set". Manning, Raghavan et al. [19] define the calculation of precision and recall mathematically using the following formulas:

$$Precision = \frac{\# \ relevant \ items \ retrieved}{\# \ retrieved \ items} = P(relevant|retrieved)$$

OR

$$Precision = \frac{|\{relevant \ items\} \cap \{retrieved \ items\}|}{|\{retrieved \ items\}|}$$

$$Recall = \frac{\# \ relevant \ items \ retrieved}{\# \ relevant \ items} = P(retrieved|relevant)$$

OR

$$Recall = \frac{|\{relevant \ items\} \cap \{retrieved \ items\}|}{|\{relevant \ items\}|}$$

Consider a search engine, for example. When a user enters a query, given enough time, a document containing exactly what the user was looking for could be returned from the set. But if the search had a high level of precision, then the number of documents returned (recalled) would be low and would take more time. Search engines, however, attempt to return results as quickly as possible. Because of this, precision is reduced and a higher number of relevant, but possibly less exact, documents are returned.

An accuracy measure relative to both the precision and recall, called an F-measure (F), may be used as the score for overall accuracy of the measured query. The equation for calculating the F-measure is defined by Russell and Norvig (2009) as:

$$F = 2 \cdot \frac{precision \cdot recall}{precision + recall}$$

3.3   Accuracy of Analysis

This work proposes that precision and recall may also be applied to the measurement of digital forensic analysis. For example, a digital examination can be considered similar to a search engine query. Digital investigators are asking a question, and their tools return a set of artifacts that may be more or less relevant to the question posed. These artifacts are normally analyzed by an investigator to further remove irrelevant artifacts. Finally, artifacts are then tested for relevance in court. For comparison, a baseline of correctness, or 'gold standard', must be established. The artifacts found (recalled) can be used to calculate the accuracy of the examination as compared to a baseline standard.

In digital forensics, peer reviewed in-depth examination of a suspect's system by an expert is the level of examination that is normally accepted for use in court. Because the ground truth about evidential artifacts is unknown, this level of examination may not accurately identify all potential artifacts; however, it is the most comprehensive examination method possible. In other words, with an unknown ground truth, an investigator cannot know what he or she has missed, if anything. In this work an artifact is defined as information that supports or denies a hypothesis. The results of an examination (a collection evidential artifacts) are evaluated for admissibility by the court, resulting in a possible subset of artifacts accepted as evidence. From this, the 'gold standard' investigators normally strive for will be defined as *the resulting set of evidential artifacts returned during a peer-reviewed examination that are accepted as admissible evidence in court.* However, in this work the gold standard will be defined as the returned and categorized artifacts after a peer-reviewed examination. With this definition, the gold standard is set at the level of a peer-reviewed human investigation. Using this standard, the results of an examination from other investigators, tools or processes may be objectively compared. Likewise, autonomous digital forensic analysis systems may also be measured against the gold standard, and compared to other processes.

Accuracy of analysis for a certain process, investigator or autonomous system can also be averaged over time to evaluate trends. For example, as software used for analysis becomes out of date, new evidential data sources may exist that the software cannot analyze. By measuring the performance of the process over time, the accuracy may decrease, signaling either an issue with the software or the investigator's knowledge about the new data sources.

Since the accuracy of tools using precision and recall has been discussed in other works, this paper will focus on a method for investigator and analysis phase accuracy calculation.

Measuring the Investigation Process. In digital forensic analysis, the ideal investigator performance is a high precision (no false positives), and a high recall (no false negatives); all found as fast as possible. Essentially, requirements for an investigator are similar to the requirements for an analysis tool, as described by Carrier [4]. An investigator that is comprehensive, accurate and whose work is deterministic and verifiable could be considered competent. This means that both high precision and high recall – high accuracy – is equivalent to high performance. This work does not take the weight of artifacts into account. That is, no one artifact is considered any more important than any other. By calculating the investigation process's precision and recall for an analysis, compared to the results of a peer-reviewed examination (or acceptance in court), the resulting accuracy measure may be calculated.

Consider an example where the results of a particular process discovered 4 inculpatory artifacts, and 3 exculpatory artifacts for a total of 7 artifacts. During a peer-reviewed examination the gold standard discovered 9 inculpatory artifacts and 1 exculpatory artifact. This means that the given process led to the discovery of 5 relevant artifacts, missed 5 artifacts, and identified two artifacts falsely compared to the gold standard. In this case, since the gold standard may not be the ultimate truth, a human investigator would need to evaluate whether the falsely identified artifacts were, in fact, not relevant. In the case that they were actually false, precision (P) for the process is found to be:

$$P = \frac{\#\ relevant\ items\ retrieved}{\#\ items\ retrieved} = \frac{5}{7} = 0.71$$

Recall (R) is found to be:

$$R = \frac{\#\ relevant\ items\ retrieved}{\#\ relevant\ items} = \frac{5}{10} = 0.5$$

Finally, the F-measure (F) is found to be:

$$F = 2 \cdot \frac{P \cdot R}{P + R} = 2 \cdot \frac{0.71 \cdot 0.5}{0.71 + 0.5} = 0.59$$

In this case the process's precision is 0.71 or 71 %. However, if the process led to the discovery of only one artifact, and that artifact was of evidential value, then the process's precision would be 100 %. In digital investigations, it may be possible that one piece of evidence is all that is necessary, but in many cases supporting information may need to be provided. This is why recall is important. A high precision with a low recall means that the process is missing evidence. In the current example the recall is 0.5 or 50 %. This means that the process missed half of the possible artifacts. The F-measure is the relative combination of the precision and recall. In this case, the examination process scored 0.59 or 59 %. This is the process's accuracy score for this analysis.

By measuring Precision, Recall and F-measure over time, departments can observe accuracy trends in the examination process, as well as calculate overall performance. Consider the fictional example shown in Table 1. By examining the F-measure, it can be seen that the process's accuracy is decreasing (Fig. 1). It can also be seen that the process is consistently missing almost half of the relevant artifacts. By using this method, it becomes easy to see if there are problem areas, and where the problem exists; either with precision (categorization) or recall (artifact extraction).

Table 1. Fictional example calculating Precision, Recall and F-measure for an investigator over time

	Precision	Recall	F-measure
Analysis 1	0.71	0.5	0.59
Analysis 2	1	0.6	0.75
Analysis 3	1	0.5	0.67
Analysis 4	0.7	0.3	0.42
Average	0.85	0.48	0.61

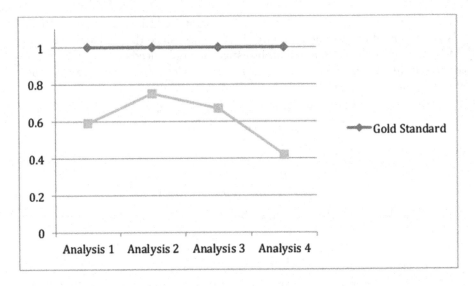

Fig. 1. Analysis accuracy over time compared to the gold standard

Other Levels of Forensic Examination. Casey, Ferraro et al. [5] describe multiple layers of digital forensic examination to help handle an ever-increasing amount of data needing to be analyzed. The use of a multiple layer investigation model has been confirmed by James and Gladyshev [11], where 78 % of respondents claimed to use some sort of preliminary analysis. Most forms of preliminary analysis involve some form of automation, and much of the time if a preliminary analysis is done, the decision to continue or stop the examination will be made based on what is found – or not – with these less in-depth processes. It also appears that in all cases if anything suspicious is found during a preliminary examination, then an in-depth analysis will normally take place [12]. Current processes, such as triage, have been shown to help reduce the number of suspect machines needing an in-depth examination; however, triage and highly automated preview examinations are not currently as effective as manual in-depth investigations in every situation [8, 16]. The issue then is that decisions to not continue analysis are being made based on a minimum amount of information. Also, investigators conducting preliminary analyses do not know what is potentially being missed since they are not conducting a full examination.

"To reduce the incidence of incorrect conclusions based on unreliable or inaccurate data it is necessary to quantify uncertainty and correct for it whenever possible" [5]. The proposed method to measure accuracy may be applied to all layers of examination. If a highly automated tool, such as a triage solution, is being used to make decisions about a system, an F-measure can be calculated for the solution or process as described and compared to the gold standard. Form this, departments can determine the limitations and benefits of their preliminary analysis techniques and particular tools, resulting in more informed decisions about their overall analysis process.

4 Implementation of Accuracy Measurement in Digital Forensic Laboratories

Current tool and process verification methods are challenging to implement in practice for the simple reason that testing is a time-consuming task for laboratories that may already be overburdened. Baggili, Mislan, et al. [2] proposed a programmatic approach to error rate calculation but also showed concerns about whether an investigator would record required data in a database. Implementing current tool testing methods usually requires a strict process and definition of scope to potentially only test one out of hundreds of functions of a tool. For tool or process testing to be practical, the measurement process must be minimally disruptive to current digital investigation processes.

While there are many ways to implement the proposed accuracy measurement method in a digital investigation, this work will give one example of how such a measurement process could be implemented in a way that is minimally disruptive to current investigation processes. The proposed measurement method was used during the implementation of a new 'Preliminary Analysis Unit' as described by James and Gladyshev [12].

One major concern with implementing a preliminary analysis phase within a real unit is that, as described, without conducting a full investigation of every piece of media the investigators do not know what may be missed. Since a preliminary analysis process is normally highly automated investigators are limited in the use their own intuition to judge whether an investigation should continue even if nothing was found. As was observed, concerns over missing potential evidence caused the investigators to be more conservative in their judgment for suspect data to receive a full investigations.

The goal of accuracy measurement in this case was to evaluate the accuracy of not only the preliminary analysis tool, but the entire preliminary analysis process. In other words, (1) how accurate was the decision for the suspect data to receive a full analysis and (2) how accurate was the quick preliminary analysis in extracting and identifying evidential data. Precision and recall was used to evaluate the latter question.

Since an entirely new process was being implemented, each preliminary analyst conducted a preliminary analysis on each test case. The output of their analysis was a decision, "yes" or "no", to conduct a full analysis of the suspect device, and the number of pieces of information that they identified as relevant to the case based on the provided output. Pieces of information would normally be extracted files, but could also be the identification of encryption or information in a log file. For example, the Windows Registry could be considered a single data source, but each key within the data source may provide a single piece of information. When implementing the measurement process, a standard definition must be made about what exactly is being measured and how different data are classified.

Each test case, regardless of the preliminary analyst's decision received a full examination. The examiner was not made aware of the preliminary analyst's decision and results. After each of the suspect test devices received a full investigation, the output of the full investigation was whether the suspect device was relevant, "yes" or "no", and the number of the pieces of information the investigator identified as relevant.

By comparing the results of the preliminary analysis with the results of the full investigation, the precision, recall and accuracy of the preliminary analysis process could be calculated. By calculating the precision and accuracy of the process, a baseline accuracy was set for the preliminary analysis process. From this it became clear that accuracy was largely analyst-specific. When the output of the tool was given to multiple investigators for analysis, each analyst classified the data – at least slightly – differently. And, as expected, the analyst with the most experience was the most accurate.

Testing all cases in a similar manner, however, is not sustainable. Once management was satisfied that the preliminary analysis process was fit for their purposes – and understood where the process failed – they opted for measurement on a sample set rather than during each case.

It was decided that each preliminary analyst would conduct a preliminary analysis will full measurement of identified pieces of information on every 10 cases. After, each suspect device would be forwarded for a full investigation regardless of the decision of the preliminary analyst. Each device would receive a full investigation (gold standard) and the results would be compared to the output of the preliminary analysis.

By choosing to conduct measurement on only a sample set, the unit could still receive the benefit examining a fewer number of suspect devices while having continual verification of the process built in.

The proposed accuracy measurement implementation process can be summarized in the following steps:

1. Identify what is being measured
2. Identify the gold standard
3. Identify how the measured process will be implemented in the current investigation work flow
4. Conduct the measured process
5. Conduct the gold standard process
6. Measure the output of the new implementation against the output of the gold standard

To fist understand the process being implemented, we found it necessary to have a test period where analysis of all suspect devices was measured. Once the process was understood, a sample (ideally a random sample) was chosen and measurement was only conducted for that random sample.

5   Case Study

In this section, two cases are given where the proposed accuracy measurement method is used. The first case will use data where an investigator was testing a triage tool against a full human investigation. The second case involves five investigators separately testing a different preliminary analysis tool. Comparisons between the investigators, as well as the tools are then evaluated.

Table 2. Summary of examination accuracy results using precision and recall to calculate the overall F-measure

	Precision	Recall	F-measure
Analysis 1	0.67	0.33	0.44
Analysis 2	0.00	0.00	0.00
Analysis 3	1.00	1.00	1.00
Analysis 4	0.07	0.53	0.12
Analysis 5	0.15	0.12	0.13
Average	0.38	0.40	0.34

5.1 Case 1

The following example case has been adapted from the work of Goss [8], where the accuracy of a newly implemented triage process is being compared to a human investigator conducting a full analysis on the given media. In this case the accuracy of automated triage analysis will be compared to the gold standard set by an in-depth manual investigation based on the analysis of a data set with an unknown ground truth. In other words, the automatic classification of objects as having evidential value is being compared to the human gold standard. Five automated triage examinations (5 different media) are given in Appendix A, with their precision, recall and F-measure calculated. In this case, the human investigator validated the gold standard. For this reason, only false positives, as compared to the gold standard, with no further validation, are given. Table 2 gives a summary of the examination accuracy results.

From Table 2, the accuracy of the triage analysis conducted varies greatly. By observing these fluctuations, their cause may possibly be determined. Analysis 2, for example, had poor results because triage is unable to take the context of the case into consideration, and out of context the results returned by a quick triage examination might be suspicious. Alternatively, analysis 3 was extremely accurate because all discovered evidence was found using a 'known-bad' hash database, and only previously known artifacts (artifacts that were in the hash database) were on the suspect system. Overall in this case it can be said that this triage tool, as configured, is good for finding known, or 'low hanging', artifacts but it is not as effective as an in-depth examination by the investigator during more complicated investigations.

Using this method, it is shown that the overall precision of the implemented triage solution in this particular case study is 38%, and that it is missing 60% of the possible evidential artifacts as compared to the gold standard. The overall accuracy 'grade' for the implemented triage analysis is 34%. From here, this measurement can be used as a baseline for improvement, comparison with other automated tools, or to focus when triage should and shouldn't be used. Also, when using this method it becomes clear in which situations triage is missing evidence. With this knowledge, the triage process could possibly be changed to be more comprehensive.

5.2   Case 2

The second case involves five pieces of suspect media that each received a full expert digital forensic analysis, and had reports written as to the findings of all evidential artifacts. Each case was an investigation into possession of suspected child exploitation material. After the suspect media received a full manual analysis by an expert investigator, five preliminary examiners conducted a blind analysis on each piece of media using a locally developed preliminary analysis tool. One preliminary examiner (examiner 1) had experience conducting in-depth digital forensic investigations, while the remaining investigators had no experience with in-depth digital forensic analysis. The goal was to determine if decisions to discard media that did not contain illegal material could accurately be made without a time-consuming full examination. To test this method, the decision error rate was examined as well as the preliminary analysis precision rate using the described method to attempt measure the precision of both the tool and the examiner. The results of each preliminary analysis are given in Appendix B.

In the context of this case study, false positives are defined as artifacts identified as suspicious, but are in fact not illegal according to the gold standard. False negatives are defined as artifacts that are illegal that were not identified according to the gold standard. It is important to note that in a preliminary analysis it is acceptable – and likely – to have false positives in both the object identification and decision for further analysis. This process, however, must have a false negative rate of 0 for the decision for further analysis, meaning that exhibits with illegal content are always sent for further analysis. This process does not necessarily need a false negative rate of 0 for illegal artifact identification, since full illegal artifact identification is the purpose of the full analysis.

Five test cases were given where the suspect media with unknown ground truth received a full manual analysis by a human investigator, from which a report of findings was created. This report is considered the gold standard for classification of artifacts as illegal or unrelated. All cases were based on charges of possession of child exploitation material. Out of the five suspect media, three (60 %) were found to not contain illegal content. Two exhibits (40 %) were found to contain illegal content, most of which were illegal images.

A preliminary examiner then used an automated tool for object extraction purposes, and manually classified objects as illegal or unrelated. Table 3 gives the overall results of the preliminary examiner's further analysis decision and accuracy rates, Table 4 shows the average artifact identification error rate per preliminary examiner compared to the gold standard, and Table 5 displays the average accuracy rate based on artifact identification per investigator compared to the gold standard.

From the Table 3, it is shown that no preliminary examiner falsely excluded suspect media containing illegal material. This means that all exhibits containing illegal material would have received an in-depth analysis. Also, Table 3 shows that the preliminary examiner with more experience – Examiner 1 – had a lower false positive rate in the decision making process. This is presumably due to a better ability to categorize and differentiate between illegal and borderline

Table 3. Further analysis decision false positive and false negative error rates per preliminary examiner

Media further analysis decision error rate				
Examiner	False positive	False positive error	False negative	False negative error
Examiner 5	2	.4	0	0
Examiner 4	2	.4	0	0
Examiner 3	2	.4	0	0
Examiner 1	1	.2	0	0
Examiner 2	2	.4	0	0

Table 4. Average artifact identification error rate per preliminary examiner

Average object identification error rate		
Examiner	Ave. false positive error	Ave. false negative error
Examiner 5	.4	.26
Examiner 4	.31	.13
Examiner 3	.35	.02
Examiner 1	.21	.24
Examiner 2	.31	.09

Table 5. Average accuracy rate based on artifact identification per preliminary examiner

Average accuracy rate	
Examiner	F-measure
Examiner 5	.35
Examiner 4	.57
Examiner 3	.80
Examiner 1	.64
Examiner 2	.55
Unit Ave	.58

content. From Table 4, it can be seen that false positive rates for artifact identification were relatively high. This was an expected outcome since the preliminary examiners are not capable of definitely categorizing borderline illegal content. A higher false positive rate may also indicate the preliminary examiners being overly cautious. Also from Table 4, the false negative rate for artifact identification is somewhat high. This is also expected since preliminary examiners are not conducting a full analysis. Artifact identification false negatives must be compared with the results in Table 3. When comparing artifact identification to the decision process, missing some of the illegal material did not have an effect on the decision process. This is because if there are suspect artifacts, there are likely multiple sources that are suspicious. However, this correlation should be continuously monitored.

5.3 Evaluation

Table 5 is the calculated average accuracy rate based on automatic artifact identification and manual classification. This is a metric that may be used for measurement and comparison in the future to ensure continued quality, where recall correlates to the ability of the tool to return related artifacts, and precision correlates to a preliminary examiner's ability to correctly categorize returned artifacts. If each preliminary examiner dropped in accuracy, it may indicate an issue with tools not extracting the required artifacts, or possibly an issue with the training of the preliminary examiner.

The calculated average accuracy rates may also be used to compare two analysis methods. As an example, consider Table 2, where the average accuracy of the Case 1 triage solution compared to the gold standard (full analysis) was .34 (34 %). If this is compared to the average calculated accuracy – .58 (58 %) – of the (mostly untrained) preliminary examiners in Case 2, it can be seen that the preliminary examiners in Case 2 are approximately .24 (24 %) more accurate than the Case 1 triage solution for making similar decisions. Other metrics, however, should also be considered, such as the time for processing and analysis. For example, the Case 1 triage solution is meant to run on-scene in approximately 2 hours or less, not including analysis. The preliminary analysis solution in Case 2 is designed to be ran in a laboratory from 24 to 48 hours, depending on the size of the suspect media. Because of this, improved accuracy may be expected, but at the cost of time.

Limitations. There are two main limitations to the proposed method, the greatest being the definition of the gold standard. The gold standard, as defined in this paper, requires an expert to verify the findings of a given analysis. While such verification is sometimes performed as a matter of course in digital forensic laboratories, not all organizations can afford to duplicate efforts, even on a random sample. Furthermore, it should be noted that a gold standard is only as good as the experts creating it. If a sub-par examiner is setting the standard, the results of measurement may look very good even for poor examinations.

The second limitation is that the accuracy measurement cannot be used when no illegal artifacts were found in the full analysis. This method is only useful in measuring when some objects – either inculpatory or exculpatory – are discovered by the gold standard.

6 Conclusions

This paper proposed the application of precision and recall metrics for the measurement of the accuracy of digital forensic analyses. Instead of focusing on the measurement of accuracy and errors in digital forensic tools, this work proposed the use of Information Retrieval concepts to incorporate errors introduced by tools and the overall investigation processes. By creating a gold standard with which to compare to, the accuracy of tools and investigation processes can be evaluated, and trends over time determined. From the calculated accuracy it can be determined whether artifact identification or categorization is leading to lower accuracy. This may allow an investigator to assess whether error may lie in the tools or the training over time. The proposed measurement may be applied to many different layers of the investigation process to attempt to determine the most accurate processes, how those processes change over time, and how the unit should change with new trends.

Appendix

A   Case 1: Results of Precision of Investigation vs. the Gold Standard

Examination 1:
   See Table 6.

Table 6. Examination 1 artifacts identified compared to the gold standard

	Inculpatory	Exculpatory	False positive	Total
Gold standard	12	0	N/A	12
Triage examination	4	0	2	6

$$P = \tfrac{4}{6} = 0.67 \quad R = \tfrac{4}{12} = 0.33 \quad F = 2 \cdot \tfrac{0.67 \cdot 0.33}{0.67 + 0.33} = 0.44$$

Examination 2:
   See Table 7.

Table 7. Examination 2 artifacts identified compared to the gold standard

	Inculpatory	Exculpatory	False positive	Total
Gold standard	0	1	N/A	1
Triage examination	0	0	5	5

$$P = \tfrac{0}{5} = 0 \quad R = \tfrac{0}{1} = 0 \quad F = 2 \cdot \tfrac{0 \cdot 0}{0 + 0} = 0$$

Examination 3:
See Table 8.

Table 8. Examination 3 artifacts identified compared to the gold standard

	Inculpatory	Exculpatory	False positive	Total
Gold standard	200	0	N/A	200
Triage examination	200	0	0	200

$$P = \frac{200}{200} = 1 \ R = \frac{200}{200} = 1 \ F = 2 \cdot \frac{1 \cdot 1}{1+1} = 1$$

Examination 4:
See Table 9.

Table 9. Examination 4 artifacts identified compared to the gold standard

	Inculpatory	Exculpatory	False positive	Total
Gold standard	30	0	N/A	30
Triage examination	16	0	200	216

$$P = \frac{16}{216} = 0.07 \ R = \frac{16}{30} = 0.53 \ F = 2 \cdot \frac{0.07 \cdot 0.53}{0.07+0.53} = 0.12$$

Examination 5:
See Table 10.

Table 10. Examination 5 artifacts identified compared to the gold standard

	Inculpatory	Exculpatory	False positive	Total
Gold standard	34	0	N/A	34
Triage examination	4	0	22	26

$$P = \frac{4}{26} = 0.15 \ R = \frac{4}{34} = 0.12 \ F = 2 \cdot \frac{0.15 \cdot 0.12}{0.15+0.12} = 0.13$$

B   Case 2: Results of Precision of Investigation vs. the Gold Standard

See Tables 11, 12, 13, 14, 15, 16, 17, 18, 19, 20, 21, 22, 23, 24, 25, 26, 27, 28, 29 and 30.

Table 11. Results of a full examination on media number 1

Fully-examined case	
Suspect objects	Notes
0	No illegal content was detected in a full analysis

Table 12. Results of preliminary analysis on media number 1 from five examiners

Examiner	Further analysis	Suspect objects	Notes
Examiner 1	Yes	4	Decision made based on found images suspicious deleted files and searching activity
Examiner 2	Yes	6	Decision made based on found images, cleaner programs, Internet activity and evidence of P2P activity
Examiner 3	Yes	4	Decision made based on found images, movies and Internet search and browser history
Examiner 4	Yes	30	Decision made based on large amount of highly suspicious images and some movie files
Examiner 5	Yes	903	Decision made based on a large amount suspicious images

Table 13. Preliminary analysis object identification error rates for media number 1

Object identification error rate				
Examiner false	Positive	False positive error	False negative	False negative error
Examiner 1	4	1	0	0
Examiner 2	6	1	0	0
Examiner 3	4	1	0	0
Examiner 4	30	1	0	0
Examiner 5	903	1	0	0

Table 14. Preliminary analysis accuracy rates for media number 1

Accuracy rate			
Examiner	Precision	Recall	F-measure
Examiner 1	n/a	n/a	n/a
Examiner 2	n/a	n/a	n/a
Examiner 3	n/a	n/a	n/a
Examiner 4	n/a	n/a	n/a
Examiner 5	n/a	n/a	n/a

Table 15. Results of a full examination on media number 2

Fully-examined case	
Suspect objects	Notes
19	All illegal objects were images

Table 16. Results of preliminary analysis on media number 2 from five examiners

Examiner	Further analysis	Suspect objects	Notes
Examiner 2	Yes	44	Decision made based on suspicious images, cookies and installed cleaner
Examiner 5	Yes	9	Decision made based on suspicious images. Note: more suspicious images available not listed in report
Examiner 1	Yes	6	Decision made based on suspicious movie, porn chat (cookies), possible disk wiping, undeleted, and nothing in the live set
Examiner 3	Yes	75	Decision made based on suspicious images, undeleted and cookies
Examiner 4	Yes	40	Decision made based on many suspicious undeleted images and trace cleaning software

Table 17. Preliminary analysis object identification error rates for media number 2

Object identification error rate				
Examiner false	Positive	False positive error	False negative	False negative error
Examiner 2	25	.56	0	0
Examiner 5	0	0	10	.47
Examiner 1	1	.05	13	.68
Examiner 3	56	.74	0	0
Examiner 4	21	.53	0	0

Table 18. Preliminary analysis accuracy rates for media number 2

Accuracy rate			
Examiner	Precision	Recall	F-measure
Examiner 2	.43	1	.60
Examiner 5	1	.47	.64
Examiner 1	.83	.26	.40
Examiner 3	.25	1	.41
Examiner 4	.48	1	.64

Table 19. Results of a full examination on media number 3

Fully-examined case	
Suspect objects	Notes
0	No evidence or trace evidence relevant to the investigation

Table 20. Results of preliminary analysis on media number 3 from five examiners

Examiner	Further analysis	Suspect objects	Notes
Examiner 3	Yes	0	Decision made based on presence of virtual machines
Examiner 5	No	0	n/a
Examiner 4	Yes	0	Decision made based on evidence that user is highly computer literate
Examiner 2	Yes	0	Decision made based on deleted files that could not be processed – user also highly computer literate
Examiner 1	No	0	n/a

Table 21. Preliminary analysis object identification error rates for media number 3

Object identification error rate				
Examiner false	Positive	False positive error	False negative	False negative error
Examiner 3	0	0	0	0
Examiner 5	0	0	0	0
Examiner 4	0	0	0	0
Examiner 2	0	0	0	0
Examiner 1	0	0	0	0

Table 22. Preliminary analysis accuracy rates for media number 3

Accuracy rate			
Examiner	Precision	Recall	F-measure
Examiner 3	n/a	n/a	n/a
Examiner 5	n/a	n/a	n/a
Examiner 4	n/a	n/a	n/a
Examiner 2	n/a	n/a	n/a
Examiner 1	n/a	n/a	n/a

Table 23. Results of a full examination on media number 4

Fully-examined case	
Suspect objects	Notes
0	No evidence or trace evidence relevant to the investigation

Table 24. Results of preliminary analysis on media number 4 from five examiners

Examiner	Further analysis	Suspect objects	Notes
Examiner 5	Yes	45	Decision made based on found images
Examiner 1	No	0	n/a
Examiner 3	No	0	n/a
Examiner 4	No	0	Images found, but appear to be non-exploitation stock photos
Examiner 2	No	0	n/a

Table 25. Preliminary analysis object identification error rates for media number 4

Object identification error rate				
Examiner false	Positive	False positive error	False negative	False negative error
Examiner 5	45	1	0	0
Examiner 1	0	0	0	0
Examiner 3	0	0	0	0
Examiner 4	0	0	0	0
Examiner 2	0	0	0	0

Table 26. Preliminary analysis accuracy rates for media number 4

Accuracy rate			
Examiner	Precision	Recall	F-measure
Examiner 5	n/a	n/a	n/a
Examiner 1	n/a	n/a	n/a
Examiner 3	n/a	n/a	n/a
Examiner 4	n/a	n/a	n/a
Examiner 2	n/a	n/a	n/a

Table 27. Results of a full examination on media number 5

Fully-Examined Case	
Suspect objects	Notes
182	More images appear to be one the machine but have yet to be categorized

Table 28. Results of preliminary analysis on media number 5 from five examiners

Examiner	Further analysis	Suspect objects	Notes
Examiner 4	Yes	66	Decision made based on found images, keywords and encryption
Examiner 3	Yes	165	Decision made based on found images, movies, keywords, Real Player history, evidence of disk wiping tools, evidence of encryption tools
Examiner 2	Yes	96	Decision made based on found images, movies, encryption software, P2P, cleaner software
Examiner 5	Yes	31	Decision made based on found images and movies
Examiner 1	Yes	85	Decision made based on found images, movies

Table 29. Preliminary analysis object identification error rates for media number 5

Object identification error rate				
Examiner false	Positive	False positive error	False negative	False negative error
Examiner 4	0	0	116	.64
Examiner 3	0	0	16	.09
Examiner 2	0	0	86	.47
Examiner 5	0	0	151	.83
Examiner 1	0	0	97	.53

Table 30. Preliminary analysis accuracy rates for media number 5

Accuracy rate			
Examiner	Precision	Recall	F-measure
Examiner 4	1	.36	.53
Examiner 3	1	.91	.95
Examiner 2	1	.53	.69
Examiner 5	1	.17	.29
Examiner 1	1	.47	.64

References

1. Anderson, T., Schum, D.A., Twining, W.L.: Analysis of Evidence. Cambridge University Press, Cambridge (2005)
2. Baggili, I.M., Mislan, R., Rogers, M.: Mobile phone forensics tool testing: A database driven approach. Int. J. Digit. Evid. **6**(2), 168–178 (2007)
3. Beebe, N.L., Clark, J.G.: Digital forensic text string searching: improving information retrieval effectiveness by thematically clustering search results. Digit. Investig. **4**, 49–54 (2007)
4. Carrier, B.D.: Defining digital forensic examination and analysis tools. In: Digital Forensic Research Workshop, Syracuse, NY, p. 10 (2002). (Citeseer)
5. Casey, E.: Error, uncertainty, and loss in digital evidence. Int. J. Digit. Evid. **1**(2), 1–45 (2002)
6. de Vel, O.: File classification using byte sub-stream kernels. Digit. Investig. **1**(2), 150–157 (2004)
7. Gogolin, G.: The digital crime tsunami. Digit. Investig. **7**(1–2), 3–8 (2010)
8. Goss, J., Gladyshev, P.: Forensic triage: managing the risk. Ph.D. thesis, Dublin (2010)
9. Guidance: EnCase Legal Journal, September 2009 Edition (2009)
10. James, J.: Survey of evidence and forensic tool usage in digital investigations (2010)
11. James, J.I., Gladyshev, P.: 2010 Report of digital forensic standards, processes and accuracy measurement (2011)
12. James, J.I., Gladyshev, P.: A survey of digital forensic investigator decision processes and measurement of decisions based on enhanced preview. Digit. Investig. **10**(2), 148–157 (2013)
13. James, J.I., Gladyshev, P.: Challenges with automation in digital forensic investigations, pp. 1–7 (2013)
14. Jones, A., Valli, C.: Building a Digital Forensic Laboratory: Establishing and Managing a Successful Facility. Butterworth-Heinemann, Oxford (2008)
15. Kim, J.S., Kim, D.G., Noh, B.N.: A fuzzy logic based expert system as a network forensics. In: Proceedings of the 2004 IEEE International Conference on Fuzzy Systems, vol. 2, pp. 879–884. IEEE (2004)
16. Koopmans, M.B., James, J.I.: Automated network triage. Digit. Investig. **10**(2), 129–137 (2013)
17. Li, B., Wang, Q, Luo, J.: Forensic analysis of document fragment based on SVM (2006)
18. Lyle, J.R.: If error rate is such a simple concept, why don't i have one for my forensic tool yet? Digit. Investig. **7**, S135–S139 (2010)
19. Manning, C.D., Raghavan, P., Schutze, H.: Introduction to Information Retrieval. Cambridge University Press, Cambridge (2008)
20. NIST: Computer forensics tool testing program (2013)
21. Obasogie, O.: Phantom of Heilbronn revealed! (2009)
22. Palmer, G.L.: Forensic analysis in the digital world. Int. J. Digit. Evid. **1**(1), 1–6 (2002)
23. Rennison, A.: Codes of practice and conduct for forensic science providers and practitioners in the criminal justice system (2011)
24. Russell, S.J., Norvig, P.: Artificial Intelligence: A Modern Approach. Prentice Hall, Upper Saddle River (2009)

25. Supreme Court: Daubert v. Merrell Dow Pharmaceuticals (1993)
26. Supreme Court: Crawford v. Commonwealth of Virginia (2000)
27. Thompson, W.C.: DNA testing. In: Levinson, D. (ed.) Encyclopedia of Crime and Punishment, vol. 2, pp. 537–544. Sage Publications Inc, Thousand Oaks (2002)
28. Yeoman, F.: The phantom of Heilbronn, the tainted DNA and an eight-year goose chase (2009)

Towards a Process Model for Hash Functions in Digital Forensics

Frank Breitinger[1]([✉]), Huajian Liu[2], Christian Winter[2], Harald Baier[1], Alexey Rybalchenko[1], and Martin Steinebach[2]

[1] da/sec - Biometrics and Internet Security Research Group,
Hochschule Darmstadt, Darmstadt, Germany
{frank.breitinger,harald.baier}@cased.de, alexryba@yandex.ru
[2] Fraunhofer Institute for Secure Information Technology, Darmstadt, Germany
{huajian.liu,christian.winter,martin.steinebach}@sit.fraunhofer.de

Abstract. Handling forensic investigations gets more and more difficult as the amount of data one has to analyze is increasing continuously. A common approach for automated file identification are hash functions. The proceeding is quite simple: a tool hashes all files of a seized device and compares them against a database. Depending on the database, this allows to discard non-relevant (whitelisting) or detect suspicious files (blacklisting).

One can distinguish three kinds of algorithms: (cryptographic) hash functions, bytewise approximate matching and semantic approximate matching (a.k.a perceptual hashing) where the main difference is the operation level. The latter one operates on the semantic level while both other approaches consider the byte-level. Hence, investigators have three different approaches at hand to analyze a device.

First, this paper gives a comprehensive overview of existing approaches for bytewise and semantic approximate matching (for semantic we focus on images functions). Second, we compare implementations and summarize the strengths and weaknesses of all approaches. Third, we show how to integrate these functions based on a sample use case into one existing process model, the computer forensics field triage process model.

Keywords: Digital forensics · Hashing · Similarity hashing · Robust hashing · Perceptual hashing · Approximate matching · Process model

1 Introduction

One of the biggest challenges in computer crime is coping with the huge amounts of data – the trend is that everything goes digital. For instance, books, photos, letters and long-playing records (LPs) turned into ebooks, digital photos, email and mp3. In addition, we have smartphones providing access to wireless Internet virtually everywhere.

To handle all this, the forensic community developed investigation models to assist law enforcement [1] which mainly describe where investigators should

© Institute for Computer Sciences, Social Informatics and Telecommunications Engineering 2014
P. Gladyshev et al. (Eds.): ICDF2C 2013, LNICST 132, pp. 170–186, 2014.
DOI: 10.1007/978-3-319-14289-0_12

start. For instance, in 2006 Rogers presented the computer forensics field triage process model (CFFTPM) which is promoted to be "an on-site or filed approach for providing the identification, analysis and interpretation of digital evidence in a short time frame" [2]. While this model precisely describes how to approach a computer crime, the author states that steps could be very time consuming due to the amount of data. Hence, it is important to reduce the amount of data to be inspected manually by automatically distinguishing between relevant and non-relevant files.

A common technology for automated file identification are hash functions. The proceeding is quite simple: calculate hashes for all files and compare these fingerprints against a reference database (e.g., NRSL [3] from NIST). Depending on the underlying database, known files are either filtered out (no further consideration) or highlighted as suspicious.

Currently, mostly cryptographic hash functions (e.g., SHA-1 [4]) are applied which are very efficient in exact duplicate detection but fail in similar file detection. However, investigators might also be interested in similarity, e.g., detect the correlation between an original image and its thumbnail, which could be solved using approximate matching.

The contribution of this paper is tripartite. Firstly, we give an overview of existing approximate matching algorithms. The second part is a brief comparison of algorithms. Besides a comparison of the same group (bytewise and semantic), we also present a sketchy comparison across groups to clearly demonstrate benefits and drawbacks. The third part of the paper shows a sample use case of how to integrate hashing and approximate matching into existing investigation models wherefore we focus on CFFTPM.

The rest of the paper is organized as follows: First, we give a summary of exiting bytewise and semantic approximate matching algorithms in Sect. 2. Next is an explanation of our test methodology in Sect. 3 followed by the experimental results and assessment in Sect. 4. Out of the assessment, we discuss a possible usage based on a sample use case in Sect. 5. Section 6 concludes the paper.

2   Hashing and Approximate Matching

Hashing has a long tradition in computer sciences and various fields of application. The impact of applying cryptographic hash functions in forensics was first analyzed by White [5] and later by Baier and Dichtelmüller [6]. While White propagates an identification rate up to 85 %, Baier and Dichtelmüller only obtained rates between 15 % and 52 %. This low detection rates result from changing files which happens during updates. Besides, it is very likely that word/excel documents, logfiles or source code changes over the time.

Hence, it is necessary to have approximate matching which is able to detect similarity between objects. In general, one distinguishes between bytewise[1] and semantic approximate matching[2]. While the former one operates on the byte

---

[1] Well-known synonyms are fuzzy hashing and similarity hashing.

[2] Well-known synonyms are perceptual hashing and robust hashing.

level and thereby follows the view of a computer, the latter one works on a perceptual level and tries to imitate the perspective of a human observer. Of course, operating on a semantic level requires a separate algorithm for each media type, i.e., there need to be algorithms for images, videos, audio, text documents etc.

2.1 Bytewise Approximate Matching

Bytewise approximate matching is a rather new area and probably had it breakthrough in 2006 with a tool called ssdeep. However, it has been proven to be useful for similar inputs detection (e.g., different versions of a file), embedded objects detection (e.g., a jpg within a Word document) or fragment detection (e.g., network packages).

To the best of our knowledge, there are currently seven different algorithms. We ignore the following algorithms:

- bbHash [7] is very slow as it takes about 2 min to process a 10 MiB file.
- mvHash-B [8] needs a specific configuration for each file type.
- SimHash [9] and MinHash [10] can handle near duplicates only.

The remaining three algorithms are briefly explained in the following:

ssdeep. In 2006 Kornblum presented context triggered piecewise hashing (abbreviated CTPH) which is based on the spam detection algorithm from Tridgell [11]. The implementation is freely available and currently in version ssdeep 2.9[3].

The overall idea of ssdeep is quite simple. CTPH identifies trigger points to divide a given byte sequence into chunks. In order to generate a final fingerprint, all chunks are hashed using FNV [12] and concatenated. To represent the fingerprint of a chunk CTPH only takes the least significant 6 bits of the FNV hash resulting in a Base64 character.

sdhash. Four years later Roussev suggested a completely different algorithm named *similarity digest hashing* which resulted in the tool sdhash[4] [13]. Instead of dividing an input into chunks the algorithm extracts statistically improbable features by using the Shannon entropy whereby a feature is a byte sequence of 64 bytes. All features are hashed by SHA-1 [4] and inserted into a Bloom filter [14]. Hence, files are similar if they share identical features.

mrsh-v2. In 2012 Breitinger & Baier proposed a new algorithm [15] that is based on MRS hash [16] and CTPH. Equal to CTPH the algorithm divides an input into chunks and hashes each chunk. In contrast to ssdeep, there are two main modifications. Firstly, we removed the condition of a maximum fingerprint length of 64 characters. Secondly, mrsh-v2 uses now Bloom filters instead of Base64 characters.

---

[3] http://ssdeep.sourceforge.net; visited 2013-Aug-20.

[4] http://roussev.net/sdhash/sdhash.html; visited 2013-Aug-20.

2.2   Semantic Approximate Matching

Semantic approximate matching can be performed for any media type, but we restrict our analysis to algorithms for images because a main application of semantic approximate matching in digital forensics is the detection of child pornographic images.

Semantic approximate image matching originates from *content-based image retrieval* (CBIR). This term dates back to 1992 [17] while research in the field has an even longer tradition. CBIR systems evaluate the similarity of images based on descriptors for color, texture and shape [18]. A standardized set of image features for CBIR applications has been defined in the MPEG-7 standard [19]. However, the calculation of multiple image features is quite time consuming. The INACT software, which is based on MPEG-7 descriptors, and which has been developed for supporting forensic investigations, requires already 10 s for processing a medium resolution image (640 × 320 pixels) [20]. This is far too slow for a usage under real-world conditions.

The analysis of maybe hundreds of thousands images in an investigation target and up to millions of images in the reference database requires very fast methods for digest calculation and comparison. Hence we focus on image features with the potential for high efficiency:

Histograms. Color histograms, lightness histograms etc. are very basic image features with a long tradition [21]. They just count how many pixels correspond to each value of the observed attribute. Robustness and compactness of the information can be increased by extracting features from the histogram like its first three moments [22], Haar wavelet coefficients (MPEG-7), or range selections [23]. However, the extent of images considered as similar in histogram-based matching approaches is more than just different versions of the same image, as the histograms do not consider any spacial information. Hence such approaches are not well suited for recognizing known images. They are more appropriate for finding images from similar scenes and for clustering images according to the depicted scene.

Low-Frequency Coefficients. While high-frequency parts of images get easily disturbed or lost due to rescaling or lossy compression, low-frequency parts are quite robust. Hence low-frequency Fourier coefficients, DCT coefficients [24], wavelet coefficients [25], etc. can be used as robust image features. The same idea can be used for deriving a key-dependent robust digest by replacing the low-frequency basis functions of the aforementioned transformations with "random smooth patterns generated from a secret key" [24]. Typically, images are scaled to a fixed, low resolution before coefficient calculation for reasons of efficiency.

Block Bitmaps. Robust features can be obtained by dividing an image into a small, fixed number of blocks and calculating one feature bit per block. The most simple version of this approach scales the image down such that it has one pixel per block and sets the bit according to whether the lightness of the pixel is above or below the median lightness [26]. An improved variant called rHash considers the median of each quadrant of the image separately and incorporates a flipping mechanism for robustness against mirroring [27]. Another approach derives an edge map from the image. Such a map can be obtained for example by thresholding the gradient magnitude calculated with the Sobel operator [28,29]. However, more sophisticated edge detection algorithms should be avoided to keep the computing time low.

Projection-Based. This class of approaches has been inspired by the Radon transform, which calculates angle-dependent, one-dimensional projections of the image by integrating the image along straight lines parallel to each projection direction. The hashing algorithm RASH calculates the integral along one radial line for each direction [30]. The proposed improvement RADISH replaces the integral by the variance of the luminance of the pixels on the line [31]. Furthermore, the low-frequency DCT coefficients of the previously calculated angle-dependent function can be used as compact, robust digest of an image [32].

Interest points are another kind of image features. Such points are corners and other prominent points in the image, and various kinds of perceptual hashing based on interest points have been proposed [33,34]. Each interest point can be attached with descriptors of the neighborhood of that point [35,36]. However, the calculation of interest points is computationally expensive – similar to sophisticated edge detection. Lv and Wang report an average processing time of 3.91 s for an image with their default size of 256×342 pixels [36].

For the evaluation in this paper we selected 4 algorithms which are potentially suitable for investigating huge amounts of images: DCT based hash [24], Marr-Hildreth filter based hash [33], radial variance based hash [32] and block mean based hash rHash [37]. A similar evaluation of the mentioned first 3 algorithms and a proof-of-concept implementation of the block bitmap approach based on [26] has been done by Zauner et al. [38,39]. In contrast to their evaluation on a relatively small number of high-resolution images, we will show results for larger collections of images and different resolutions.

3   Test Methodology

In order to grade the aforementioned approaches, we need criteria. These criteria are mainly borrowed from existing literature (e.g., [39,40]).

Firstly, we focus on the general efficiency properties of approximate matching algorithms like compression, runtime efficiency and fingerprint comparison in Sect. 3.1. These properties are derived from traditional/cryptographic hash functions and play an important role. The tests for bytewise and semantic approximate matching are explained in Sects. 3.2 and 3.3, respectively.

3.1 Efficiency

The efficiency tests analyze the two main aspects of approximate matching algorithms named compression and ease of computation. It is composed of the following three sub-tests:

Compression: The output of each algorithm is either of a fixed length or variable. In the latter case we simply compare the input against the output size and present a ratio.

Runtime efficiency: Runtime describes the time needed to process an input. Simply put, the time for generate a similarity digest.

Fingerprint comparison: Once similarity digests are created, they are usually compared against a set. To estimate the performance for large scale scenarios, we discuss the complexity of indexing/ordering them.

3.2 Bytewise Approximate Matching

Bytewise approximate matching is especially helpful when analyzing similar files, file fragments and embedded objects. Compared to semantic approximate matching, it is file type independent and therefore also applicable for multiple, different or unknown file types.

In order to classify existing algorithms, there is a framework called FRASH [40] which tests algorithms by the following sensitivity and robustness tests:

Single-common-block correlation (sensitivity) calculates the smallest object that two files need to have in common for which the algorithm reliably correlates two targets. An example is comparing two similar documents.

Fragment detection (sensitivity) quantifies the smallest fragment for which the similarity tool reliably correlates the fragment and the original file. Examples are network packet analysis or RAM analysis.

Alignment robustness analyzes the impact of inserting byte sequences at the beginning of an input by correlating the size of the change to changes in the comparison output. Examples may be logfiles, source code files, office documents or emails.

Random noise resistance analyzes the impact of random edits on the correlation capabilities of the algorithm. An example may be source code files where the name of a variable is changed.

3.3 Semantic Approximate Matching

Semantic approximate matching has two essential properties: robustness and discriminability. Robustness refers to the ability to resist content-preserving processing and distortions, while discriminability is the ability to differentiate contents, i.e. to avoid collisions [41].

Content-preserving processing includes the manipulations that only modify the digital representation of the image content and that apply insignificant perceptual changes on the image content. To evaluate the robustness the following manipulations are applied:

- mirroring: flipped horizontally
- resizing: 61 % downscaling
- cropping: remove outer 10–15%
- rotation: 90 degree clockwise

- blurring: Gaussian filter with 20px radius
- color modification: red and blue plus 100
- compression: JPEG with 5 % quality
- stretching: horizontally 20 % downscaling.

The discriminability can be measured by the false positive rate (FPR) and the false negative rate (FNR). FPR refers to the probability that different contents result in similar hash values, i.e. non-relevant contents are identified as relevant, while FNR denotes the possibility that the same or similar contents produce significantly different digests, i.e. relevant contents are missed in the identifying process. For investigating huge amount of images, low FPR is of essential importance, which must be kept as close as possible to zero in order to reduce the amount of data for the manual inspection followed [37].

4   Experimental Results and Assessment

Our assessment is based on the cryptographic hash function SHA-1 and the bytewise approximate matching algorithms ssdeep, sdhash and mrsh-v2. On the semantic approximate matching side, we run DCT based hash (dct), Marr-Hildreth operator based hash (mh), radial variance based hash and block mean value based rHash. The pHash C library[5] offers implementation of the first three functions. The implementation of rHash is based on the improved block mean value based hash algorithm in [37].

4.1   Infrastructure

All tests were performed on a conventional business notebook having an Intel Core 2 Duo T9400 CPU clocked at 2.53 GHz with 4 GB RAM.

We used 3 different test sets of images for our experiments: TS_{2000} is a set of 2197 low resolution images (400×266 pixels) having a total size of 53.3 MB; TS_{1500} is a set of 1500 medium resolution images (approximately 1000×800 pixels) having a total size of 603 MB; TS_{1000} is a set of 998 high resolution images (3000×2250 pixels) having a total size of 719 MB.

To define the runtime efficiency we measured the real time which is wall clock time - time from start to finish of the call. This is all elapsed time including time slices used by other processes and time the process spends blocked (for example if it is waiting for I/O to complete).

4.2   Efficiency

Compression. Actually, a fixed length fingerprint is a basic property of hash functions. However, approximate matching only partly fulfills this issue, i.e. ssdeep has a maximum length of 108 bytes (but might be shorter) and sdhash has proportional length between 1.6 % and 2.6 % (depending on the mode). All perceptual algorithms and SHA-1 have a fixed length output as shown in Table 1.

---

[5] http://phash.org; visited 2013-Aug-20.

Table 1. Fingerprint length for different algorithms (compression).

dct	mh	radial	rHash	ssdeep	sdhash	mrsh-v2	SHA-1
64 bit	576 bit	320 bit	256 bit	~600 bit	1.6–2.6 %	~1 %	160 bit

Runtime Efficiency. The assessment of the runtime efficiency is based on all test sets. The time for building a hash database out of a test set and the time for checking a test set against a database are tested respectively. For hash database building, the original images in each test set are used; for hash checking, the images (except ssdeep) in each set are downscaled by 25 % and compressed by JPEG 20 %.

Table 2. Time for processing test sets (in seconds).

Test Set	TS_{2000}		TS_{1500}		TS_{1000}	
Algorithm	Build	Check	Build	Check	Build	Check
mh	471.39	514.96	436.21	396.52	1015.06	647.06
radial	32.26	114.53	179.87	111.12	799.23	450.44
dct	54.69	30.17	281.24	132.92	1601.42	854.64
rHash	18.37	10.88	92.33	41.55	415.08	220.41
sdhash	6.86	5.90	47.81	30.09	55.49	97.17
ssdeep	5.57	5.79	41.43	48.33	47.16	52.02
mrsh-v2	1.36	6.17	3.83	35.37	4.56	102.83
SHA-1	0.84	0.72	2.35	0.84	2.81	1.12

As shown in Table 2, the cryptographic hash function is the fastest for all test sets, followed by bytewise approximate matching. For all test sets, SHA-1 takes less than three seconds to build hash databases and around one second to check the attacked images. For TS_{2000}, SHA-1 is about 5–8 times faster than ssdeep and sdhash, and for medium and high resolution images, SHA-1 is orders of magnitudes faster than others.

Regarding bytewise approximate matching only, mrsh-v2 is far the fastest for generating. However, ssdeep becomes approximately 6–10x faster when checking the attacked images instead of the original ones. This is because the hash database generated by ssdeep features a file size comparison which significantly speeds up the hash checking process when comparing against files of different sizes.

Among the four semantic algorithms, rHash has the best runtime for images of any resolution. The DCT based hash is very fast for low resolution images but becomes the slowest one while hashing high resolution images, where it takes about 4 times longer than rHash. Comparing with other perceptual hashes, mh is not efficient for low resolution images, but its speed is comparable with radial when coming to large images. The checking process for radial is much slower than the building process, which indicates that peak of cross correlation is not so efficient as hamming distance for hash comparison.

Fingerprint Comparison. While designing the algorithms all developers pay attention on simple hash values and thus they could be compared easily. For instance, the hash comparison time for all the perceptual hashing functions stay below $4\,\mu s$, with the exception of radial variance based function, which needs an average of $16\,\mu s$ for the comparison.

However, the focus of this subsection is the behavior of querying large scale databases on a theoretical level (it is not based on own empirical tests).

Let n be the amount of fingerprints in the database. Cryptographic hash values are stored within hash tables or binary trees and hence their lookup complexity is $O(1)$ or $O(\log n)$, respectively. Considering approximate matching, it was not possible to sort or index the fingerprints for a while. Recently, both algorithms were extended and now have a possibility for indexing. In case of ssdeep the authors propagate an improvement of a factor of almost 2000 which is 'practical speed'. For instance, they decrease the time for verifying 195,186 files against a database with 8,334,077 entries from 364 h to 13 min [42]. With respect to sdhash we could not find any numbers describing the improvement.

The fingerprint comparison for perceptual hashes is similar to approximate matching – it is not trivial to sort or order them. In the worst case a lookup is an all-against-all (bruteforce) comparison and thus a complexity of $O(n)$. First experimental results using locally sensitive hashing and binary trees showed that minor improvements are possible [43]. However, this is ongoing work and final results are unclear.

To conclude, besides cryptographic hash functions only ssdeep offers a possibility to reduce the comparison against large databases down to a practical time.

4.3 Bytewise Approximate Matching

As mentioned in Sect. 2.1, our evaluation focuses on ssdeep, sdhash and mrsh-v2. The former two approaches were already deeply analyzed [40,44] with the main result that sdhash outperforms ssdeep in all points beside compression.

For instance, assuming a practical relevant file size of 2 MiB, sdhash correlates them if they share a common subsequence of 170 bytes while ssdeep needs 368 bytes. Regarding fragment detection, ssdeep can only reliably detect similarity down to 50 % (in 94 % of all cases) whereas sdhash works nearly perfect down to 20 % pieces (in 97 % of all cases). The alignment test which inserts up to 400 % of the original file size only beaks down ssdeep that worked acceptable for inserts smaller than 100 % (detection rate of 73 %). The last test described in [40] is random-noise-resistance. While ssdeep only works acceptable for less than 0.026 % changes, sdhash allows to change over 1.100 % of all bytes and still has a higher detection rate. mrsh-v2 showed very similar results than sdhash and thus we won't give more details.

Due to the fact that we now have at least two algorithms nearly on the same level, we need further comparison criteria. An important aspect is always the false positive and false negative rate.

4.4 Semantic Approximate Matching

To test the robustness of semantic approximate matching, ten images are randomly selected out of TS_{1000} and compose a new test set TS_{10}. Next, we applied the manipulations listed in Sect. 3.3. For easier comparison, the matching scores of different algorithms are represented by a normalized score varying from 0 to 100.

The score of each algorithm after resizing and blurring is always above 95 except mh which produces scores between 90 and 95. The color modification yields similar scores but both mh and dct produce slightly lower scores (90–95) than the others (95–100).

The results of the remaining five manipulations vary enormously and are presented in Fig. 1. For rotation and mirroring, the scores of all algorithms are around 50 except that rHash performs very well for mirroring. Cropping is a challenging manipulation, where radial performs best, followed by dct, and mh and rHash are not robust. Both radial and rHash are very robust to compression, where dct and mh are inferior. Regarding stretching all algorithms deliver scores around 98 except radial which is only at 55.

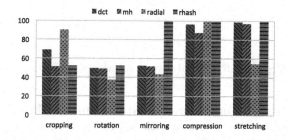

Fig. 1. Average scores for five most influencing perceptual changes on TS_{10}.

As mentioned in Sect. 3.3, the false positive rate (FPR) and the false negative rate (FNR) can be used to measure the discriminability. Hence, we further evaluate the recall precision of different algorithms using TS_{2000} as the known image set and a new test set consisting of 2197 other similar images, called $TS_{2000}U$, as the unknown image set. The 4394 images in TS_{1000} and $TS_{2000}U$ contain similar scenes of cheerleaders.

First, each algorithm builds a hash database out of TS_{2000}. Then, all images in the known image set, TS_{2000}, are downscaled by 25 % followed by JPEG compression with a quality factor of 20. Finally, digest matching is performed on the modified TS_{2000} and $TS_{2000}U$ respectively.

The results are plotted in Fig. 2. The x-axis denotes FPR and the y-axis FNR. All algorithms obtain fairly good results except dct. Among the four algorithms, only rHash achieves zero FPR together with zero FNR. Under the requirement of zero FPR, dct has the worst result, whose FNR reaches as high as 0.245, while mh and radial obtain a FNR of 0.027 and 0.0045. For dct algorithm, the best tradeoff is to achieve a FPR of 0.0009 with a FNR of 0.0396.

To conclude, all algorithms show good robustness in case of format conversion, blurring, color modification, resizing, compression and stretching (except radial), but are not robust against rotation, cropping (except radial) and mirroring (except rHash). Furthermore, under combined manipulation of downscaling and compression, all algorithms (except dct) achieve good discriminability between known images and unknown images.

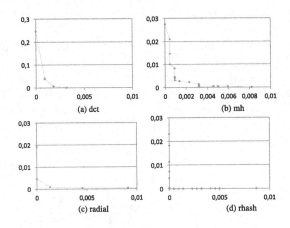

Fig. 2. FNR/FPR of perceptual hashes on TS2000.

Byte Level Changes for Semantic Approximate Matching. Here we briefly analyzed the behavior of semantic approximate matching for byte level changes which corrupt the files. More precisely, we did the following byte level modifications:

- broken data: randomly manipulates 10 bytes all in the file body.
- broken/missing header: deletes the first 128 bytes of the image file.
- missing content: deletes 128 bytes in the middle of the image file.
- missing end: deletes the last 128 bytes of the image file.
- inserting data: inserts 128 bytes from a random image file in the middle.

Real life scenarios are where these manipulations could happen are: transmitting errors, defect hard disk sectors, ram analysis or deleted, fragmented files.

'Missing end' does not influence the score at all–all algorithms output a score of 100. Considering 'missing content' and 'broken data' the scores were still high at round about 90. The lowest scores were returned by 'inserting data' lying between 72 and 82. In all cases the algorithms warn about corrupt JPG data. Regarding 'broken/header' all algorithms failed to produce meaningful results, either by aborting, crashing or delivering out of range errors.

4.5 Summary of Experimental Results

All algorithms have a good to very good compression. Most of them produce a fixed length output or have a upper limit expect `sdhash` and `mrsh-v2` with a proportional length.

As shown in Table 2 the crypto hash SHA-1 is the fastest algorithms followed by the bytewise approximate matching algorithms. Regarding perceptual hashing, there are huge differences in the processing time where `rHash` is far the fastest.

Considering the fingerprint comparison, it is obvious that the lookup complexity with $O(1)$ for crypto hashes is best followed by `ssdeep`. Currently it is unclear what improvement can be obtained for `sdhash` indexing. For now, the worst fingerprint comparison is for perceptual hashing.

The sensitivity & robustness is hard to decide. On the one hand we have the semantic approximate matching algorithms which are very robust against domain specific attacks. However, they do not allow fragment detection (e.g., the header is missing) or embedded object detection (e.g., JPG in a Word document) which are the benefits of bytewise approximate matching. In addition, semantic approximate matching is file domain bound, each domain needs its own algorithm, e.g., images, movies or music.

5 Sample Use Case: Analyzing a USB Hard Disk Drive

In this section we present a reasonable utilization of the three different hash function families on base of the use case *allegation of production and ownership of child abuse pictures*. During a house search the police and IT forensic special agents find besides different computers and DVDs a USB hard disk drive of size 40 GiB (presumably an old backup device).

Following Marcus Roger's process model CFFTPM "time is of the essence" and the search for evidence should start at the crime scene [2]. His key argument is that accused persons tend to be more cooperative within the first hours of an investigation.

During the planning phase of the CFFTPM the forensic investigator chooses hardware (e.g., a forensic workstation equipped with a hardware write blocker for USB devices) and software (implementation of at least one hash function of each family together with respective databases of incriminated pictures) to examine a device onsite for pictures of child abuse. The identification software is configured to run silently in the background and notify the investigator, if potential evidence is found or if the software terminates. An overview of our sample process model for the use case at hand is given in Fig. 3.

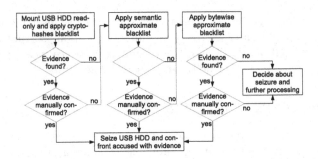

Fig. 3. Process model in case of onsite search for pictures of child abuse.

In our sample use case the investigator decides that an analysis of a 40 GiB volume is feasible at scene. He mounts the USB HDD read-only into the file system of his forensic workstation and starts the automatic identification of evidence.

Due to their superior efficiency with respect to runtime, compression and fingerprint comparison (see Sect. 4.2), the identification software first applies a blacklist of *crypto-hashes* (e.g., PERKEO[6]) to all files on the USB HDD. If there is a match the identification software notifies the investigator, who manually inspects the potential evidence. If it turns out to be a picture of child abuse, he seizes the USB HDD and informs the police to confront the accused person with the evidence.

If the blacklist crypto-hashes do not yield a trace or if the alert turns out to be a false-positive, the identification software turns to *semantic approximate hashing*. We favor semantic approximate matching, because we expect a higher recall in this specific use case. However, this claim has to be confirmed. The investigator and the software operate analogously in case of a true-positive and false-positive, respectively.

Finally, if after the second step no evidence is found, the software performs file carving on the USB HDD and applies *bytewise approximate matching* to all extracted files/fragments. Please note that in contrast to semantic approximate matching, the final bytewise approximate matching may find fragments or embedded pictures of non-image data files (e.g., pdf, doc). If after all no evidence is found, the investigator decides about a seizure of the device and the further processing, e.g., in the lab.

6   Conclusion and Future Work

In this paper we analyzed the impact of different hashing technologies for forensic investigations. We discussed the three families of crypto hashes, semantic approximate matching algorithms and bytewise approximate hashing functions. We showed that all approaches have different strengths and weaknesses and hence all families are of relevance.

---

[6] http://perkeo.com; visited 2013-Aug-20.

Semantic approximate hashing functions have proven to be most powerful in the area of content identification. Compared to cryptographic hashing or approximate matching, they offer significantly higher detection quality in the areas of image (or other media) copyright violations or illegal material such as child pornography. However, they are bound to their file domain and it is thus necessary to run perceptual hashing for multiple domains, e.g., images and movies – additional processing time. In addition, these approaches are by default slower than there bitwise opponents.

The key strength of approximate matching is that is able to detect embedded objects, e.g., detect a JPG within a Word document. In addition, it allows fragment detection, which is especially important when dealing with network traffic or defect file systems, e.g., one may analyze the hard disk on the sector or block level.

We identified benefits of cryptographic hash functions, too. The algorithms are superior to their competitors with respect to efficiency (runtime, compression, fingerprint comparison). They are the most recognized in court (yet) and the US NIST provides a comprehensive database containing approximately 100 million hash values. Finally they do not err, i.e., their security properties allow to identify equal files with nearly 100 % probability, which is very important for whitelisting.

We finally presented a sample order of applying the hash function families within a sample use case of investigating a USB HDD at crime scene. However, an actual process model to optimize the operation of hash functions and its validation is still missing. Our next step is to identify typical use cases and propose a reasonable order of application of hash functions (both inside a family and between different families), respectively. Then we validate our proceeding with respect to efficiency and sensitivity and try to abstract from the use cases to a more general model.

Finally we think that it is also necessary to consider the defendants where we have two possibilities. On the one hand the defendant is the 'normal user' and not very familiar with the personal computers. Thus, the files reside somewhere unencrypted on the device. Maybe they are processed with a tool to all have the same size. On the other hand the defendant is an 'expert' and files might be encrypted. Hence, investigators can try to find fragments in the RAM[7] or in unallocated HDD sectors.

Acknowledgments. This work is supported by CASED (Center for Advanced Security Research Darmstadt).

References

1. Pollitt, M.M.: An ad hoc review of digital forensic models. In: Second International Workshop on Systematic Approaches to Digital Forensic Engineering, SADFE 2007, pp. 43–54 (2007)

---

[7] Live response.

2. Rogers, M.K., Goldman, J., Mislan, R., Wedge, T., Debrota, S.: Computer forensics field triage process model. In: Conference on Digital Forensics, Security and Law, pp. 27–40 (2006)

3. NIST: National Software Reference Library, May 2012. http://www.nsrl.nist.gov

4. NIST: Secure Hash Standard. National Institute of Standards and Technologies, FIPS PUB 180–1 (1995)

5. White, D.: Hashing of file blocks: When exact matches are not useful. Presentation at American Academy of Forensic Sciences (AAFS) (2008)

6. Baier, H., Dichtelmueller, C.: Datenreduktion mittels kryptographischer Hashfunktionen in der IT-Forensik: Nur ein Mythos? In: DACH Security 2012, pp. 278–287, September 2012

7. Breitinger, F., Baier, H.: A Fuzzy Hashing Approach based on Random Sequences and Hamming Distance. In: ADFSL Conference on Digital Forensics, Security and Law, pp. 89–101, May 2012

8. Breitinger, F., Åstebøl, K.P., Baier, H., Busch, C.: mvhash-b - a new approach for similarity preserving hashing. IT Security Incident Management & IT Forensics (IMF), vol. 7, March 2013

9. Sadowski, C., Levin, G.: Simhash: Hash-based similarity detection, December 2007. http://simhash.googlecode.com/svn/trunk/paper/SimHashWithBib.pdf

10. Broder, A.Z.: On the resemblance and containment of documents. In: Compression and Complexity of Sequences (SEQUENCES'97), pp. 21–29. IEEE Computer Society (1997)

11. Tridgell, A.: Spamsum, Readme (2002). http://samba.org/ftp/unpacked/junkcode/spamsum/README

12. Noll, L.C.: Fowler/Noll/Vo (FNV) Hash (2001). http://www.isthe.com/chongo/tech/comp/fnv/index.html

13. Roussev, V.: Data fingerprinting with similarity digests. Int. Fed. Inf. Process. **337**(2010), 207–226 (2010)

14. Bloom, B.H.: Space/time trade-offs in hash coding with allowable errors. Commun. ACM **13**, 422–426 (1970)

15. Breitinger, F., Baier, H.: Similarity Preserving Hashing: Eligible Properties and a new Algorithm MRSH-v2. In: 4th ICST Conference on Digital Forensics & Cyber Crime (ICDF2C), October 2012

16. Roussev, V., Richard, G.G., Marziale, L.: Multi-resolution similarity hashing. Digital Forensic Research Workshop (DFRWS), pp. 105–113 (2007)

17. Kato, T.: Database architecture for content-based image retrieval. In: Image Storage and Retrieval Systems. Proc. SPIE, IS&T, SPIE Electronic Imaging, San Jose. California, 9–14 February, vol. 1662, pp. 112–123, April 1992

18. Eakins, J., Graham, M.: Content-based image retrieval. University of Northumbria at Newcastle, JTAP report 39, October 1999

19. MPEG: Information technology - multimedia content description interface - part 3: Visual. ISO/IEC, Technical Report 15938–3 (2002)

20. Grega, M., Bryk, D., Napora, M.: INACT–INDECT advanced image cataloguing tool. Multimedia Tools and Applications, July 2012

21. Swain, M.J., Ballard, D.H.: Color indexing. Int. J. Comput. Vis. **7**(1), 11–32 (1991)

22. Stricker, M., Orengo, M.: Similarity of color images. In: Storage and Retrieval for Image and Video Databases III. Proc. SPIE, IS&T, SPIE Electronic Imaging, San Jose, California, 5–10 February, vol. 2420, pp. 381–392, March 1995

23. Xiang, S., Kim, H.J.: Histogram-based image hashing for searching content-preserving copies. In: Shi, Y.Q., Emmanuel, S., Kankanhalli, M.S., Chang, S.-F., Radhakrishnan, R., Ma, F., Zhao, L. (eds.) Transactions on DHMS VI. LNCS, vol. 6730, pp. 83–108. Springer, Heidelberg (2011)
24. Fridrich, J.: Robust bit extraction from images. In: IEEE International Conference on Multimedia Computing and Systems, vol. 2, pp. 536–540. IEEE Computer Society (1999)
25. Venkatesan, R., Koon, S.-M., Jakubowski, M.H., Moulin, P.: Robust image hashing. In: 2000 International Conference on Image Processing, vol. 3, pp. 664–666. IEEE (2000)
26. Yang, B., Gu, F., Niu, X.: Block mean value based image perceptual hashing. In: Intelligent Information Hiding and Multimedia Multimedia Signal Processing. IEEE Computer Society (2006)
27. Steinebach, M.: Robust hashing for efficient forensic analysis of image sets. In: Gladyshev, P., Rogers, M.K. (eds.) ICDF2C 2011. LNICST, vol. 88, pp. 180–187. Springer, Heidelberg (2012)
28. Queluz, M.P.: Towards robust, content based techniques for image authentication. In: Multimedia Signal Processing, pp. 297–302. IEEE (1998)
29. Xie, L., Arce, G.R.: A class of authentication digital watermarks for secure multimedia communication. IEEE Trans. Image Process. 10(11), 1754–1764 (2001)
30. Lefèbvre, F., Macq, B., Legat, J.-D.: Rash: radon soft hash algorithm. In: EUSIPCO'2002, vol. 1. TéSA, pp. 299–302 (2002)
31. Stanaert, F.-X., Lefèbvre, F., Rouvroy, G., Macq, B., Quisquater, J.-J., Legat, J.-D.: Practical evaluation of a radial soft hash algorithm. In: ITCC, vol. 2, pp. 89–94. IEEE Computer Society (2005)
32. De Roover, C., De Vleeschouwer, C., Lefèbvre, F., Macq, B.: Robust image hashing based on radial variance of pixels. In: ICIP, vol. 3, pp. 77–80. IEEE (2005)
33. Bhattacharjee, S., Kutter, M.: Compression tolerant image authentication. In: 1998 International Conference on Image Processing, vol. 1, pp. 435–439. IEEE Computer Society (1998)
34. Monga, V., Evans, B.L.: Perceptual image hashing via feature points: performance evaluation and tradeoffs. IEEE Trans. Image Process. 15(11), 3453–3466 (2006)
35. Lowe, D.G.: Object recognition from local scale-invariant features. In: International Conference on Computer Vision, no. 2, pp. 1150–1157. IEEE Computer Society (1999)
36. Lv, X., Wang, Z.J.: Perceptual image hashing based on shape contexts and local feature points. IEEE Trans. Inf. Foren. Sec. 7(3), 1081–1093 (2012)
37. Steinebach, M., Liu, H., Yannikos, Y.: Forbild: Efficient robust image hashing. In: SPIE 8303. Security, and Forensics, Media Watermarking (2012)
38. Zauner, C.: Implementation and benchmarking of perceptual image hash functions, Master's thesis, University of Applied Sciences Upper Austria, July 2010
39. Zauner, C., Steinebach, M., Hermann, E.: Rihamark: perceptual image hash benchmarking. In: Media Watermarking, Security, and Forensics III. Proc. SPIE, IS&T/SPIE Electronic Imaging, San Francisco, California, 23–27 January, vol. 7880, pp. 7880 0X-1-15, Feb 2011. http://dx.doi.org/10.1117/12.876617
40. Breitinger, F., Stivaktakis, G., Baier, H.: FRASH: a framework to test algorithms of similarity hashing. In: 13th Digital Forensics Research Conference (DFRWS'13), Monterey, August 2013
41. Weng, L., Preneel, B.: From image hashing to video hashing. In: Boll, S., Tian, Q., Zhang, L., Zhang, Z., Chen, Y.-P.P. (eds.) MMM 2010. LNCS, vol. 5916, pp. 662–668. Springer, Heidelberg (2010)

42. Winter, C., Schneider, M., Yannikos, Y.: F2S2: fast forensic similarity search through indexing piecewise hash signatures. http://www.anwendertag-forensik.de/content/dam/anwendertag-forensik/de/documents/2012/Vortrag_Winter.pdf
43. Giraldo Triana, O.A.: Fast similarity search for robust image hashes, Bachelor Thesis, Technische Universität Darmstadt (2012)
44. Roussev, V.: An evaluation of forensic similarity hashes. In: Digital Forensic Research Workshop, vol. 8, pp. 34–41 (2011)

Automation in Digital Forensics

An Automated Link Analysis Solution Applied to Digital Forensic Investigations

Fergal Brennan$^{(\boxtimes)}$, Martins Udris, and Pavel Gladyshev

University College Dublin, Dublin, Ireland
{fergalbrennan,martins.udris}@gmail.com,
pavel.gladyshev@ucd.ie

Abstract. The rapid growth of computer storage, new technologies, anti-forensics and hacking tools, as well as cheaper and easily accessible powerful computing equipment, has led to digital crimes becoming more frequent and often more sophisticated. These challenges have led to digital examinations becoming increasingly time-consuming and laborious, resulting in an urgent need for the automation of digital forensic analysis. In addition to in-depth analysis of particular digital devices, it is often necessary to establish that two devices and hence their owners are linked. This need arises, for example, when a suspect is apprehended and the investigator needs to establish grounds for the detention of a suspect. This paper proposes a methodology and a software solution to automate the detection of information linkage between two or more distinct digital devices.

Keywords: Forensic tools · Link analysis · Social network analysis · Software engineering · Automation · Profiling · Visualisation · Keywords

1 Introduction

Technological advances have led to an increasingly networked society, with criminal and terrorist networks thus becoming more sophisticated and increasingly difficult to analyse. Social network analysis tools can provide a quantitative or qualitative understanding of the performance of networks and their ability to meet their goals, to identify networks characteristics and key individuals, as well as establish how quickly information flows within networks.

Jacob L. Moreno is widely credited for being the founder of what we now know as social network analysis [1]. Moreno's 1934 publication *Who Shall Survive?* [2] developed a methodology known as Sociometry, which measures social relationships between individuals and the impact of these relationships on small groups. Although there were various articles published prior to Moreno's work, such as Almack [3] and Bott [4], which explored network structures, it was Moreno who first began to explore the use of graphs as a visualisation tool to depict social networks [5]. Wassermann and Stanley's excellent publication Social Network Analysis: Methods and Applications [1] provide an excellent overview of the subject as well as an in-depth exploration of social network analysis.

© Institute for Computer Sciences, Social Informatics and Telecommunications Engineering 2014
P. Gladyshev et al. (Eds.): ICDF2C 2013, LNICST 132, pp. 189–206, 2014.
DOI: 10.1007/978-3-319-14289-0_13

The time-consuming nature of manual social network analysis had limited applicability to criminal or terrorist investigations [6]. Due to the benefits of social network analysis, the need for the automation of this process to address the challenges faced by investigators was urgently required [7]. This led to a number of tools being developed that were capable of interrogating large data sets and automatically producing graphical representations of the entities and relationships within a network. These tools included functionality for filtering based on entity type and they employed the spring embedder algorithm [8]. The most popular of these tools were Netmap [9] and early versions of both COPLINK [10] and Analyst's Notebook [11].

This initial wave of new analysis tools was a breakthrough in the field of automated social network analysis. It led to the development of advanced analytical functionality that can determine important network characteristics in tools such as Analyst's Notebook, COPLINK and the recently released Maltego [12] which leverages Open Source Intelligence [13] to discover relationships between entities based on public information. These tools provide the investigator with the ability to determine principles such as centrality, betweenness, closeness, patterns of interaction and the ability to identify individuals of most importance in a social network [1]. However, these tools rely on structured relational data already in place within an organisation or data that is publicly available. Therefore, to prove or disprove the existence of a relationship between various individuals potentially involved in a crime remains a time consuming and challenging task.

Traditional forensic tools like EnCase [14] or XWays [15] are designed to allow investigators to manually traverse the file structure of a forensic image in order to discover relevant digital evidence. Additionally, certain forensic artefacts require bespoke extraction and presentation using a variety of tailored forensic tools. Performing analysis in this fashion particularly in a multiparty case where each artefact repository would ordinarily have to be examined independently, the findings then manually correlated requires significant manual effort. This may lead to crucial data links connecting certain parties being overlooked.

The possibility of automating the discovery of relational data among forensic artefacts, on the other hand, may lead investigators to crucial evidence – for example, by searching the computers of a criminal and their suspected accomplice for common data items, such as email addresses, documents, etc., the investigator can quickly and automatically determine that the two persons know each other, which may be sufficient grounds for the detention of the suspect for further questioning. Automated discovery of common data items, such as a specific email addresses, keywords, or internet history entries on multiple devices may allow the investigators to identify criminal rings and focus their investigation on the individuals whose devices have the most relational data linking them to other devices in the case.

To the authors' knowledge there are currently no publicly available open source forensic tools that would provide such functionality. This paper summarises the results and the lessons learned from a project aimed at the development of a prototype of such a forensic tool.

2   Solution Overview

The solution provides investigators with a platform to compare data from multiple data sources for purposes of comparison and presentation with the goal of revealing any relationships that exist between the digital forensic evidence sets. To facilitate this fundamental objective, the solution provides a number of libraries that enable the acquisition, normalisation, comparison and presentation of forensic artefact data from the Windows and Linux platforms. While the solution provides a considerable amount of functionality, it also facilitates an extensible platform with which investigators can develop libraries to meet their needs by logically separating the core functions of the solution into three tasks, as described below and presented in Fig. 1.

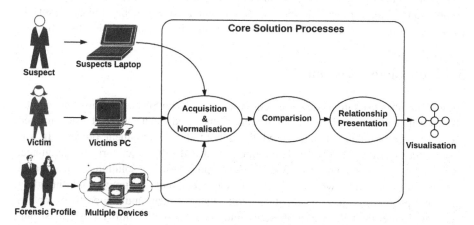

Fig. 1. External user interaction and presentation of solutions core processes separated by each processes' singular functional concern.

1. The acquisition and normalisation of forensic data.
2. The comparison of forensic data.
3. The presentation of forensic data.

If a case involves a device that the solution does not currently support the acquisition of data from, but the investigator wishes to compare its data to the rest of their case data, they can write their own library which can be integrated into the solution for use.

Due to the increasing number and complexity of cases investigators are required to handle, a logically structured intuitive user interface is available where investigators can organise their current and historical case data. A number of search and sorting functions are available to allow easy access to relevant case data and real time statistics. The solution's interface follows a logical digital forensic case paradigm whereby data sources and evidence can be attributed to individuals within a case.

This structure also enables the creation of digital profiles which allows investigators to logically group acquired forensic artefacts. For example, if an investigative department seizes disk images from a number of convicted paedophiles, the investigator can generate a profile based on the entirety or subsections of these disk images. The investigator can then run the data associated with a single individual or multiple individuals against a digital profile which will highlight any relationships that exists between them and the created paedophile profile, as well as potentially identifying new leads or individuals of interest in the case. Given enough processing power, a police department could build up a profile repository similar to that of a finger-print/DNA database currently in use throughout the world.

The user interface allows the investigator to execute any of the available libraries. In the event of long running tasks, the solution's interface provides an acceptable level of responsiveness and up to date information regarding the status of those tasks. On completion of appropriate libraries to acquire and compare the forensic artefacts associated with a case the resulting data is presented in a graphical visualisation.

3   Technology Decisions

All technologies used in the development process are Open Source and freely available, allowing the solution to be distributed without the need for licensing. Python formed the core programming language used throughout the development process. It was chosen because it is a freely available, interpreted and fully object-oriented language, which will allow for continued modular development of the solution. Python has a simple and clear syntax which increases development speed, supports multithreading and multiprocessing, has excellent memory management and supports exception handling. PostgreSQL is the database engine provider that is utilized to persist and store normalised forensic data. It is a highly scalable object-relational Open Source database and runs on all major operating systems. PyQt was chosen for the first development phase of the user interface. PyQt is a set of Python wrappers for Nokia's Qt application framework, it provides a rich graphical widget toolkit, has extensive drawing capabilities and runs on all major operating systems.

The solution architecture, as presented below in Fig. 2, is distributed among a number of logical tiers to promote ease of continued development and testing.

4   Functional Design Implementation

Six core features were identified to create an intuitive environment to allow digital forensic artefact correlation. These are: 1. Create an investigative case, 2. Create a digital profile, 3. Acquire information sources, 4. Extract forensic artefacts, 5. Compare individuals and profiles and 6. Visualise the results.

To support the identified features, a number of plugin libraries were developed. Plugin libraries are the functional building blocks registered for use within the solution based on their classification, which is defined by their role (acquisition, extraction, comparison or visualisation). The solution structure is logically separated by a number

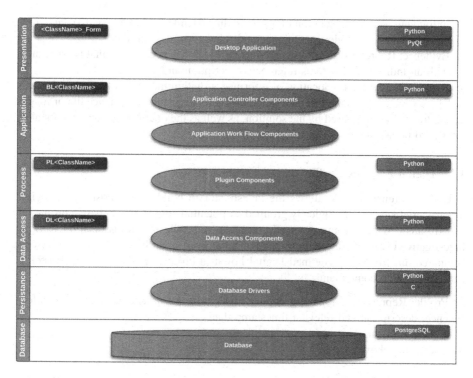

Fig. 2. High level solution architecture enabling flexibility and reusability, extending or replacing an entire layer can be done in isolation without affecting other components.

of packages. When the investigator develops a library to perform the required function, it can be then copied to the relevant package, based on the library's classification. When executed each Plugin library is launched in a separate process using the Python multiprocessing package allowing the solution to be fault tolerant. In the event of a crashing or faulting library, the solution will function as normal and no critical data will be affected. The solution monitors the newly spawned process, reporting the progress of the library back to the main application, so the user is informed at all times of its status. Once the library has completed successfully with no errors, the data generated is persisted to the database.

4.1 Investigative Case

An Investigative Case is a concept which allows investigators to logically organise their forensic case data under a structure with which they are already be familiar with. An Investigative Case consists of four components:

1. Case: The parent object underneath which all other case data is organised. Contains the case reference, overall description and relevant timestamp data.

2. Individual: The representation of a person directly involved in a case. Contains first name, surname, individual reference and relevant timestamp data.
3. Evidence: Represents the physical evidence which has been seized that is associated with an individual. Contains reference, description and timestamp data.
4. Source: Represents the location of information within the piece of seized evidence. The source contains the full path to the data directory, encase evidence file or image file that is to be acquired by the solution, as well as the operating system from which it is to be acquired.

4.2 Digital Forensic Profile

A Digital Forensic Profile allows the investigator to build up a repository of digital forensic artefacts that are logically grouped. A potential approach is to base a profile on already attained data from convicted criminals. A profile has no association with an Investigative Case. Therefore, individuals who are part of an Investigative Case can be compared directly to a predefined Digital Forensic Profile. A Digital Forensic Profile consists of three components:

1. Profile: Represents a logical grouping of digital forensic artefacts. Contains reference, description and relevant timestamp data.
2. Evidence (as above).
3. Source (as above).

4.3 Acquiring a Data Source

Once an Investigative Case structure has been created, data sources can then be acquired. The solution currently supports the acquisition of undeleted data from Windows as well as data from encase evidence and image files while running the solution on the Linux platform. When a user chooses to acquire a Source, the relevant acquisition library is executed. The location property of each Source object is used by the acquisition library to recursively extract undeleted file and folder information, which is then saved by the solution for further use by other components.

4.4 Extracting Forensic Artefacts

Once data has been acquired, libraries can be executed to extract forensic artefacts from it. The solution currently classifies forensic artefacts into three types, as displayed in Table 1. This is in order for the artefacts extracted from an application to be compared against those from a similar application such as comparing Skype to Messenger data.

Table 1. Forensic artefact classification

Type	Description
Keywords	Keywords that can be searched across a data source
Action	Artefacts extracted based on actions performed by the user. i.e. started an application, connected an external device, opened a URL, sent an IM, etc.
System	Operating system artefacts. i.e. Windows version, programs installed, etc.

The solution currently supports the extraction of Keywords, Firefox, Internet Explorer and Skype digital forensic artefacts from acquired Sources using already developed extraction libraries. Each extraction library creates a generic forensic Artefact object for each artefact discovered. This generic object contains priority, type and time stamp information and a reference to all other data associated with that artefact type.

4.4.1 Action Artefacts

Artefacts such as Internet Explorer, Mozilla Firefox and Chrome history are classified as action artefacts. For each browsing history entry, web form entry or a cookie object created by these applications, an equivalent Artefact Action object is created. This object is used to identify the type of action artefact, as well as to determine when the action began and ended. This normalised object structure, as presented in Fig. 3 allows the application to for example, compare the browsing history of Chrome to the browsing history of Firefox regardless of the data format that either application utilises. For each Artefact Action object created a referenced Artefact Action Payload object is also created which contains key data associated with each artefact.

4.4.2 Keyword Artefacts

Keyword searching is a powerful technique already used in many forensic investigations which involves the systematic searching of file systems for occurrences of specified keywords. The nature of keyword data allows it to be normalised with ease from popular and proprietary platforms. The ability to compare and visualise keyword data from multiple sources is a primary feature of the solution due to already established benefits of keyword comparison.

To acquire keyword data from the Windows platform the solution utilises a programme called strings.exe [16] (packaged with solution), while acquiring keyword data from the Linux platform utilises the Linux command *strings*. Each acquisition library searches through a set of data specified by the location property of a Source object for word strings. Each string is compared against an already predefined set of false positives attained from clean operating system installs to filter out any redundant keywords. If the string passes the false positive test an Artefact Keyword object is generated. This object represents each keyword extracted from a given location, as well as the number of occurrences within that location.

4.5 Comparing Individuals and Profiles

Once the investigator has created the necessary case structure, acquired data sources and extracted forensic artefacts using their own or solution-provided libraries, they can begin to compare the forensic data obtained. The solution currently supports the comparison of Keyword and Action artefact objects.

4.5.1 Keyword Comparison

The keyword comparison library evaluates each keyword forensic artefact associated with an individual or a profile and attempts to create a link to an artefact of the same

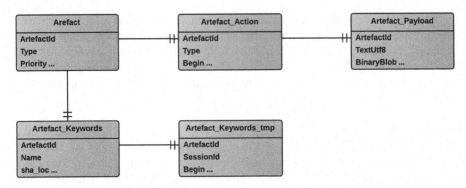

Fig. 3. Entity relationship diagram detailing the relationships between the Artefacts objects used to generate the desired architecture to facilitate the comparison of forensic artefacts.

type associated with another individual or profile by the use of a number of SQL inner joins. If there is a matching hit an Edge object is created.

4.5.2 Action Comparison

Action artefact comparisons are performed in a similar manner. The difference is that action artefacts of the same type can be compared directly against each other, regardless of the application that the artefact originated from, for example, an instant message is compared against an instant message. Based on the artefact action payload data, an attempt to create a link between each action artefact associated with an individual or a profile and another individual or a profile is performed through a number of SQL joins. If a match is found, an Edge object is created.

4.5.3 Edge

An Edge object represents a relationship and its significance that exists between two individuals or profiles, based on a digital forensic artefact they have in common. This process is repeated until all combinations have been discovered and therefore all relationships have been created as Edge objects. When an Edge object is created, a reference to the artefact which caused the creation of the Edge object is generated. Linking each relationship to a digital forensic artefact in this manner provides visibility to how each relationship was established.

4.5.4 Weighting

Artefact matches that are discovered are weighted to emphasise their importance in the context of the data set being analysed. Due to the large volumes of data that can be analysed there is potential for information overload if a large number of insignificant links are discovered and are presented to an investigator to be of equal importance. The first stage is to perform an aggregation process to discover actions or keywords with the same properties among compared parties which facilitates the calculation of the overall artefact weight.

Each action artefact discovered during extraction is created with a priority weight, this allows for the weighting of artefacts extracted by a plugin to be higher than those of others. The priority weight of an action artefact is inserted by the running plugin either in code or through the user interface in accordance with the weight that the investigator deems appropriate. Additionally, a configurable action artefact type weight is applied which is not inserted by a plugin when an artefact is extracted, but by the solution to differentiate between various action artefacts. For example, if a plugin extracts Skype forensic data, each artefact discovered may have a priority weight of 2 as applied by the plugin, the action artefact type weight applies to the particular type of Skype artefact extracted such as a Skype contact or a Skype instant message. This allows weighting granularity of particular types of artefacts extracted using one plugin. The significance of action artefacts is calculated as follows:

$$((\text{Individual1.OccurrenceOfMatch} * \text{ArtefactPriorityWeight}) + (\text{Individual2.}$$
$$\text{OccurrenceOfMatch} * \text{ArtefactPriorityWeight})) *$$
$$(\text{Individual1.OccuranceOfMatch} + \text{Individual2.OccuranceOfMatch}) *$$
$$\text{ArtefactsTypeWeight}$$

When a keyword match is discovered a count of the number of files that the keyword was discovered in is taken into account to determine its significance, the more a keyword appears the more significant it is. The total count of each keyword occurrence is multiplied with the number of files it has been discovered in. The keyword weighting formula is as follows:

$$(\text{Individual1.OccurancesOfKeywordMatch} +$$
$$\text{Individual2.OccurancesOfKeywordMatch}) *$$
$$(\text{Individual1.NumberOfFilesKeywordFoundIn} +$$
$$\text{Individual2.NumberOfFilesKeywordFoundIn})$$

The presented weighting scheme assumes that the more occurrences of an artefact that individuals have in common the more significant it is. This may not be the case depending on the context and scope of the investigation. The solution can be extended to override the presented weighting scheme by abstracting the weighting calculation into a runnable plugin library. This provides flexibility allowing users to create their own weighting libraries or use already established scientific weighting schemes.

4.6 Comparison Visualisation

Once the data sets of individual's have been compared, they can be visualised in order to provide a quantitative understanding of it. The initial execution of the default visualisation plugin displays an overview of the comparison data. This is a collection of all of the Edge objects that have been created between individuals. Yellow nodes represent individuals while blue nodes represent the relationships between them, an example of which is displayed in Fig. 5.

4.6.1   Filtering Visualisation

Visualisations can become cluttered if a large numbers of relationships are discovered. However nodes which have a high degree of Edge objects associated with one another will be drawn closer together indicating a strong relationship. Additionally, users can filter artefact nodes by their weight and individual nodes based on the total weight of all artefacts between individuals which will display nodes with a higher degree of artefact relations.

5   Test Case Execution

Given below is a summary of a simulated case, created by Dr. Cormac Doherty, Dr. Pavel Gladyshev, and Mr. Ahmed Shosha for the 1st Interpol/UCD Summer school in cybercrime investigation, which was held in Dublin, Ireland in July/August 2011. It consists of 4 disk images and associated documents.

Simulated case synopsis. John Smith, who is a postdoctoral researcher in Digital Forensics Investigation Research Laboratory (DigitalFIRE) developed and patented a highly successful algorithm, which earned him millions, received a ransom letter for his son, Toby Smith. Toby is eighteen and a computer science undergraduate student at UCD. John Smith paid the requested ransom using his personal laptop without contacting An Garda Síochána. Toby was not released and An Garda Síochána were contacted regarding the case. John's laptop's HDD was then imaged. One of the prime suspect's was Mr. Paeder Patterson, John Smith's manager. The Gardaí searched the studio apartment of Paeder Patterson in UCD Residences at Belfield, where two laptops were discovered and both HDD's imaged. Mr. Patterson was not available for questioning. An Garda Síochána were then called to an address where an individual fitting the description of Toby Smith had been seen. When officers called at the address, a male ran from the building, leaving behind a laptop. The laptop was seized and the HDD imaged.

A new case with each appropriate object was created in the tool as represented below in Fig. 4. Due to the fact that Mr. Patterson was unavailable for questioning, ownership could not be established of the laptops found at his address. Therefore, two individuals marked Patterson - Image 2 and Patterson - Image 3 were created to encompass this data. One Source object is created for each evidence item. The location property of each Source object points to the user directory of each image associated with an individual.

Each Source was acquired using the appropriate acquisition library, the results of which are displayed below in Table 2.

Skype Extraction, Comparison and Visualisation. The Skype forensic artefacts' extraction library was executed against each acquired Source associated with each individual to facilitate comparison. Displayed in Table 3 are the results of the Skype artefact extraction process for each individual.

Three of the four disk images contained Skype artefacts. These artefacts can be compared to determine if there are any matches between the data sets. Displayed in Table 4 are the Skype comparison results of the three applicable individuals.

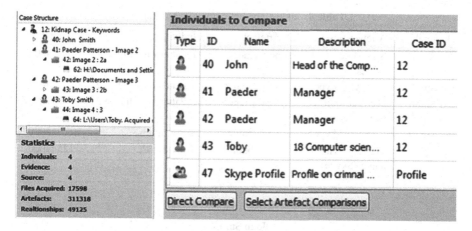

Fig. 4. Solution workbench displaying the created test case Investigative Case structure as well as important case statistics associated with the case. The compare individuals/profiles component allows users to directly compare already generated forensic data or specifically select the forensic artefact data they wish to compare.

Table 2. Acquired kidnap case data

Individual	Image name	Files acquired
John Smith	1_john	10747
Paeder Patterson – Image 2	2a	939
Paeder Patterson – Image 3	2b	3587
Toby Smith	3	2325

Table 3. Skype artefact extraction results

Individual	Image name	Skype artefacts
John Smith	1_john	61
Paeder Patterson – Image 2	2a	30
Paeder Patterson – Image 3	2b	0
Toby Smith	3	182

Once the Skype artefact data has been compared, it can be visualised using the default visualisation plugin, the results of this operation are displayed below in Fig. 5.

Each of the blue nodes displayed in Fig. 5 were expanded to display the artefacts that created the relationship, the results of which are displayed below in Fig. 6.

Firefox Extraction, Comparison and Visualisation. The Firefox forensic artefacts' extraction library was executed against each acquired Source to facilitate comparison, the results of which are displayed in Table 5.

Table 4. Skype artefact comparison results

Individual	Artefact type	Artefact	Individual	Weight
John Smith	Nickname (Skype)	novye.dengi	P Patterson – Image 2	4000
John Smith	Contact (Skype)	tobyskeeper	P Patterson – Image 2	4000
John Smith	Message sent to name (Skype)	tobyskeeper	P Patterson – Image 2	361000
John Smith	Contact (Skype)	lorna.bubbles	Toby Smith	4000
John Smith	Message sent to name (Skype)	lorna.bubbles	Toby Smith	12544000

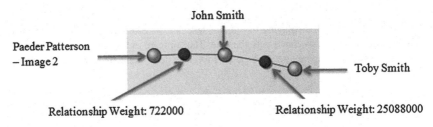

Fig. 5. Visualisation based on the Skype data that the relevant parties have in common.

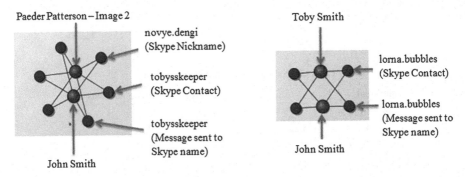

Fig. 6. Skype artefact visualisation displaying the artefact's that created the relationships.

Table 5. Firefox artefact extraction results

Individual	Image name	Firefox artefacts
John Smith	1_john	1192
Paeder Patterson – Image 2	2a	0
Paeder Patterson – Image 3	2b	0
Toby Smith	3	779

Two of the four disk images contain Firefox artefacts. These artefacts were compared to determine if any artefacts match and then visualised as displayed in Fig. 7.

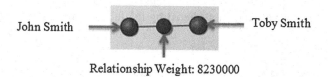

John Smith   Toby Smith

Relationship Weight: 8230000

Fig. 7. Overview visualisation based on the Firefox data that both parties have in common.

The artefact relationship node is expanded to display the Firefox browsing artefacts that the individuals have in common, the results of which are displayed in Fig. 8.

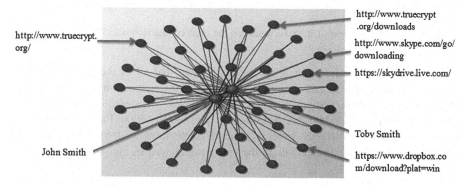

http://www.truecrypt.org/

http://www.truecrypt.org/downloads

http://www.skype.com/go/downloading

https://skydrive.live.com/

Toby Smith

John Smith

https://www.dropbox.com/download?plat=win

Fig. 8. Firefox artefact visualisation displaying artefact's that created the relationship (nodes of significance highlighted).

Keyword Extraction, Comparison and Visualisation. The keyword forensic artefacts' extraction library was executed against each acquired Source to facilitate comparison, the results of which are displayed in Table 6.

Table 6. Keyword artefact extraction results

Individual	Image name	Keyword artefacts
John Smith	1_john	202376
Paeder Patterson – Image 2	2a	4141
Paeder Patterson – Image 3	2b	54996
Toby Smith	3	49805

Once keyword data has been extracted and filtered against a defined set of false positives, the data associated with each individual can then be compared. Once the comparison data is generated it will be presented in the text results view of the solution from where it can then be visualised, an example of which is displayed below in Fig. 9. The text results of these comparisons operations are displayed in Appendix A. This data has been ordered by individual and weight and additionally manually filtered to protect individual's personal information, remove IP addresses, UCD infrastructure information and irrelevant data not filtered by the false positives process to improve readability.

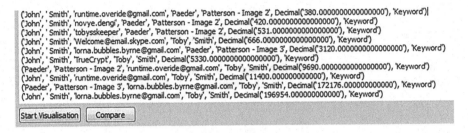

('John', ' Smith', 'runtime.overide@gmail.com', 'Paeder', 'Patterson - Image 2', Decimal('380.0000000000000000'), 'Keyword')|
('John', ' Smith', 'novye.dengi', 'Paeder', 'Patterson - Image 2', Decimal('420.0000000000000000'), 'Keyword')
('John', ' Smith', 'tobysskeeper', 'Paeder', 'Patterson - Image 2', Decimal('531.0000000000000000'), 'Keyword')
('John', ' Smith', 'Welcome@email.skype.com', 'Toby', 'Smith', Decimal('666.0000000000000000'), 'Keyword')
('John', ' Smith', 'lorna.bubbles.byrne@gmail.com', 'Paeder', 'Patterson - Image 3', Decimal('3120.0000000000000000'), 'Keyword')
('John', ' Smith', 'TrueCrypt', 'Toby', 'Smith', Decimal('5330.0000000000000000'), 'Keyword')
('Paeder', 'Patterson - Image 2', 'runtime.overide@gmail.com', 'Toby', 'Smith', Decimal('9690.0000000000000000'), 'Keyword')
('John', ' Smith', 'runtime.overide@gmail.com', 'Toby', 'Smith', Decimal('11400.000000000000'), 'Keyword')
('Paeder', 'Patterson - Image 3', 'lorna.bubbles.byrne@gmail.com', 'Toby', 'Smith', Decimal('172176.000000000000'), 'Keyword')
('John', ' Smith', 'lorna.bubbles.byrne@gmail.com', 'Toby', 'Smith', Decimal('196954.000000000000'), 'Keyword')

Start Visualisation   Compare

Fig. 9. Text results view of the tool based on the total comparison data of the test case.

When this data is visualised it can be easily seen that all of the individuals are connected in some way to each other, despite some of the connections being of minor relevance while others display a much greater degree of weighting significance. However if the person weight threshold filter is adjusted to 15000, Paeder Patterson – Image 2 can be seen to only have significant connections to John Smith and no connections to the other individuals in the case as displayed in Fig. 10.

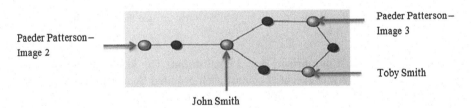

Paeder Patterson –
Image 2

Paeder Patterson –
Image 3

Toby Smith

John Smith

Fig. 10. Keyword overview visualisation regenerated based on increased threshold.

6   Conclusion

The tool successfully acquired, extracted and compared the various data sets associated with the individuals in this test case. The investigator is provided with compressive text data results, as well as functionality to visualise the comparison data in order to offer various perspectives of the data that would not ordinarily be available. The investigator can quickly view each relationship discovered between the various individuals and see which forensic artefact caused the relationship. Each artefact was weighted according to its significance, allowing the investigator to focus on forensic artefacts that are possibly of greater importance and thus potentially leading them to the most critical piece of forensic data sooner. The test case results presented clearly highlight a number of significant findings.

1. No matches of any importance were discovered between artefacts associated with the individuals marked P Patterson – Image 2 and P Patterson – Image 3.
2. A keyword of runtime.overide@gmail.com with a heavy weighting was matched on the images taken from John and Toby Smith as well as the image marked 2a (Paeder Patterson – Image 2).
3. A large number of Skype messages sent between a Skype alias of novye.dengi originating from John Smith's laptop to a Skype alias of tobyskeeper originating from Paeder Patterson – Image 2.
4. John Smith is identified as a Gatekeeper entity (individual within a network which has the ability to control information between different network segments) in this social network due to a number of significant relationships being discovered between him and all other individuals involved in the case.
5. An individual with an alias of Lorna Bubbles has had contact with John and Toby Smith as well as the data present on the image marked 2b (Paeder Patterson – Image 3). This could represent a new lead in the case.
6. A large number of common browsing locations between John and Toby Smith.

Based on the findings presented by the prototype, the investigator can now narrow the scope of their investigation and focus on the areas of greater relationship density. Further detailed analysis into these results would have established:

- That the forensic image marked 2a taken from the laptop discovered at Mr. Patterson's was used by the kidnapper.
- That the forensic image marked 2a taken from the laptop discovered at Mr. Patterson's apartment was in fact planted at that address and not owned by Mr. Patterson.
- The forensic image marked 2b taken from the laptop discovered at Mr. Patterson's apartment was owned by Mr. Patterson.
- No links of any significance between the forensic images 2a and 2b taken from both of the laptops at Mr. Patterson's address.
- The Skype alias of novye.dengi found to be the Skype account that John Smith used to communicate with the kidnaper. Tobyskeeper found to be the Skype account used by the kidnaper to communicate with John Smith.
- The user of runtime.overide@gmail.com found to be a contact of Toby Smith with direct involvement in the kidnap case.

7 Evaluation and Further Research

Without performing any preliminary investigation into the test case using traditional or other forensic tools, the solution generated a substantial amount of information with which the investigator can strategically plan the rest of their investigation. This data was available within minutes, which ordinarily would have taken days if not weeks to manually generate. No special expertise to make inferences regarding the graphical data presented is required, as visual patterns are easily understood.

The prototype has the potential to save an investigator a vast amount of time and resources. This has particular relevance where many law enforcement units are under resourced and are struggling to deal with the increasing number of digital forensic cases involving huge amounts of digital evidence as well as an already substantial backlog of digital forensic cases in some instances.

The tools primary application should be as a preliminary information gathering solution prior to using traditional digital forensic tools. The results generated should be used to conduct a more targeted and focused digital forensic examination. Greater value can be attained from the results when comparing digital forensic artefact data which can be attributed to a device or an individual. The tool is of is most benefit if used to discover relationships in multiparty digital forensic cases, such as child exploitation, financial fraud, paedophile rings or cases involving a number of suspect's and victim's.

In digital forensic cases involving a single individual or a number of individuals who have no relationship in the context of the case, the prototype is less applicable. However, the support for digital profiles allows investigators to compare data attributed to a single device or individual against a predefined set of forensic artefacts. This can be of benefit if the investigator has no background knowledge of the case they are investigating and wishes to establish some initial findings. However, the discovery of no relational information in a single or multiparty case is still a valid finding and would have taken a significant amount of time to establish.

Further research and development is required to enhance the digital forensic prototype's functionality. The further addition of acquisition, extraction and visualisation libraries to process common digital forensic artefacts, as well as developing the support for comparing operating system artefacts such as programs installed, installation information and mounted devices would result in a more complete solution. Incorporating the concept of graph theory centrality into the prototype's default visualisation would provide the investigator with a greater understanding of the underlying structural properties of visualised networks. Further research into the area of artefact relationship discovery is required in order to develop the substantial benefits from automating the digital forensic investigation process.

Appendix A – Keyword Comparison Results

Individual	Keyword	Individual	Weight
John Smith	tobysskeeperTobys	P Patterson – Image 2	96
John Smith	novye.denginovye	P Patterson – Image 2	102
John Smith	tobysskeeperN7	P Patterson – Image 2	114
John Smith	runtime.overide@gmail.com	P Patterson – Image 2	380
John Smith	novye.dengi	P Patterson – Image 2	420
John Smith	Tobysskeeper	P Patterson – Image 2	531
John Smith	paeder.patterson@mobileemail.vodafone.ie	P Patterson – Image 3	294
John Smith	paeder.ucd	P Patterson – Image 3	330

(*Continued*)

(Continued)

Individual	Keyword	Individual	Weight
John Smith	skype.outbound.ed10.com	P Patterson – Image 3	351
John Smith	lorna.bubbles@gmail.com	P Patterson – Image 3	513
John Smith	paeder.patterson @ucd.ie	P Patterson – Image 3	22644
John Smith	paeder.ucd@gmail.com	P Patterson – Image 3	64005
John Smith	Patterson	P Patterson – Image 3	75504
John Smith	lorna.bubbles.byrne@gmail.com	P Patterson – Image 3	203194
John Smith	john.ucd@gmail.com	P Patterson – Image 3	415692
John Smith	john.smith@ucd.ie	P Patterson – Image 3	44818818
John Smith	smithtoby.smith	Toby Smith	6
John Smith	lorna.bubblesLorna	Toby Smith	6
John Smith	lorna.bubblesA	Toby Smith	6
John Smith	toby.smithToby	Toby Smith	10
John Smith	lorna.bubbles.byrne@gmail. comByrne	Toby Smith	36
John Smith	novye.dengi	Toby Smith	60
John Smith	skype.com	Toby Smith	68
John Smith	TrueCrypt.exe	Toby Smith	80
John Smith	skype.outbound.ed10.com	Toby Smith	80
John Smith	toby.smithN1	Toby Smith	92
John Smith	lorna.bubbles	Toby Smith	220
John Smith	Welcome@email.skype.com	Toby Smith	666
John Smith	toby.smith	Toby Smith	1352
John Smith	TrueCrypt	Toby Smith	5330
John Smith	runtime.overide@gmail.com	Toby Smith	11400
John Smith	lorna.bubbles.byrne@gmail.com	Toby Smith	196954
John Smith	john.ucd@gmail.com	Toby Smith	230971
John Smith	toby.paul.smith@gmail.com	Toby Smith	796500
P Patterson – Image 2	novye.dengi	Toby Smith	1176
P Patterson – Image 2	runtime.overide@gmail.com	Toby Smith	42560
P Patterson – Image 2	skype.outbound.ed10.com	Toby Smith	337
P Patterson – Image 2	lorna.bubbles.byrne@gmail.com	Toby Smith	569204

References

1. Wassermann, S., Faust, K.: Social Network Analysis: Methods and Applications. Cambridge University Press, New York (1994)
2. Moreno, J.L.: Who Shall Survive? Foundations of Sociometry, Group Psychotherapy and Sociodrama. Beacon House, New York (1934, 1953, 1978)

3. Almack, J.C.: The influence of intelligence on the selection of associates. Sch. Soc. **16**, 529–530 (1922)

4. Bott, H.: Observation of play activities in a nursery school. Genet. Psychol. Monogr. **4**, 44–88 (1928)

5. Scott, J.: Social Network Analysis: A Handbook, 2nd edn. Sage Publications Ltd., London (2000)

6. Xu, J., Chen, H.: Criminal network analysis and visualization: a data mining perspective. Commun. ACM **48**(6), 101–107 (2005)

7. Sparrow, M.K.: The application of network analysis to criminal intelligence: an assessment of the prospects. Soc. Netw. **13**, 251–274 (1991)

8. Eades, P.: A heuristic for graph drawing. Congressus Numerantium **42**, 149–160 (1984)

9. Verisk Analytics: NetMap. http://www.iso.com/Products/NetMap-Suite-of-Products/NetMap-Suite-visual-link-analysis-to-fight-insurance-fraud.html. Accessed 16 Apr 2012

10. IBM i2: COPLINK Accelerating Law Enforcement. http://www.i2group.com/us/products/coplink-product-line. Accessed 4 Apr 2012

11. IBM i2: Analysts Notebook. http://www.i2group.com/us/products/analysis-product-line/ibm-i2-analysts-notebook. Accessed 2 Mar 2012

12. Paterva: Maltego. www.paterva.com/web5/. Accessed 1 Mar 2012

13. Bazzell, M.: Open Source Intelligence Techniques: Resources for Searching and Analyzing Online Information, CreateSpace Independent Publishing Platform (2013)

14. Guidance Software: EnCase Forensic V7. http://www.guidancesoftware.com/encase-forensic.htm. Accessed 2 May 2012

15. X-Ways Software Technology AG: X-Ways Forensics: Integrated Computer Forensics Software. http://www.x-ways.net/forensics/index-m.html. Accessed 2 May 2012

16. Microsoft: Strings v2.5, Microsoft. http://technet.microsoft.com/en-us/sysinternals/bb897439.aspx. Accessed 15 Apr 2012

Computer Profiling for Preliminary Forensic Examination

Andrew Marrington[1]([✉]), Farkhund Iqbal[1], and Ibrahim Baggili[2]

[1] Advanced Cyber Forensics Research Laboratory, College of Technological Innovation, Zayed University, P.O. Box 19282, Dubai, United Arab Emirates
marrington@computer.org, farkhund.iqbal@zu.ac.ae
[2] Tagliatela College of Engineering, University of New Haven, 300 Boston Post Road, West Haven, CT 06516, USA
ibaggili@newhaven.edu

Abstract. The quantity problem and the natural desire of law enforcement to confront suspects with evidence of their guilt close to the time of arrest in order to elicit a confession combine to form a need for both effective digital forensic triage and preliminary forensic examination. This paper discusses computer profiling, a method for automated formal reasoning about a computer system, and its applicability to the problem domain of preliminary digital forensic examination following triage. It proposes an algorithm for using computer profiling at the preliminary examination stage of an investigation, which focusses on constructing an information model describing a suspect's computer system in the minimal level of detail necessary to address a formal hypothesis about the system proposed by an investigator. The paper concludes by discussing the expanded utility of the algorithm proposed when contrasted to existing approaches in the digital forensic triage and preliminary examination space.

Keywords: Computer profiling · Triage · Formal methods · Preliminary examination

1 Introduction

The *quantity problem* in digital forensics was described by Carrier as the large amount of data which needs to be analyzed in the course of a digital investigation [1]. The quantity problem is necessarily addressed in digital investigations through data reduction techniques. A well-known example of such a technique in the investigation of a computer hard disk is the elimination of files known to be of no interest to the investigation from the examiner's view of the file system through the use of known file filters. The quantity problem contributes significantly to the time needed to complete any digital investigation, and consequently is a cause of significant delay to law enforcement. This problem becomes acute when an investigation incorporates numerous computers, storage media and other digital devices, many of which may be of no evidentiary value.

© Institute for Computer Sciences, Social Informatics and Telecommunications Engineering 2014
P. Gladyshev et al. (Eds.): ICDF2C 2013, LNICST 132, pp. 207–220, 2014.
DOI: 10.1007/978-3-319-14289-0_14

Unfortunately, a time consuming complete forensic examination may be required simply to find that the device in question contains no relevant digital evidence. It is more efficient for the examiner's time and effort to be focused on the devices and media which are considered to have the greatest potential evidentiary value. This is analogous to the paramedic, whose ministrations must first be focused on the injured person with the best chance of survival given timely treatment. In the medical domain, this allocation of medical resources is called *triage*. Even once the examiner's efforts have been focussed on the devices and media which have the greatest evidentiary value, there is a further need to quickly examine those devices and media in enough detail necessary to inform the rest of the investigation and/or to provoke an earlier confession from a suspect, both of which may be significantly delayed by waiting for a length in-depth examination in the lab.

Casey et al. argue that simply defaulting to in-depth forensic examination alone risks unacceptably delaying investigations involving digital evidence, and consequently argue for three stages to digital forensic investigations [2]:

1. Survey/Triage Forensic Inspection.
2. Preliminary Forensic Examination.
3. In-depth Forensic Examination.

As defined in [3], in medical terms triage is "a process for sorting injured people into groups based on their need for or likely benefit from immediate medical treatment." In the field of digital forensics, triage means identifying the digital devices or media which contain evidence relevant to the investigation at hand [2]. After this stage is completed, the devices and media identified can be examined. An in-depth forensic examination will produce the most complete results, but will take a long time, and may be subject to further delays due to backlogs at the digital forensics laboratory (which could stretch into the months or even years). Such a delay in the forensics lab can delay the entire investigation, and the impact the digital evidence may have to the course of that investigation may be reduced if it is not available in the early stages of the investigation. For example, a suspect may be less likely to confess if they have had a number of months to anticipate the discovery of certain files on their computer hard disk and have had time in the meantime to seek legal counsel. Consequently, Casey et al. argue for a stage between triage and in-depth examination, called *preliminary forensic examination*, "with the goal of quickly providing investigators with information that will aide them in conducting interviews and developing leads" [2].

In this work we propose the application of automated and formal *computer profiling* to the triage and preliminary examination stages described by Casey et al. [2]. The term *profiling* is used to describe many different approaches conceived for many different purposes in the digital investigations literature, such as criminal profiling [4], or user log transaction profiling [5]. In this work, profiling means that the computer system will be automatically described according to a formal model to support formal reasoning for the purpose of allowing an investigator to quickly answer questions about the computer system as a preliminary examination activity. The result of this process, the computer profile, can be tested against an investigator's formally stated hypothesis. The computer profile can also be used by the investigator to test other evidentiary statements, such as witness testimony, against the digital evidence recovered from the computer system. The results of this evaluation of hypotheses and evidentiary statements against the computer profile can both inform the decision to conduct and guide a subsequent thorough forensic examination of the system. Unlike the triage stage, some prior evidence (e.g. witness statement) or suspicion is assumed in this preliminary examination stage process. We believe that profiling may have particular utility in the evaluation of theories of the crime, and in interviewing witnesses and suspects, as both can be expressed formally and evaluated against the profile.

The approach we take in this work is based on a model for the forensic description of computer systems (i.e. profiling) described by Marrington et al. [6] and extended and improved upon by Batten and Pan [7]. This provides the basis for the description of a computer system to support formal reasoning. The formalism is useful as it provides for practical implementation which can support preliminary forensic examination in a generic sense, rather than in the form of a case-specific implementation. The contribution of this work is to describe algorithms for the implementation of a computer profiling tool for preliminary forensic examination, to support efficient querying of a computer profile to answer key questions about a computer system prior to a manual forensic examination of that computer system. In Sect. 2, we discuss the literature about both digital forensic triage and preliminary examination (Subsect. 2.1) and formal models for digital forensics (Subsect. 2.2).

2   Related Work

2.1   Triage and Preliminary Examination in Digital Forensics

In any criminal investigation, a suspect is more likely to confess to a crime when caught in the act or confronted with some evidence of their guilt. Much of the existing digital forensics literature describes all forensic activities designed to produce results more quickly (especially for the purposes of provoking an earlier confession) has described those activities as forensic triage activities. We believe that some of these techniques are either equally or more properly activities which could belong in Casey et al.'s preliminary forensic examination stage [2], or which at the very least inform the investigator's activity in the preliminary stage. Consequently, all of these activities, whether they are strictly triage or preliminary examination stage activities, or a combination of the two, are related to the work described in this paper.

Much of the existing literature in the digital forensic triage domain has considered the scenario of a fast, on-scene automated or semi-automated examination of the system to allow law enforcement officers to confront suspects with evidence of guilt in situ – a sort of "digital forensics breathalyzer". Such triage approaches are case specific – for example, in a child pornography case, a graphical triage utility might display thumbnails of image files on the screen [8].

Confronted with the illicit material they are alleged to have downloaded, a suspect may confess at the scene to law enforcement officers. Subsequently, the suspect's computer system will still be examined manually in the usual fashion, and the evidence produced by this "traditional" digital forensic examination will be the evidence produced in court.

The breathalyzer analogy is useful to illustrate the relationship between the on-scene triage examination and the more thorough examination in the laboratory. In many jurisdictions, once a suspect blows over the legal blood-alcohol limit on the breathalyzer, a blood test is taken to verify the results of the breathalyzer. It is this subsequent blood test which is considered to produce more reliable scientific evidence, but the initial breathalyzer results are often enough to provoke a suspect to confess to driving under the influence.

A forensic examiner needs to first identify various primary and secondary sources of evidence including computer internal memory and external storage media [8]. The internal memory of a computer is volatile in nature and its' contents may be lost if not handled immediately after the confiscation of a suspect's computer. Volatile memory may contain traces of forensically crucial information including open DLL files, function calls, references to called functions, system's files and processes, and operating system's utilities and artefacts. Therefore, once a crime-scene is cordoned off, it is imperative to start data acquisition first from fragile volatile containers and then from static storage devices.

Unlike traditional file-based data acquisition practice where most of the internal salient features of potential evidence are obscured, bulk-based evidence collection is best suited to triage. Garfinkel has developed *bulk_extractor*, a tool that facilitates evidence extraction and feature identification from confiscated computers with applications in both triage and preliminary examination [9].

2.2   Formal Models in Digital Forensics

Gladyshev and Patel proposed the use of a finite state machine (FSM) model for the purposes of reconstructing the history of a computer system [10], an approach also employed by Carrier and Spafford [11]. A finite state machine is a general computational model composed of a finite set of states, the transitions between those states, and various actions. A finite state machine is usually described as follows:

$$M = (Q, \Sigma, \delta, q_0, F)$$

where Q is the finite set of states of the machine, Σ is the input alphabet (or the finite set of possible events), $q_0 \in Q$ is the initial state of the machine, $F \subseteq Q$ is the set of final states, and δ is the transition function mapping $Q \times \Sigma$ to Q. At any given point in its history, a computer system can be in only one state. When an event (such as user input) happens, the computer system may change state or may stay in the same state – as expressed by the transition function $\delta(q, \sigma)$, which gives a state for each state $q \in Q$ and each event $\sigma \in \Sigma$. The state of the system at the time of the investigation can be considered to be the final state $f \in F$, and event reconstruction is fundamentally about tracing back the history of the machine from f to q_0 [10].

Gladyshev and Patel employ transition back-tracing to enumerate all of the possible scenarios leading to the final state q. A scenario is a run of finite computations, producing a series of transitions (that is, a series of events and states at the time of those events) leading the system M to end in state q. Essentially, a scenario describes some hypothesis explaining the evidential statement. Those scenarios arriving at the final state q which are inconsistent with the rest of the evidential statement (for example, witness statements, print-outs, trusted logs) can be discarded. This leaves only those scenarios which are consistent with the evidential statement. The evidential statement can be expanded to include investigative hypotheses, such that scenarios which disprove those hypotheses would be discarded by the expansion of the evidential statement to include them. Evidential statements are built from non-empty chronological sequences of observations. An observation is a statement to the effect that some property p was observed over time. Each observation is expressed as a triple $o = (P, min, opt)$, where P is the set of all computations of M possessing the observed property p, and min and opt are positive integers specifying the duration of observation. Each computation performed by the computer system includes an event $\sigma \in \Sigma$ and a state $q \in Q$, and causes the system to transition into another state (or back into the same state). A run of computations is a sequence of computations such that each computation causes the system to transition into the state which is part of the next computation in the run. A run of computations r is said to explain the observation o if every element of the run r possesses the observed property p (that is, for all i where $0 \leq i < |r|, r_i \in P$), and if $min \leq |r| \leq (min + opt)$ [10]. In this way, hypotheses are tested for computational feasibility.

It is difficult, however, to describe a complete practical computer system according to the finite state machine based-models. The problem of mapping the complete state space of a practical computer system is extremely computationally demanding. The models and techniques they describe could still be used in this fashion where the digital system under investigation (or a simplified model or subsection of it) is simple enough, given realistic computational limits, to be modelled as a finite state machine, but then this requires some degree of abstraction, which risks abstraction error [1].

Marrington et al. describe another model to describe computer systems for forensic purposes, one based on information available to investigators rather than a computational model which may be difficult to construct in practice [6]. In this model, the computer system is described as a 4-tuple cp:

$$cp = (O, AR, T, \text{EVT})$$

where O is the set of all the objects on the computer system (encapsulating users, groups, files, applications, and so on), AR is the set of relations on O capturing the relationships between different objects on the computer system, T is the set of all the times in the computer system's history (which need not be explicitly populated but which is included for the sake of completeness), and EVT is the set of all events in the computer system's history. Batten and Pan refine this model, allowing for the dynamic resizing of the set of all objects on the computer system O as the investigation progresses [7]. All components of this computer profiling model are constructed from the information which can be retrieved from the computer system at the time of its seizure. Although it lacks the power of computational models, this information-based model is practical, and the concept of relationships in particular provides for quite useful querying by an investigator, as shown in [7].

In the profiling model there are different types of relationships, built from binary predicates, which capture the nature of the connection between two objects [6]. A generic relation R on O is a set of ordered pairs of $O \times O$, and if the predicate $related(a, b)$ is true, where $a \in O, b \in O$), then we say aRb. Relations describing more specific predicates, such as $author(a, b)$ (i.e. that a is the author of some document b), are represented with more specific relationship types in [6], such as $aRAUTHORb$. Relations also have different properties [6,7]:

1. A relation R on O is *reflexive* if $\forall o \in O, oRo$.
2. A relation R on O is *symmetric* if aRb implies bRa for all objects $a \in O$ and $b \in O$.
3. A relation R on O is *transitive* if aRb and bRc implies aRc for all objects a, b and c in O.

Batten and Pan also prove that if a relation is reflexive, symmetric and transitive, then it is an *equivalence* relation by transitive closure (i.e. that if aRb is reflexive, symmetric and transitive, then $(a) = (b)$) [7]. As should be obvious from the discussion of objects and relationships in logical terms, computer profiling happens at a high level of abstraction, equivalent to a high-level of abstraction in Carrier's Complex Computer History Model [11] as opposed to the low-level Primitive Computer History Model. This means that profiling is prone to abstraction error as discussed in [1]. However, as we are applying profiling to the preliminary examination stage, we expect that the issue of abstraction error will be mitigated by subsequent forensic examination of the file system.

Our work builds on the work of Marrington et al. in [6] and of Batten and Pan in [7], employing the computer profiling model to the problem of preliminary examination. In so doing, we hope to practically provide some of the features of the FSM-based models of Gladyshev and Patel [10] and Carrier and Spafford [11], specifically with regard to testing hypotheses and evidentiary statements against the model. The principle difference is that we test these statements against a practically populated information model rather than a powerful, complete but unobtainable (or extremely abstracted) computational model.

3   Profiling for Preliminary Examination

Hard disk drive capacities are growing far in excess of the rate of improvement in bus speeds and seek times. This has informed our design for profiling-based preliminary forensic examination, because it means that it is desirable to extract the least information necessary from the suspect computer system to sustain or refute an evidentiary statement. Batten and Pan demonstrate the utility of dynamically resizing the set of all objects on the computer system O throughout the course of an investigation in order to more efficiently answer questions about the computer system's profile [7]. We apply this theoretic approach to the problem domain of preliminary examination, as we believe it supports the selective extraction of evidence from the hard disk (as opposed to requiring the examiner to acquire a complete disk image).

We suggest an iterative profiling/querying process for preliminary forensic examinations. At each iteration we build a computer profile, query it, and if the query does not return a result, we expand the profile and repeat. It is envisioned that this process would be repeated for a maximum number of iterations, which we shall simply refer to as n. At each iteration, we build a computer profile cp_i:

$$cp_i = (O_i, AR_i, T, \text{EVT}_i).$$

Note that we anticipate that the times in T will not change between iterations of the profiling triage process, although the other sets may expand each iteration. T will not change between iterations because it refers to all the times in the history of the computer system, which does not vary, nor do we anticipate that in practice T would have to be explicitly populated during the profiling process. In Subsect. 3.2 we start to describe the construction of this model, and expand on it with each subsequent iteration as described in Subsect. 3.3.

3.1 Setup

In order to minimize how much data must be read from the hard disk, each profiling iteration only reads from a portion of the disk. The complete disk will only be read if the profiling process reaches iteration n (the final iteration). The objective for triage is to build a profile which is complete enough at an early enough iteration to address the investigator's queries about the computer system without requiring n iterations.

In order to support iterative profiling, our algorithm requires that the computer's hard disk/s be divided into n "slices". Other than defining what should be included in the first slice ($slice_0$), our approach does not specify how the hard disk should be divided into these slices. If profiling is taking place on a live system, then it makes sense to divide the hard disk into slices according to the logical structure of the file system. If profiling is taking place on a previously acquired hard disk image, then it might make sense to divide the disk according to disk geometry (e.g. by sector). In the context of a preliminary forensic examination, we believe that the best approach would be to apply profiling to the original media through a write-blocker device – in this way, we avoid completely acquiring the media, but we do not give up the ability to search unallocated space. The exact mechanism chosen is an implementation issue – we simply specify that:

1. $slice_0$ includes the user home directories and main system log storage location; and
2. $slice_1$ to $slice_{n-1}$ are roughly equal in size to each other (but not necessarily to $slice_0$).

3.2 Initial Iteration

We start by building a very small set O_0 at our initial iteration, recording some metadata about each object in a database (roughly corresponding to the properties of objects discussed in [6]). This metadata includes, for each object, any associated timestamps and their descriptions, and source locations. Metadata can be a rich source of digital evidence, and can answer "Who, What, Where, When, How?" questions about files [12]. In terms of the profiling model, metadata can help us to discover relationships and events. At this stage, the set O_0 consists of a handful of important objects which can be identified from $slice_0$ of the suspect's hard disk/image:

1. The computer system's users (derived from the Windows registry, /etc/ password or other sources).
2. The userland applications installed on the system (derived from the Windows registry or walking common directories like c:\Program Files\ or /usr/bin).
3. The files in each user's home directory.

We then build AR_0, the set of relations on O_0. This set initially consists of relationships which we can derive simply from the metadata from the file system of the objects discovered in O_0. We should also determine the type of each relationship thus discovered. Relationship type can be derived from the metadata – if metadata is arranged as a set of keyword/value pairs, then the keyword indicates of the relationship type, whereas the value indicates the other object in the relationship.

For example, if an application or file, (x), is owned by the user y, then xRy, so we add (x, y) to R. In this example, the type of the relationship would be ROWNER, as the file x belongs to the user y, as indicated by the keyword/value pair $(owner, y)$ in the metadata of the file x. This relation is *symmetric* as the reverse is also true – x belongs to y and y is the owner of x.

The set EvT_0 is constructed out of the events in the system logs (e.g. the Windows Event Logs), and out of events inferred from the timestamps stored in the metadata for each object in O_0. Each of the common file system metadata timestamps (modified, accessed, created) provides some indicator of an event relating to the file [12]. The set EvT may be expanded in future iterations.

This completes cp_0, which is now queried by the investigator according to the method described in Sect. 4. If the query returns a result, then the investigator's query statement has been sustained, and the investigator may chose to either switch to another query statement for testing, or finish with the preliminary examination activity. If no match was found, or the investigator chooses to continue to test another query statement, then we proceed to the next iteration.

3.3 Iteration i

At iteration i (where $0 < i < n$), we expand upon the profile produced in the previous iteration to add more information. Adapting the three-stage approach per iteration employed by Batten and Pan [7], we expand the set of all objects and the set of all relationships as they allow, but we also expand the set of all events. Unlike Batten and Pan's work, which permits resizing in both directions, our sets grow with each iteration – they are not reduced. All of the elements of cp_i have the initial value at the start of this iteration of the elements of cp_{i-1} – e.g. O_i starts as O_{i-1} and has new objects added to it during this iteration.

There are two distinct components to our expansion of the profile in each iteration i:

1. Searching $slice_i$ for new objects.
2. Searching the metadata of the objects in $(O_i - O_{i-1})$ for new relations and new events.

After completing both of these steps, cp_i is completed, and queried. If the query returns a result, then the profiling process finishes at this iteration unless otherwise directed to continue to test other statements. If no match was found, or the investigator chose to continue profiling, then we proceed to the next iteration.

Searching the Disk Slice. At this stage we enumerate or carve all of the files in the section of the disk $slice_i$, depending on whether we are conducting a live analysis of a hard disk or examining a disk image. A new object is created for each file discovered in $slice_i$, and the file metadata is recorded in a database for later reference. We add new objects to O_i.

Searching File Metadata. For all of the objects in the set given by $(O_i - O_{i-1})$ (i.e. all of the objects discovered in this iteration), we search the metadata of each object and create events and relationships. Assuming that the metadata is a set of keyword/value pairs, then:

- When the value takes the form of a timestamp, the keyword describes some event which took place at that time, which can be added to EvT_i.
- When the value takes the form of another file's name, an application, a username (or other person's name), etc., the keyword describes the type of a relation between the object and another object described by the value, which can be added to AR_i.

4   Querying the Computer Profile

After the computer profile has been constructed, it can be queried with statements formally expressing hypotheses or evidentiary statements. These statements are formed in a similar fashion to the approach described by Gladyshev with respect to his FSM-based model [10], but instead of being tested for computational feasibility, the statements are tested for consistency with the profile.

Since a computer profile consists of objects, relationships, times and events, it can be queried for any of these things. A query may be as simple as a statement for evaluation that a particular object, relationship, time or event exists within the profile:

- $o \in O$ if the file, user or application being searched for was found.
- aRb if the objects a and b are found and are related.
- $t \in T$ if the computer was in operation at time t.
- $evt \in \text{EVT}$ if the event being searched for was found.

Each of these can be extended and combined so that a query need not test whether a single object exists in the profile – instead, the query can combine multiple substatements along these lines. There are two sets which we believe will be of particular interest for querying: R and EVT.

Querying a profile to see whether a sequence of events occured within the system's history is relatively straightforward. We use the *happened-before* relation as described by Lamport [13]. A sequence of events with wildcard timestamps or bounded potential times instead of timestamps (e.g. after 6:27pm but before 8:30pm) is provided by the invesigator as a statement for evaluation. Then we test that each timestamp $t_i \in T$ in the sequence of events provided in the investigator's query *happened-before* the timestamp t_{i+1}, i.e., that:

$$t_i \rightarrow t_{i+1}.$$

Relationships provide the richest source for querying. An investigator might posit any relationship between any two objects. The statement would be sustained if such a relationship already existed in AR. Otherwise, a statement like aRb may still be sustained depending on the properties of the relationship type (see Sect. 3). For example, if the posited relationship type is *transitive* and the relation includes $((a,c),(c,d))$ then we can also say that aRb and the statement is therefore sustained.

5   Use in Preliminary Forensic Examination

Profiling exists as an activity in the preliminary examination stage to be deployed primarily when an investigator has suspicions or witness statements (or other statements of evidence), expressed as formal hypotheses, which may involve the computer system to be examined. These hypotheses may arise from the digital forensic triage stage, or from interviews with suspects, or from other leads. As formalized observations, the profiles produced at each iteration may be of some use to an investigator with no prior knowledge of a computer system, however, as the process continues through multiple iterations, we anticipate that the profile will grow too large to be manually digestible. This anticipation is based on the numbers of objects reported in profiles constructed according to an early version of the model described by Marrington et al., where for an average office desktop PC circa 2007, the profile constructed by prototype software included nearly 4600 objects and over 44,000 events [14]. The profiling implementation described in that paper was not iterative, so the profile constructed would be analogous to the profile cp_n in this work. If the computer profile is ever useful as a set of human-digestible observations about an unknown computer system, then, we suggest that it will only be so during the early iterations, as the numbers of objects, relationships and events are likely to be too large to be practical for manual interpretation as the profiling process nears iteration n. The real utility of profiling for preliminary forensic examination, then, is to test suspicions or evidentiary statements to support investigators as they form leads and as they interview suspects.

Profiling could be employed as a preliminary activity either on a live system, a write-blocked hard disk removed from a suspect system, or on an already acquired disk image. As we discussed in Sect. 3, one of our objectives is to reduce access to the disk by constructing the profile progressively in iterations, rather than all at once in a single step. Obviously, if executed on a live system, then profiling as a triage activity may produce a result without the necessity of imaging an entire disk. However, live forensics of all types have serious drawbacks [15], and any profiling software which was run on a live system would likely cause modifications to the system's hard disk. For this reason, a more forensically sound approach to preliminary examination using profiling may involve acquiring an image of the suspect's hard disk, and then subsequently analyzing the image, or, as we have said in Sect. 3, removing the suspect's hard disk, connecting it to a write blocker, and conducting a preliminary examination on a forensic workstation plugged into the write protected disk. Both of these approaches will ensure that the profiling tool can recover objects from unallocated space, and thus produce more complete results, while protecting the suspect's hard disk from modification. The latter approach will avoid the need to completely acquire the media.

Whether executed on a "live" system or an already acquired disk image, we envision that the iterative profiling process described in this work would be executed after triage tools have been employed to identify the most relevant media, but where a preliminary forensic examination is still necessary. In some cases, the triage tools alone may be adequate and avoid the need for a preliminary forensic examination altogether – for example, a child pornography investigation would be well served by a triage tool which simply displayed all the image files found on the suspect computer system to the screen, as discussed in Subsect. 2.1. Rogers et al. discuss the different sorts of data files which investigators should focus on retrieving first in the triage stage of an investigation into a wide variety of case types [8]. Beyond case-specific triage tools, when an investigator is searching for the presence of particular files, hash values pre-computed for known files can be computed for hash values of files found on the suspect's hard disk. Similarity hashing is an advanced hashing technique which aims to still compute a match when only minor differences exist between known files and the files on the suspect's hard disk [16]. Recent work into sector hashing also means that target files may even be identified on disks where the file system has been destroyed or otherwise cannot be referenced [17]. Computer profiling exists to supplement these triage techniques – not to replace them.

There is an inherent inefficiency in the approach described in Sect. 3, concerning the case of computer systems whose disks contain no evidence of interest to the forensic investigator. The inefficiency is that while the profiling process may be ended at an iteration $i < n$ in the case where a query returns a result of interest, for an uninteresting computer system (i.e. one containing no evidence), the profiling process will continue until iteration n, by which point the entirety of the computer's disk/s (or image/s of the disk/s) will have been read. This is unsatisfactory, but does not mean that iterative profiling is unsuited to triage, as for an uninteresting system, even though all n iterations of the profiling process will be executed, they will constitute the entirety of the examination of the system, bypassing the need to manually examine the file system in the traditional fashion.

One point to bear in mind is that forensic science is a search for both *inculpatory* and *exculpatory* evidence. Since the profile generated by the process we discuss in Sect. 3 generates as minimal a profile as is necessary, the querying process we discuss in Sect. 4 will only likely discover inculpatory evidence (i.e. evidence of a suspect's guilt), since a query will only be answered in the positive (or not at all). A complete examination of the computer system being profiled subsequent to the triage stage of the investigation may, however, uncover exculpatory evidence which explains away the results of this query. It is important to note that we propose profiling as a preliminary examination activity only – we do not suggest that it replace manual in-depth forensic examination, only that it supplements it.

6 Future Work

We are in the process of implementing a practical computer profiling preliminary examination tool which applies the approach described in this work to live computer systems, physical disks addressed through a write blocker, and also to images acquired before the profiling process. We are particularly interested in building a profiler tool which reads in a DFXML file (introduced in [18]), in order to enhance the inoperability between our profiling tool and existing open source forensic tools.

Once a practical profiling triage tool has been implemented, we would like to use it to generate computer profiles for data mining puposes. Data mining computer profiles to produce patterns which we associate with particular illicit usage scenarios. These patterns could be included with future versions of the profiling triage tool, so that similar patterns in the target hard disk's computer profile could be identified. Once a likely pattern match is identified, the profiling tool could characterize the target computer's profile according to the matching pattern. For instance, the tool might alert the investigator to the similarity between the system they are currently examining and a system they examined before.

Finally, we wish to expand upon the basic approach of testing for a particular sequence of events. We are interested in allowing investigators to specify large hypotheses which are chained together, and even including multiple slightly divergent timelines. This would allow for the expression of still more powerful queries than those discussed in Sect. 4.

7   Conclusion

In this work, we have proposed the use of computer profiling for the problem of preliminary digital forensic examinations. We have designed an iterative profiling process which gradually expands the computer profile as it progresses. Due to this iterative approach, the computer profile is immediately useful for some querying early on, before the examination is complete. This makes the computer profile functional straight away, and thus minimizes the chance that the entire disk will need to be read/written to before any useful results are produced by the profiling tool.

The approach is not without limitations. Like most triage and preliminary examination applications, some knowledge of the target computer sytem is required. In the case of this work, enough knowledge of the target system is required to compose formal evidentiary statements about the system for testing via computer profiling. Counter-intuitively, our approach takes longer (at least, takes more iterations) for the computers on which no interesting evidence is found than it does on systems which are interesting, as discussed in Sect. 5.

References

1. Carrier, B.: Defining digital forensic examination and analysis tools using abstraction layers. Int. J. Digital Evid. **1** (2003)
2. Casey, E., Ferraro, M., Nguyen, L.: Investigation delayed is justice denied: proposals for expediting forensic examinations of digital evidence. J. Forensic Sci. **54**, 1353–1364 (2009)
3. The American Heritage Dictionary of the English Language. Houghton Mifflin, Boston (2000)
4. Rogers, M.: The role of criminal profiling in the computer forensics process. Comput. Secur. **22**, 292–298 (2003)
5. Abraham, T., de Vel, O.: Investigative profiling with computer forensic log data and association rules. In: Proceedings of 2002 IEEE International Conference on Data Mining, ICDM 2002, pp. 11–18 (2002)
6. Marrington, A., Mohay, G., Morarji, H., Clark, A.: A model for computer profiling. In: Third International Workshop on Digital Forensics at the International Conference on Availability, Reliability and Security, Krakow, IEEE, pp. 635–640 (2010)
7. Batten, L.M., Pan, L.: Using relationship-building in event profiling for digital forensic investigations. In: Lai, X., Gu, D., Jin, B., Wang, Y., Li, H. (eds.) Forensics in Telecommunications, Information, and Multimedia. LNICST, vol. 56, pp. 40–52. Springer, Heidelberg (2011)
8. Rogers, M.K., Goldman, J., Mislan, R., Wedge, T., Debrota, S.: Computer forensics field triage process model. In: Proceeding of the Conference on Digital Forensics Security and Law, pp. 27–40 (2006)
9. Garfinkel, S.: Digital media triage with bulk data analysis and bulk-extractor. Comput. Secur. **32**, 56–72 (2013)
10. Gladyshev, P., Patel, A.: Finite state machine approach to digital event reconstruction. Digital Invest. **1**, 130–149 (2004)

11. Carrier, B., Spafford, E.: Categories of digital investigation analysis techniques based on the computer history model. Proc. Sixth Ann. Digital Forensic Res. Workshop (DFRWS '06) **3**, 121–130 (2006)
12. Buchholz, F., Spafford, E.: On the role of file system metadata in digital forensics. Digital Invest. **1**, 298–309 (2004)
13. Lamport, L.: Time, clocks, and the ordering of events in a distributed system. Commun. ACM **21**, 558–565 (1978)
14. Marrington, A., Mohay, G., Clark, A., Morarji, H.: Event-based computer profiling for the forensic reconstruction of computer activity. In: Clark, A., McPherson, M., Mohay, G. (eds.) AusCERT Asia Pacific Information Technology Security Conference 2007 Refereed R&D Stream, Gold Coast, pp. 71–87 (2007)
15. Carrier, B.D.: Risks of live digital forensic analysis. Commun. ACM **49**, 56–61 (2006)
16. Roussev, V., Richard III, G., Marziale, L.: Multi-resolution similarity hashing. Digital Invest. **4**, 105–113 (2007)
17. Young, J., Foster, K., Garfinkel, S., Fairbanks, K.: Distinct sector hashes for target file detection. Computer **45**, 28–35 (2012)
18. Garfinkel, S.: Digital forensics XML and the DFXML toolset. Digital Invest. **8**, 161–174 (2012)

Digital Forensics and the Cloud

Determining Training Needs for Cloud Infrastructure Investigations Using I-STRIDE

Joshua I. James[1]($\boxtimes$), Ahmed F. Shosha[2], and Pavel Gladyhsev[2]

[1] Digital Forensic Investigation Research Group: ASP Region,
Soon Chun Hyang University, Shinchang-myeon, Asan-si, South Korea
joshua@cybercrimetech.com
[2] Digital Forensic Investigation Research Group: Europe,
University College Dublin, Belfield, Dublin 4, Ireland

Abstract. As more businesses and users adopt cloud computing services, security vulnerabilities will be increasingly found and exploited. There are many technological and political challenges where investigation of potentially criminal incidents in the cloud are concerned. Security experts, however, must still be able to acquire and analyze data in a methodical, rigorous and forensically sound manner. This work applies the STRIDE asset-based risk assessment method to cloud computing infrastructure for the purpose of identifying and assessing an organization's ability to respond to and investigate breaches in cloud computing environments. An extension to the STRIDE risk assessment model is proposed to help organizations quickly respond to incidents while ensuring acquisition and integrity of the largest amount of digital evidence possible. Further, the proposed model allows organizations to assess the needs and capacity of their incident responders before an incident occurs.

Keywords: Digital forensic investigation · Incident response · Capability assessment · Cloud forensics · I-STRIDE · Asset-based risk assessment · Security policy

1 Introduction

New concepts in cloud computing have created new challenges for security teams and researchers alike [27]. Cloud computing service and deployment models have a number of potential benefits for businesses and customers, but security and investigation challenges – some inherited from 'traditional' computing, and some unique to cloud computing – create uncertainty and potential for abuse as cloud technologies proliferate.

According to a survey from Ponemon Institute [19], only 35 % of IT respondents and 42 % of compliance respondents believe their organizations have adequate technologies to secure their Infrastructure as a Service (IaaS) environments. The report shows that respondents believe IaaS is less secure than their on-premise systems, however, "[m]ore than half (56 %) of IT practitioners say that security concerns will not keep their organizations from adopting cloud services".

© Institute for Computer Sciences, Social Informatics and Telecommunications Engineering 2014
P. Gladyshev et al. (Eds.): ICDF2C 2013, LNICST 132, pp. 223–236, 2014.
DOI: 10.1007/978-3-319-14289-0_15

A drive towards cloud service offerings is reiterated by Gartner [10], who forecasts that spending on cloud computing at each service model layer will more than double by 2016. At the same time Ernst and Young [9] found that there is a perceived increase in risk by adopting cloud and mobile technologies, and many respondents believe that these risks are not currently being adequately dealt with. However, North Bridge [23] suggests that confidence in cloud computing is increasing, even though maturity of the technologies remains a concern.

An increased confidence in cloud computing and a drive to improve business processes while reducing costs are leading to security of such systems sometimes being a secondary concern. This attitude has somewhat been carried over from traditional computing, which could possibly result in the same, or similar, security challenges, such as those presented by the Computer Research Association [6] in the *Four Grand Challenges in Trustworthy Computing*. If both security and insecurity from traditional computing are inherited by cloud computing, both may be augmented with the increased complexity of the cloud model, the way that services are delivered, and on-demand extreme-scale computing. Each cloud deployment and service model has its own considerations as far as security and liability are concerned. For example, in a private, single-tenant cloud where all services may be hosted on-premise, the risks are similar to on-premise, non-cloud hosting. The organization has end-to-end control, can implement and target security systems, and can control critical data flow and storage policies. A challenge with this model is that the organization must have the capability to be able to create, implement, and maintain a comprehensive security strategy for increasingly complex systems.

Several works have previously examined some cloud security concerns [3, 4, 7, 12, 15, 21, 28]. This work, however, is concerned with an organization's ability to assess the investigation and response capability of their investigators considering the organization's unique needs. Security groups, such as the National Institute of Standards and Technology, have previously called for digital forensic readiness to be included in incident response planning [13]. However, determining the required capabilities of investigators has not been directly addressed. Prior works, such as Kerrigan [14] proposed a capability maturity model for digital investigations. Such maturity models essentially focus on assessing how standardized knowledge and processes are in a particular organization, and how well these organizations actually conform to these standards. While technical capability of digital investigators is a factor, this model does not include assessment of specific technical needs of an organization. Pooe and Labuschange [20] proposed a model for assessing digital forensic readiness that includes identification of more specific technical challenges; however, this model too does not help guide an organization in specifically defining their internal digital investigation capability needs in regards to the technical skills.

1.1 Contribution

This work proposes a method to guide organizations in determining the technical skills needed for incident response and digital investigations that are tailored specifically to the organization. The proposed method uses an extension of a previously known asset-based risk assessment model to help guide an organization and prepare for digital investigations, including determination of technical training that is specifically required for investigators within the organization.

The remainder of this paper first discusses related prior work for assessing risk to cloud infrastructure. After, a method is described for assessing investigation capability based on an organizational risk assessment. A case study is then given applying the proposed model to cloud infrastructure. In-house knowledge can be questioned based on the identification and prioritization of risks, and gaps in knowledge may be identified from which specified training areas can be defined. Finally, conclusions are given and potential future work is discussed.

2   Assessing Risk to Cloud Infrastructure

To help in the identification of threats, their impact on a system, potential evidential traces and technical skill needed by investigators, an extension to the six-category, threat categorization model – 'Spoofing, Tampering, Repudiation, Information Disclosure, Denial of Service, and Elevation of Privilege' (STRIDE) [26] – is proposed. The STRIDE model is a threat categorization model that can be used to help understand the impact of a specific threat being exploited in a system [17]. It helps to determine vectors of attack, the impact of an attack on data, and the overall impact to the organization due to the altered - or loss of - data. The STRIDE model has previously been applied to probabilistic risk assessment in cloud environments [22], threat modeling using fuzzy logic [24], among others.

James, Shosha et al. [11] previously proposed an extension to the STRIDE model beyond risk assessment and potential exploitation results, to add the identification of possible investigation-relevant traces produced by the exploitation, named the "Investigation STRIDE model", or I-STRIDE.

As shown in Fig. 1, the I-STRIDE process is conducted by first deconstructing a service into its dependent components. A risk assessment is conducted per component, and risk mitigation techniques are derived. Each risk identified by I-STRIDE has associated investigation-relevant data sources. When a threat to a component has been identified, an investigator may determine what data is likely to be effected by the threat. From this subset of affected data, specific data sources that may be of evidential value can be identified. These potential evidential data sources may then be used for pre-investigation planning and data targeting purposes.

Determining forensic investigation knowledge required to investigate a particular threat can be modeled using risk analysis and assessment techniques. In particular, risk assessment models such as Root Cause Analysis (RCA) [25] can be used to help identify required training. Broadly speaking, RCA is used to identify the root cause of an event that causes a phenomena of interest. Thus, RCA in combination with the proposed I-STRIDE model can be used as a basis to identify training related to the investigation of identified threats (Fig. 2).

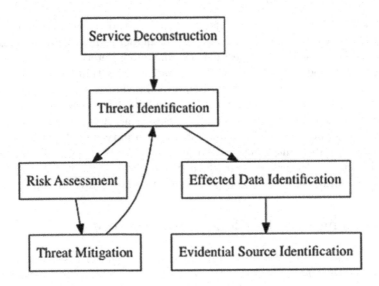

Fig. 1. The I-STRIDE process model for risk assessment, mitigation and investigation

Utilizing methodologies such as RCA benefits not only the process of training identification, or gaps in knowledge, but also training efficacy. When considering investment in training, organizations attempt to determine whether a specific training meets their unique needs. By identifying gaps in knowledge related to prioritized organizational risks, training can be more focused at areas the organization specifically needs. As such, training can be audited according to the identified training objectives and scope based on the needs of the organization.

3   Incident Response Planning and Capability Assessment

An important step in Incident Response – if not the most important – is the readiness phase. In the integrated digital investigation process (IDIP) model, Carrier and Spafford [5] state that "the goal of the readiness phases is to ensure that the operations and infrastructure are able to fully support an investigation". The operations readiness phase involves the on-going training of personnel, such as first responders and lab technicians, and the procurement and testing of equipment needed for the investigation. However, while general training may be applicable to each organization, an organization may have specific training needs that need to be identified.

For example, operational readiness in cloud environments should include education in cloud-related technologies, such as hypervisors, virtual machines and cloud-based storage, but may specifically depend on what services the organization is providing. Personnel should have general knowledge of how to interact with cloud technologies at the infrastructure, platform and software layers, and understand the effect their actions have on the environment. They should understand the methods and tools available to collect investigation-relevant data in

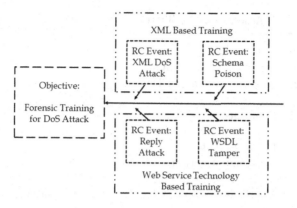

RC: Root Cause

Fig. 2. Root Cause Analysis to guide forensic investigation training Stephenson, Peter. "Modeling of post-incident root cause analysis." International Journal of Digital Evidence 2.2 (2003): 1–16.

each layer of the cloud. Different Cloud Service Providers (CSP) may have proprietary systems, so training on the use and investigation of these proprietary systems should be considered. However, determination of exactly what skills and knowledge are necessary to ensure quality investigations may be difficult. Further, identifying what technologies should be the focus of technical training may not be fully known.

The training of personnel, identification of potential risks, and identification of potential data sources before an incident occurs can greatly help in efficient incident response, and with the timely and sound acquisition of relevant data. For this reason this work recommends organizations model threats, their potential impact, and potential evidential trace data sources before an incident occurs. This will assist the CSP in preserving potential evidence during incident response, and will help law enforcement have a better idea of what data will be available, and how to handle such data, if a particular incident occurs.

4   Methodology

The proposed knowledge identification method is broken into two areas of assessment: Technology (security) risk and Knowledge (training/education) risk. Assessment of 'knowledge risk' is necessary because simply knowing a technical vulnerability exists will not aid in incident response or investigation unless the responder/investigator has knowledge of concepts such as where relevant evidential data may exist and how to properly acquire such data. Below are both the Technology risk and knowledge risk assessment processes.

- Technology Risk Assessment (I-STRIDE)
  1. Identify Assets
  2. Identify Threats to Assets
  3. Determine Potential Threat Impact
  4. Determine Potential Evidential Data Sources (Pre-Investigation)
  5. Prioritize Threats
     - Organizational needs
     - Common Vulnerability Scoring System (CVSS) [18]
- Knowledge Risk Assessment
  1. Identify required investigation knowledge
  2. Assess current in-house knowledge
     - Knowledge of the collection/analysis of associated evidential data sources
  3. Compare in-house knowledge with risk prioritization.

Knowledge risk in this case can be assessed based on Bloom's Taxonomy [2]. Using Bloom's Taxonomy in-house knowledge could be assessed, either through self-assessment or a more formal process. The Taxonomy would allow an organization to understand the level of knowledge they possess about the investigation of breaches caused by the specific vulnerability.

Bloom's Taxonomy has 6 'verbs' that correspond to a level of knowledge: remembering, understanding, applying, analyzing, evaluating, and creating. Knowledge of a vulnerability or evidential data sources can be assessed based on these levels of knowledge. As such, a score can be assigned to each level (1–6), which can be considered the knowledge risk score. Such a score implies that higher-level knowledge such as an ability to analyze and evaluate a topic is preferred over simple remembering.

If an organization is also using a threat prioritization metric – such as the CVSS – then these scores can be combined to create a 'knowledge prioritization' model. For example, with CVSS a score of 1 indicates a low risk, where a score of 10 indicates a high risk. In Bloom's taxonomy a score of 1 indicates low knowledge, and a score of 6 indicates higher-level knowledge. Assume CVSS is used to assess the severity of a threat (1 being least severe, 10 being the most severe). Bloom's taxonomy measures can be scaled to the same scale as CVSS, and the knowledge risk can be subtracted from the technology risk as so:

$$T_s - ((K_s \div K_{max}) \cdot T_{max})$$

where:

- T_s is the technology risk score
- K_s is the knowledge risk score
- K_{max} is the maximum knowledge risk score
- T_{max} is the maximum technology risk score.

In this case, if the technology risk score is high (10 out of 10), and the knowledge risk score is also high (6 out of 6), then the *knowledge priority* will be low (0) in terms of training or education needs. If the technology risk score is low (2 out of 10), and the knowledge risk score is also low (1 out of 6), then the overall knowledge priority will still remain low (0.33). The threats with the highest priority will be high-scoring technology risks that the organization has little knowledge about. Further, as knowledge is updated (either gained or lost) knowledge risk can also be updated to reflect the current state of knowledge in the organization.

Again, this prioritization is used to identify areas where investigation education or training is lacking and supplementation may be necessary due to technology risk, not to imply that a high knowledge of a vulnerability will reduce an organization's risk of that vulnerability being exploited.

5   Case Studies

To show the applicability of the I-STRIDE model for determining training needs, assessment of cloud computing infrastructure based on Eucalyptus [8] and OpenStack will be given as examples.

5.1   Case 1: Eucalyptus Cloud

This case will specifically look at a deployed Eucalyptus Cloud. The components of this platform will be explained, and an analysis using the I-STRIDE model will be conducted against this deployment.

The Eucalyptus architecture is composed of five high-level components that are essentially standalone web services. These components include:

- Cloud Controller (CLC): The cloud controller is the main entry point for the cloud environment. CLC is responsible for "exposing and managing the underlying virtualized resources".
- Cluster Component (CC): CC is responsible for managing the execution of VM instances.
- Storage Controller (SC): Provides block-level network storage that can be dynamically attached by VMs instances.
- Node Controller (NC): Executed on every node that is designated for hosting and allows management of VM instances.
- Walrus: Allows the storage and management of persistent data.

Figure 3 shows the Eucalyptus components and their connection and communication channels.

The scope of this case will be limited to asset-centric threat modeling. The assets in this case will be defined as each of the Eucalyptus components which can be thought of as the Cloud Service Provider (CSP), and will also include a cloud client. In this case, threats (Table 1) were identified and exploited in the deployed Eucalyptus architecture. Per the I-STRIDE model, an analysis of affected assets was conducted. An investigation was then conducted to determine potential evidential data sources. Identified threats, the threat description, the

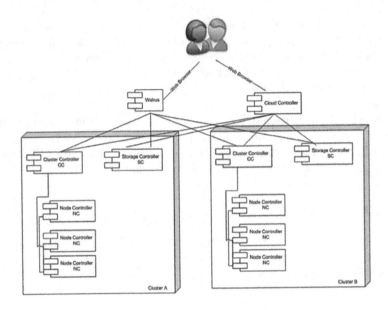

Fig. 3. Deployed Eucalyptus architecture

affected asset, the impact on the asset, and the location of potential evidential data sources are listed in Table 1. Information in this table may normally be used to assess threats, and, if a threat is exploited, help to collect potential evidential traces during the incident response phase.

Using the I-STRIDE model could help CSPs and law enforcement identify an investigation starting point during Incident Response (IR). This level of readiness would potentially allow for improved pre-planning, first response and cooperation once an incident occurred. While I-STRIDE may help to determine data sources interesting to an investigation, this information is only useful if the responders understand how to properly access, acquire and preserve such data. The output of the I-STRIDE model can be considered the knowledge the organization needs. For example, if the Cluster Component is compromised then incident responders need knowledge of the Cluster Component to be able to make use of the knowledge of associated evidential data sources. The I-STRIDE model can be used to guide training and education development plans based on the needs of an assessed organization.

Case 1: Knowledge Prioritization. Consider again Table 1. If denial of service was found to be a priority risk in an organization, then at least 4 threats have an impact defined as denial of service. The threat vector, and already known potential evidential sources can be used to define the type of training necessary to thoroughly investigate breaches using such vectors of attack. For example, the first priority threat as shown in Table 2 uses XML as an attack vector. XML parser logs were identified as potential evidential sources at the cloud controller.

Table 1. Identified threats, the estimated threat impact and potential evidential data sources identified for a Eucalyptus that is the result of the proposed I-STRIDE model

Threat	Description	Asset	Threat impact	Potential evidential sources
XML Denial of Service	Attacker crafts XML message with a large payload, recursive content or with malicious DTD schema.	Cloud Controller, Cloud Client	Denial of Service	XML parser logs at the cloud controller
Replay Attack Flaws	Attacker could issue recurrence overloaded Simple Object Access Protocol (SOAP) messages over HTTP to overwhelm the CSP and stop the service	Cloud Controller, Cloud Client	Denial of Service	SOAP message timestamp and message payload to identify the message flaws
WSDL Parameter Tampering	Attacker could embed command line code into WSDL documents or command shell to execute the command	Cloud Controller, Cluster Controller, Node Controller, Cloud client	Denial of Service	Detailed investigation of WSDL file could identify parameter tampering
Schema Poisoning	Attacker could compromise the XML schema grammar and manipulate the data	Cloud Controller, Cloud Client	Denial of Service	Detailed investigation of XML parser logs at the cloud controller may contain evidence of XML schema tampering

The organization can apply the methodology described in Sect. 4 to determine knowledge risk. Notice, in Table 2 the organization did not use CVSS, but instead chose a low-medium-high technology risk prioritization scheme. In this case, since each technology risk is a high priority (3 out of 3), the organization can now assess their knowledge about the investigation of each technology risk. For this case, let's assume that the organization has a great understanding of XML attack vector investigations (5 out of 6), and very little knowledge of SOAP exploit prevention and investigation (1 out of 6). Knowledge prioritization can then be assessed as follows

Table 2. Threat prioritization (in this case, based on the organization's subjective decision) and required investigation knowledge identification based on identified threats that cause a particular class of threat impact

Priority	Threat	Asset	Threat impact	Potential evidential sources	Knowledge
High	XML Denial of Service	Cloud Controller, Cloud Client	Denial of Service	XML parser logs at the cloud controller	XML attack vector investigation
High	Replay Attack Flaws	Cloud Controller, Cloud Client	Denial of Service	SOAP message timestamp and message payload to identify the message flaws	SOAP exploit prevention and investigation
High	WSDL Parameter Tampering	Cloud Controller, Cluster Controller, Node Controller, Cloud client	Denial of Service	Detailed investigation of WSDL file could identify parameter tampering	WSDL Security and Investigation
High	Schema Poisoning	Cloud Controller, Cloud Client	Denial of Service	Detailed investigation of XML parser logs at the cloud controller may contain evidence of XML schema tampering	XML attack vector investigation

- XML investigation training priority: $3 - ((5 \div 6) \cdot 3) = 0.5$
- SOAP investigation training priority: $3 - ((1 \div 6) \cdot 3) = 2.5$

If an organization can answer questions about in-house knowledge for high priority technology risks, then the organization can identify associated knowledge risk, and invest in training of personnel more effectively based on their unique needs. Once these knowledge priority areas have be en identified, they can be fed directly into training development models such as the Successive Approximation Model [1] for rapid training development. This will allow organizations to quickly target and close gaps in knowledge based on prioritized organizational risks.

5.2   Case 2: OpenStack

The next case concerns the assessment of OpenStack, an open source cloud infrastructure project. This example will use vulnerabilities identified in CVE Details [16], along with the threat's identified CVSS score. From CVE, an organization running OpenStack may assess their specific technology and knowledge risk in relation to new vulnerabilities.

The knowledge required for each of the technology risks identified in Table 3 can be identified using the I-STRIDE process, and specifically by simulating an incident and determine where data relevant to the investigation may be found. In this case, the required knowledge has been defined as parts of the swift architecture.

Table 3. Identified threats, the estimated threat impact and potential evidential data sources identified for OpenStack that is the result of CVE details and the I-STRIDE model

Threat	Description	Asset	Threat impact	CVSS	Potential evidential sources	Knowledge
Issue requests with an old X-Timestamp value	Authenticated attacker can fill an object server with superfluous object tombstones	Swift Cluster	Denial of Service	4.0	Tombstone files	Swift Object Servers
Re-auth deleted user with old token	When an actor claims to have a given identity, the software does not prove or insufficiently proves that the claim is correct	Keystone	Security Bypass	6.0	Instance and user logs	Swift Proxy
Generate unparsable or arbitrary XML responses	Unchecked user input in Swift XML responses	Swift account servers	Security Bypass	7.5	Account server logs	Account server

The CVSS in this case represents the technology risk if the vulnerability has not been patched yet, or for some reason cannot be. The organization must conduct an internal knowledge risk assessment based on the identified knowledge areas for newly identified vulnerabilities. In this case, assume an organization has moderate (3 out of 6) knowledge about swift proxy and account servers, and little (1 out of 6) knowledge of swift object servers. The investigation knowledge priority for each threat can be calculated as so:

- Object server investigation training priority: $4 - ((1 \div 6) \cdot 10) = 2.33$
- Proxy server investigation training priority: $6 - ((3 \div 6) \cdot 10) = 1$
- Account server investigation training priority: $7.5 - ((3 \div 6) \cdot 10) = 2.5$.

In this case, because the account server has the highest technology risk and the organization only has a moderate level of knowledge about the investigation of such a risk, it is given the highest priority. It is then followed by a technology risk that is relatively low, but is a risk which the organization does not have much knowledge about.

6   Conclusions

Cloud computing has a number of benefits, such as high availability, potentially lower cost, and potentially improved security. However, cloud computing also has a number of associated risks. Some of these risks have been inherited from traditional computing models, while the cloud business model introduces others. As more businesses and end users move their data and processing to cloud environments, these environments will increasingly become the target, or even the originator, of malicious attacks. By taking an asset-based risk assessment approach, and specifically using the I-STRIDE model, organizations can identify and prioritize threats, determine threat impact and potential evidential sources, and ultimately identify gaps in investigator knowledge before a threat is exploited. By implementing the proposed technology and knowledge risk assessment metrics, and organization can at least be better positioned to make training and education investment decisions based on observed deficiencies. I-STRIDE can act as a base for CSPs and law enforcement to more effectively work together before and during the investigation of incidents in cloud environments, and not only in the discussion of vulnerabilities but in the discussion of required knowledge.

While this work proposed a naive model for determining investigator training needs specific to the organization, future work will attempt to evaluate the model with real organizations rather than a researcher-created case study. For example, the model, as proposed, integrates prevention (security) and investigation (post incident) to attempt to improve both. However, such a model takes a considerable amount of effort and pre-planning to implement. In large organizations, even communication between investigators and security officers may be difficult. Such real-world case studies are needed to evaluate the practicality of the proposed training-guidance method.

References

1. Allen, M.W.: Creating Successful E-Learning: A Rapid System for Getting it Right the First Time, Every Time. Pfeiffer & Co, San Francisco (2006)
2. Anderson, L.W., Krathwohl, D.R., Bloom, B.S.: A Taxonomy for Learning, Teaching, and Assessing. Longman, New York (2005)
3. Armbrust, M., Fox, A., Griffith, R., Joseph, A.D., Katz, R.H., Konwinski, A., Lee, G., Patterson, D.A., Rabkin, A., Stoica, I., Zaharia, M.: Above the clouds: a Berkeley view of cloud computing. Science 53(UCB/EECS-2009-28), 07–013 (2009)
4. Balduzzi, M., Zaddach, J., Balzarotti, D., Kirda, E., Loureiro, S.: A security analysis of amazon's elastic compute cloud service (2012)
5. Carrier, B.D., Spafford, E.H.: Getting physical with the digital investigation process. Int. J. Digital Evid. 2(2), 1–20 (2003)
6. CRA and Computing Research Association. Four grand challenges in trustworthy computing. Technical report (2003)
7. Dykstra, J., Sherman, A.T.: Acquiring forensic evidence from infrastructure-as-a-service cloud computing: exploring and evaluating tools, trust, and techniques. Digital Invest. 9, S90–S98 (2012)
8. Eucalyptus. Eucalyptus: The Open Source Cloud Platform (2013)
9. EY and EYGM Limited. Into the cloud, out of the fog: Ernst & Young's 2011 global information security survey. Technical report (2011)
10. Gartner. Forecast: public cloud services, Worldwide, 2010–2016, 2Q12 Update. Technical report (2012)
11. James, J.I., Shosha, A.F., Gladyshev, P.: Digital forensic investigation and cloud computing. In: Ruan, K. (ed.) Cybercrime and Cloud Forensics: Applications for Investigation Processes, pp. 1–41. IGI Global, Hershey (2013)
12. Jansen, W.A.: Cloud Hooks: Security and Privacy Issues in Cloud Computing, pp. 1–10. IEEE, Washington, DC (2011)
13. Kent, K., Chaevalier, S., Grance, T., Dang, H.: Guide to integrating forensic techniques into incident response. Technical report SP800-86 (2006)
14. Kerrigan, M.: A capability maturity model for digital investigations. Digital Invest. 10(1), 19–33 (2013)
15. Kui, R., Cong, W., Qian, W.: Security challenges for the public cloud. IEEE Internet Comput. 16(1), 69–73 (2012)
16. MITRE. OpenStack Security Vulnerabilities
17. MSDN. The STRIDE Threat Model (2005)
18. NIST. Common Vulnerability Scoring System
19. Ponemon and L L C Ponemon Institute. The security of cloud infrastructure: survey of U.S. IT and compliance practitioners. Technical report (2011)
20. Pooe, A., Labuschagne, L.: A conceptual model for digital forensic readiness. In: 2012 Information Security for South Africa, pp. 1–8. IEEE, August 2012
21. Ruan, K., Carthy, J., Kechadi, T., Baggili, I.: Cloud forensics definitions and critical criteria for cloud forensic capability: an overview of survey results. Digital Invest. 10(1), 34–43 (2013)
22. Saripalli, P., Walters, B.: QUIRC: A Quantitative impact and risk assessment framework for cloud security, pp. 280–288. IEEE (2010)
23. Skok, M.J.: Future of Cloud Computing 2012 (2012)
24. Sodiya, A.S., Onashoga, S.A., Oladunjoye, B.: Threat modeling using fuzzy logic paradigm. J. Issues Inf. Sci. Technol. 4(1), 53–61 (2007)

25. Stephenson, P.: Modeling of post-incident root cause analysis. Int. J. Digital Evid. **2**(2), 1–16 (2003)
26. Swiderski, F., Snyder, W.: Threat Modeling. Microsoft Press, Redmond (2004)
27. Vouk, M.A.: Cloud computing-Issues, research and implementations, pp. 31–40. IEEE (2008)
28. Zissis, D., Lekkas, D.: Addressing cloud computing security issues. Future Gener. Comput. Syst. **28**(3), 583–592 (2012)

Cloud Forensic Readiness: Foundations

Lucia De Marco[1,2]([✉]), M-Tahar Kechadi[1], and Filomena Ferrucci[2]

[1] School of Computer Science and Informatics,
University College Dublin, Dublin, Ireland
lucia.de-marco@ucdconnect.ie, tahar.kechadi@ucd.ie
[2] Department of Management and Information Technology,
University of Salerno, Fisciano, Italy
fferrucci@unisa.it

Abstract. The advances of the ICT industry in recent years has led to huge popularity of Cloud Computing Services. Due to the fact that the Cloud is distributed and hosts numerous users, its use to commit crimes becomes a critical issue. Proactive cloud forensics becomes a matter of urgency: its capability to collect critical data before crimes happen, thus saving time and energy for the investigations is its primary objective. In this paper, we discuss the basis of Cloud Forensic Readiness, because we believe that such a system is of huge necessity. We begin by carefully defining Digital Forensic Readiness in the Cloud Computing context. We propose a reference architecture for a Cloud Forensic Readiness System (CFRS) together with its features, components, and challenges.

Keywords: Forensic Readiness · Cloud forensics · Cybercrimes · Cyber-Security

1 Introduction

Cloud Computing (CC) is a real evolution in the manner in which information systems are conceived and located. Its main features and opportunities [10] represent the motivations for its rapid diffusion in the last years. Unfortunately, CC currently presents some weak points, which are exploited by criminals, thus leading to serious Cloud incidents [3].

Digital Forensics [12] has evolved through the years, and has been dealing with the collection and management of evidence from several types of devices, from single computers to computer networks and mobile devices. In single machine forensics, the evidence contained within the media are under the control of law enforcement from the time of seizure; in Network Forensics (NF) [12] this remains true, even though the media to consider are both individual machines and network path devices, e.g., routers, access points, switches and server machines. Cloud Forensics (CF) [18] was born from the necessity of managing digital crimes in the architecture of Cloud Computing services.

The paper is structured as follows: Sect. 1 introduces Cloud Computing (CC) and Digital Forensics (DF); in Sect. 2 the Digital Forensic Readiness System

© Institute for Computer Sciences, Social Informatics and Telecommunications Engineering 2014
P. Gladyshev et al. (Eds.): ICDF2C 2013, LNICST 132, pp. 237–244, 2014.
DOI: 10.1007/978-3-319-14289-0_16

(DFRS) literature review is provided; in Sect. 3 Digital Forensic Readiness (DFR) is introduced and a definition for Forensic Readiness System is provided; in Sect. 4 the architecture for the Cloud Forensic Readiness System (CFRS) is presented, together with its features and challenges; finally, in Sect. 5 we will discuss conclusions and future work.

2   Literature Review

Digital Forensic Readiness focuses on rendering existing computing environments capable of pro-actively collecting and preserving potential digital evidence for later use in digital crime investigations. Several problems arise in this context. One of the constant issues regards the evolving nature of digital forensic investigation procedures; this derives both from the innovations of technological progress and from the skills and techniques adopted by the digital criminals, thus proper techniques for defeating them are necessary. Technical forensic standardization both in industry and academia is missing; in fact, a great variety of customized investigation process models are presented in literature [1,14]. This variety of approaches does not help facilitate the design and implementation of Digital Forensic Readiness Systems (DFRSs). The issues examined in [15] dealt with human, technical, and departmental management problems for implementing a DFRS in large organizations; the proposed solution involved the implementation of frameworks rather than ad-hoc solutions, thus, a novel DFR Management System architecture was proposed and proven by a prototype. Similarly, in [5] the necessity of a structured approach for DFR was presented; it must comply with the legislation and protect the privacy of the users; such an approach seeks to pro-actively configure the existing systems for collecting and preserving the potential evidence; the proposal took into account relevant and established standards and best practices, and considered that the organizations already collected data (though for other purposes), and that they can experience security critical events. Grobler et al. in [7] examined the overlap between Digital Forensics (DF) and Information Security (IS), summarizing that some DF aspects can be considered as IS best practices that miss events prosecution procedures. In the opinion of the authors a DFRS can enrich the security strategies of an organization; its main feature is providing a way to prepare the existing system for an incident by collecting digital evidence and minimizing the cost of investigations. Thus, DFR will become a component of the IS best practices, demonstrating that protecting valuable company information resources is critical [6].

3   Forensic Readiness

Some Digital Forensic Readiness advantages were investigated in literature; an important milestone is the set of guidelines presented by Rowlingson in [16], designed to facilitate the implementation of a DFRS; this work places emphasis on the features that a DFRS must respect to be effective. Again, the impact of

DFR in a corporate context was analysed in [13], where some positive aspects were highlighted, e.g., the help for enhancing the security strategy of an organization, the reduction of security incidents, the availability of evidence, and the derived effectiveness of an investigation. Finally, another DFRS proposal involves Wireless Sensors Networks [8], where a forensic readiness prototype was conceived as an additional layer that does not modify the original architecture of an existing IEEE 802.15.4 network.

3.1 Definition

DFR was defined in [16, 19] as "the ability of an organization to maximize its potential to use digital evidence whilst minimizing the costs of an investigation", but we consider it as one of the features of a DFRS to achieve a certain aim. To the best of our knowledge, DFR means implementing an information system capable of recording the potential evidence for the investigations, encrypting and storing them for being accessed after a crime happens. We define DFR as *"an Information System implemented into another system architecture with the aim of collecting and monitoring sensitive and critical information related to digital crimes before they happen, leading to save time and money for the investigations. The data is closely related to the system artifacts and logging tools available at the moment. The data is then encrypted in order to guarantee more protection and, eventually, stored on a third party server that will act as a safe, only accessible to selected subjects"*. This definition is considered general and adaptable to every computing context, thus we can affirm that it is valid both for the past and the future, as well as for CC.

4   Cloud Forensic Readiness

The main purpose of this paper is to provide a reference architecture for a Cloud Forensic Readiness System (CFRS) by designing it. The potential evidence collected by a DFRS have the same utility of CCTV recordings: preventively saved and when necessary accessed. This facility must be given to Cloud Computing, because, due to its huge popularity, it is also object of several attacks, thus a way to conduct forensic investigations effectively, e.g., saving time, money and resources, must be designed. In a recent survey [17] almost the 90 % of the interviewees, who were familiar with digital forensics, stated that "a procedure and a set of toolkits to proactively collect forensic-relevant data in the cloud is important". For a Cloud Forensic Readiness System, we believe that an accurate definition and model must be provided, in order to clarify the tasks, the activities and the stakeholders to consider.

4.1   Technical Challenges

Cloud Computing architecture unfortunately presents several technical challenges related to Forensic Readiness [2]; no standard is present, and no structured manner to perform an investigation has yet been defined. CC obfuscates physical access to the servers, leading users and data owners to be unaware of the physical location of the machines on which their data is stored, and creating uncertainty regarding the provenance of data and processes. Furthermore, the logs from network components are impossible to retrieve, because no routing information is available. Some digital evidence sources are missing, such as the customer's browser logs, which could provide a great deal of clues to reconstruct a case timeline; also the synchronization of timestamps is necessary for a correct case timeline reconstruction, as affirmed also in [17]. Moreover, due to the fact that logs and encryption processes running on virtual machines (VMs) can be controlled by malicious or corrupted hypervisors, an open challenge concerned with determining how a VM can be protected by compromised VM Monitors. Furthermore, defining both a procedure and a set of tool-kits for recording and maintaining a Chain of Custody (CoC) [9] into the Cloud investigations is a challenge to be addressed. Another technical challenge is related to the variety of log formats to be investigated. Finally, because the current international legal structure is far away from managing data segmented and duplicated all over the world, a CFRS must also manage the multiple jurisdictions issue.

4.2   CFRS Reference Architecture

The proposed CFRS will be implemented into a Cloud Computing architecture without modifying its structure, as well as done in [8]. The proposed reference architecture is composed of several subsystems, as illustrated in Fig. 1, which need to communicate and exchange data with each other. The OVF standard language [11] is suitable for the creation of communication channels: OVF is capable of creating and distributing software applications to be executed on VMs, independently from hypervisors and from CPUs architectures; it exploits the XML standard to establish the configuration and the installation parameters, and it can be extended for future hypervisor developments. In our system, an OVF module between the CC architecture and the CFRS components is necessary: it will convert the Cloud data formats into a new defined and appropriate XML one, in order to render readable and usable the necessary information by the several system components, listed in Fig. 1.

– Monitored Data: includes CC common features and tools [4] involving monitored information, which are: Database and File Activity Monitoring, URL Filtering, Data Loss Prevention, Digital Rights Management, and Content Discovery. The Database and File Activity Monitoring tools are capable of recognizing whenever a huge amount of data is pushed into the Cloud or replicated, thus indicating a data migration; the Data Loss Prevention facility is used for monitoring data in motion; it also manages policies and rights. URL Filtering controls the customer's connections to the Cloud Services, thus it can be useful during the construction of a case timeline. Finally, we can integrate the Digital Rights Management System and the Content Discovery System, where the former is responsible for implementing and monitoring the

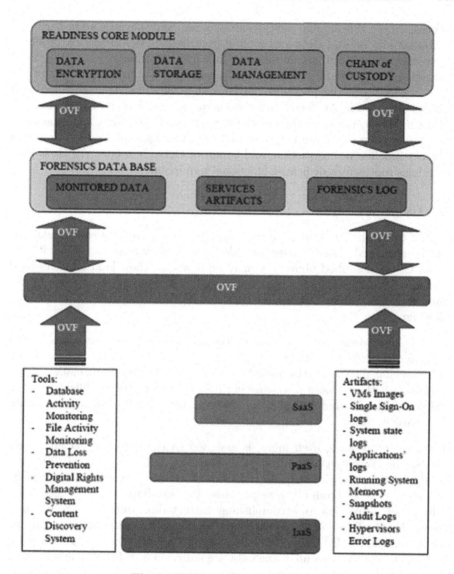

Fig. 1. CFRS reference architecture

customers' rights and restrictions on data, as stated by the SLA's clauses and terms of use contracts co-signed by CSPs and customers; the latter includes tools and processes aimed to identify sensitive information in storage, allowing us to define policies for them and to identify their violations;

– Services Artifacts: this component includes a significant quantity of CSPs artifacts, i.e., from SaaS clouds, the VM images and the Single Sign-On logs; from PaaS clouds, the system states and applications logs; and from IaaS clouds, the snapshots and the running system memory;

- Forensic Log: this module collects suitable logs, and they are: audit logs from Cloud Auditors; and error logs coming from hypervisors indicating problematic events. Both of them are relevant for incident response;
- Readiness Core Module: this module is dedicated to the computation of the data collected in the previously listed system modules, i.e., the Monitored Data, the Service Artifacts, and the Forensic Logs. We can affirm that the Core module contains all the functional requirements of the readiness system, e.g., data encryption, data storage, and data management for the purpose of events timeline reconstruction, and Chain of Custody report. All these sub-modules represent a dedicated functional requirement.

4.3 Usage of CFRS

In order to obtain the most from the proposed system, some recommendations must be respected. The CC must provide the necessary features for monitoring by the CFRS described above. As mentioned above, the Cloud artifacts used by the system are common Cloud features [4], therefore their presence at the moment of the system installation must be verified. They are essentially the following:

- Components dedicated to the monitoring of both databases and files, necessary for detecting data migrations.
- Features for filtering URLs, aimed to verifying the connections made.
- Tools with the purpose of controlling policies and rights established by the SLAs, Contracts, and Terms of Use, and possibly capable of creating new ones for sensitive data.

The same importance, even more, is assigned to the potential evidence data sources; this encompasses several logs types, for which logging facilities are already present; likewise snapshots, for which running system memory image tools are necessary. From all these premises, the installation and the usage of a CFRS is very important for accomplishing distinct aims. Implicitly, the first aim is rendering the Cloud environment ready for digital forensics, by executing the functionalities included into the Readiness Core Module; hence, data encryption functions have to be executed; the data are stored in a dedicated environment, which has to be physically prepared; the aim of reconstructing the case timeline and establishing the chain of custody [9] in case an incident occurs. The system's added value is in the provision of more control over data, on the access to services, and on the usage rules and constraints.

5   Conclusions and Future Work

The principal aim of this paper is to provide the basis for Cloud Forensic Readiness; its main contribution involves two distinct proposals; with the first proposal, we attempted to clarify what must be intended for Digital Forensic Readiness: we provided a definition adaptable to several different computing environments; with the second proposal, we proposed a CFRS reference architecture in order to corroborate our research work direction. We presented a proposal that must be considered a greenfield software engineering product, because there is no similar proposal in literature. At the same time, our proposal both takes advantage of several CC aspects specified by the Cloud Security Alliance, common to various CSPs, and integrates them in specific system components that implement dedicated functions. In the future, we will continue our research in this and we will provide more details about the CFRS reference architecture, for the purpose of prototyping it.

References

1. Alharbi, S., Weber-Jahnke, J., Traore, I.: The proactive and reactive digital forensics investigation process: a systematic literature review. In: Kim, T., Adeli, H., Robles, R.J., Balitanas, M. (eds.) ISA 2011. CCIS, vol. 200, pp. 87–100. Springer, Heidelberg (2011)
2. Birk, D.: Technical challenges of forensic investigations in cloud computing environments. In: Workshop on Cryptography and Security in Clouds, pp. 1–6 (2011)
3. Choo, K.K.R.: Cloud computing: challenges and future directions. Trends Issues Crime Crim. Justice **400**, 1–6 (2010)
4. Cloud Security Alliance: Security Guidance for Critical Areas of Focus in Cloud Computing (2011)
5. Danielsson, J., Tjostheim, I.: The need for a structured approach to digital forensics readiness. In: IADIS International Conference e - Commerce (2004)
6. Endicott-Povsky, B., Frinckle, D.A.: A theoretical framework for organizational network forensic readiness. J. Comput. **2**(3), 1–11 (2007)
7. Grobler, C.P., Louwrens, C.P.: Digital forensic readiness as a component of information security best practice. In: Venter, H., Elofif, M., Labuschagne, L., Elofif, J., von Solms, R. (eds.) New Approaches for Security, Privacy and Trust in Complex Environments. IFIP, vol. 232, pp. 13–24. Springer, Boston (2007)
8. Mouton, F., Venter, H.S.: A prototype for achieving digital forensic readiness on wireless sensor networks. In: AFRICON, pp. 1–6 (2011)
9. National Institute of Justice: Electronic Crime Scene Investigation: A Guide for First Responders (2008)
10. National Institute of Standards and Technology: NIST Definition of cloud computing v15. NIST Editor. Gaithersburg, MD (2009)
11. Open Virtualization Format: OVF Standard. http://www.dmtf.org/standards/ovf
12. Palmer, G.: A road map for digital forensics research. In: Report From the First Digital Forensics Research Workshop (2001)
13. Pangalos, G., Ilioudis, C., Pagkalos, I.: The importance of corporate forensic readiness in the information security framework. In: 19th IEEE International Workshop on Enabling Technologies: Infrastructures for Collaborative Enterprises (WET-ICE), pp. 12–16 (2010)
14. Pollitt, M.: An ad hoc review of digital forensic models. In: Second International Workshop on Systematic Approaches to Digital Forensic Engineering, pp. 43–54 (2007)
15. Reddy, K., Venter, H.S.: The architecture of a digital forensic readiness management system. Comput. Secur. **32**, 73–89 (2013). ISSN: 0167-4048

16. Rowlingson, R.: A ten step process for forensic readiness. Int. J. Digital Evid. **2**(3), 1–28 (2004)
17. Ruan, K., Baggili, I., Carthy, J., Kechadi, T.: Survey on cloud forensics and critical criteria for cloud forensic capability: a preliminary analysis. In: Proceedings of the 6th Annual Conference on Digital Forensics, Security and Law (2011)
18. Ruan, K., Carthy, J., Kechadi, T., Crosbie, M: Cloud forensics: an overview. In: IFIP International Conference on Digital Forensics, vol. 7 (2011)
19. Tan, J.: Forensic Readiness. @Stake, Cambridge (2001)

Poster Presentation

Mozilla Firefox Browsing Artifacts in 3 Different Anti-forensics Modes

Deepak Gupta[1] and Babu M. Mehtre[2(✉)]

[1] School of Computer and Information Science,
University of Hyderabad, Hyderabad, India
Deepkguptal989@gmail.com
[2] Institute for Development and Research in Banking Technology
(Established by Reserve Bank of India), Hyderabad, India
BMMehtre@idrbt.ac.in

Abstract. There are several techniques which can assist a user to avoid leaving traces (Digital Evidence) of Internet activity so that one can frustrate forensic investigation. In this paper we examined three different usage scenarios of Internet browsing using Mozilla Firefox. These different usage scenarios were a sandbox environment, browsing with portable tools, and browsing with virtual box. We tried to find the artifacts created and left by web browsing activities in each of these usage scenarios. In our experiments, we performed identical web browsing activity for each of the three scenarios and investigated whether the traces were left behind.

Keywords: Forensics investigation · Digital evidences · Artifacts · Anti-forensics techniques · Portable environment · Virtual box · Sandboxie

1 Introduction

Various software products are now available on the Internet, both free and commercial. Many products can be used either to carry out malicious activity or assist in doing so. Software artifacts are by-products produced during installation and/or use of these software products which can be used as evidence during the crucial investigation. Software artifact forensics is the collection of these byproducts to investigate and/or prove a theory of a crime. Unfortunately in the past couple of years, many tools and techniques have been made available which can help a user to get rid of these traces and to frustrate a digital investigation. These tools provide an ostensibly trace-free environment for criminals to carry out their malicious intent without leaving any trails on their computer.

This paper aims to investigate the artifacts created by the web browsing activities of Mozilla Firefox in three different anti-forensics modes: using a portable web browser version, browsing inside a sandbox environment, and browsing inside a virtual machine. For investigation purposes we started with a traditional digital forensics approach in which we search common places in which artifacts are generally found. Next we used the forensics tool EnCase for deep investigation. Physical memory (RAM) was also captured and analyzed for evidence.

© Institute for Computer Sciences, Social Informatics and Telecommunications Engineering 2014
P. Gladyshev et al. (Eds.): ICDF2C 2013, LNICST 132, pp. 247–251, 2014.
DOI: 10.1007/978-3-319-14289-0_17

2 Related Work

In this paper we have mainly focused on 3 different techniques to use various browsers without leaving activity traces on the host's hard disk. We could have chosen any browser for experimental purposes, but our main focus was on these techniques, so we chose only one browser, Mozilla Firefox, due to its worldwide popularity. Here we will first discuss all these three techniques in brief and how can they serve as anti-forensics mechanisms.

A **sandbox** is an isolated environment initially used by software developers to test new programming code. Various software products like *Sandboxie* [1] can now be used to create isolated environments for general users. It allows various computer programs to run in an isolated environment and prevent them from making any permanent change to other programs and data in computer. Once Sandboxie is closed along with the program running within it, it will automatically dump all the changes made by that program in such a manner that they will not be reflected anywhere else in the computer. By using a sandbox environment one can avoid leaving various activity traces like browsing history, cookies, cache, temporary files and many more. For this experiment's purposes, we used the tool Sandboxie version 3.76.

Portable software is an executable program that runs independently without any need for installation on the host computer's hard disk drive. These kinds of applications can be stored on removable storage media such as USB flash drives or portable hard disks. After storing a portable application on a portable device it can be used on any number of compatible machines. These applications do not leave program files or data on the host system. Generally they also do not write to the Windows registry or configuration files of the user's profile on the host system. There are lots of portable tools available on the Internet for various functions. For our experiment we used *Firefox Portable* [2] for web browsing.

A **virtual machine (VM)** is essentially a simulation of a computer within a physical computer. A VM is a computer application which creates a virtual environment which allows a user to run any number of operating systems on a single computer at the same time. A VM can be carried on removable media and can be accessed on nearly any computer. These VMs can be encrypted and disposing of them is a very easy task compared to disposing of a physical computer. When a person wants to carry out any malicious activity, it is possible to simply setup a VM and perform all activities using this VM only [3]. Thus by using virtual machines and disposing of them successfully, one can avoid creating almost all of the artifacts that could be used to prove a crime had taken place.

In recent years, some papers have been published which use advanced forensics analysis to discover evidence left behind despite the use of various anti-forensic techniques. Said et al. [4] uses RAM forensics to find traces of activities done in private browsing mode while [5] uses advanced forensics to find out the password of an encrypted volume by analyzing the hibernation file. To the best of our knowledge nobody has addressed the issue of all three of the techniques we employ in this paper so far. This is the first attempt to address such kinds of anti-forensic mechanisms by investigating the artifacts left by using these modes.

3   Investigation Methodology

This section describes the tests that we conducted on the three different anti-forensics usage scenarios. We used three workstations with the same hardware and software configuration. To perform the experiments we used an IBM compatible PC with an Intel Core i5 CPU, 4 GB RAM and 160 GB hard disk running Windows 7 Professional and the NTFS file system. We used various software products including- Sandboxie V3.76, Mozilla Firefox 20.0, FTK Imager Lite 3.1.1.8 for capturing physical memory (RAM), Hex Workshop 6.7 for analyzing RAM, Encase 7.06 for advance analysis and Oracle VirtualBox V4.1.18 to create a virtual machine.

On workstation one, we installed Sandboxie, on the second workstation, we used a portable version of Mozilla Firefox hosted on a USB drive and on the third workstation, we created a Windows 7 virtual machine using Oracle VirtualBox. We then performed the same Internet activity on all three machines using Firefox.

For experimental web browsing activity, we made a small list of URLs (to be entered in browser's address bar) and keywords (to be used as search queries in different search engines) to be entered in the web browsers on all three workstations. Table 1 shows the lists of URLs and keywords that we used for experiments.

Table 1.   Unique URLs and keywords used in our experiments.

URLs	Keywords
Mandiant.com	Secret123—google.com
Osforensics.com	Artifactsinv—yahoo.com
Isro.org	Kammaro – bing.com

After performing these experiments, we terminated the respective mode and then for each session, physical memory (RAM) was captured using FTK Imager and finally images of the complete hard disks were captured using Encase for further analysis.

4   Evidence Analysis and Results

For all three techniques, we started our analysis by examining the artifacts in common places [6] for web browsing history. In all cases no traces were found in these common places. Next we searched for evidence using Hex Workshop on physical memory (RAM) that we captured during experiments. We did a string search of all the URLs and keywords used in experiments and we were able to find various instances of each URL and Keyword of all browser activities for all three cases. For example, in the case of *Sandboxie,* we found 7 entries for the URL "mandiant.com" and 16 entries for the keyword "Secret123". In the case of "Portable mode", we were able to find 19 entries for the URL "osforensics.com" and 12 entries for the keyword "Artifactsinv". In comparison to the other two modes, for the "virtual machine mode", the numbers of hits were very large in the RAM capture. For example, we were able to find 94 hits for the URL "isro.org" and 260 entries for the keyword "kammaro" and 592 entries for "secret123". For all three cases we were also able to retrieve blocks of HTML code from the web sites we visited.

Finally Encase was used for forensics analysis of the captured image of the hard disk. In the case of "Sandboxie", we were able to find various hits at different locations on the hard disk. Some URL entries were also retrieved from *pagefil.sys*. Also entries of URLs and keywords used during tests were also found in many files such as some *dat* files, *lex* files and some other files. It appeared to us that during sandbox mode web pages and cache files are stored on the hard disk and then deleted once the sandbox environment is terminated. Thus the files still reside on the hard disk and could be recovered until they are overwritten. For "Portable mode", again several traces, scattered all over the hard disk were found. We were able to get the search hits for the entered URLs and keywords from various kinds of files such as.*dat*, *MFT*, *pagefil.sys*, *hiberfil.sys*. Finally for "VM mode", we found various evidence scattered all over the hard disk, but most hits for URLs and keywords were in unallocated clusters. Figures 1 and 2 demonstrate some of our findings.

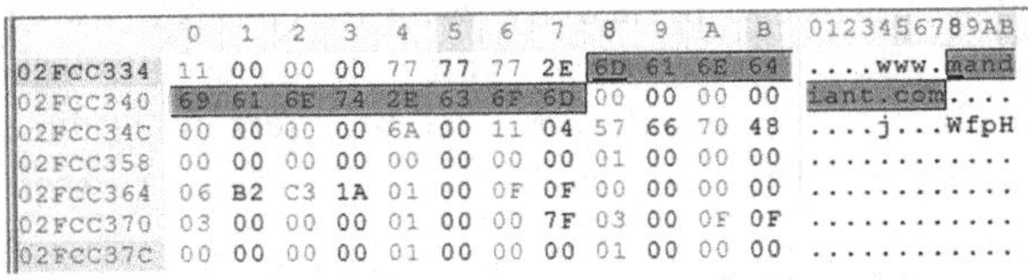

Fig. 1. "Mandian.com" found in RAM in "Sandboxie" case

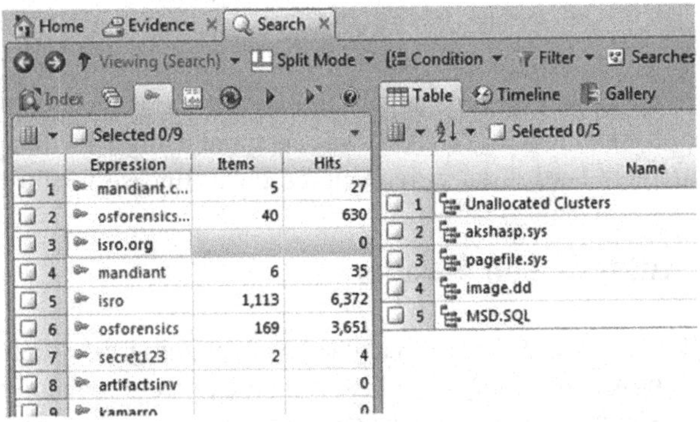

Fig. 2. Evidences in the Encase in "Portable mode" case

For common storage location analysis, no traces for any activity were found for any of the three modes. All of our findings are summarized in Table 2 such that we can also compare the results. RAM forensics and Encase forensics provided a good number of traces. Browsing within a virtual machine leaves the most number of traces in RAM, as shown in the results, while the sandbox environment leaves a lesser quantity of traces in RAM. With the help of Encase, we were able to find a good number of traces for all three usage scenarios in different locations on the hard disk.

Table 2. Summary of Results

Mode	Analysis of physical memory	Advanced analysis using the Encase
Sandboxie	- 7 entries for "mandiant.com" - 6 entries for "isro.org" - 1 entries for "osforensics.com" - 16 entries for "secret123" - 12 entries for "kammaro" - 18 entries for "artifactsinv"	- Results were scattered all over the hard disk in different files, including .dat, .lex, pagefile.sys and many more. -We were able to reconstruct pages partially
Portable	- 58entries for "mandiant.com" - 8 entries for "isro.org" - 19 entries for "osforensics.com" - 151 entries for "secret123" - 18 entries for "kamarro" - 12 entries for "artifactsinv"	-Results were scattered all over the hard disk in different files, including .MFT, hibefil.sys, pagefi-le.sys and many more -We reconctructed few page partially
Virtual Machine	- 401 entries for "mandiant.com" - 94 entries for "isro.org" - 70 entries for "osforensics.com" - 592 entries for "secret123" - 260 entries for "kammaro" - 136 entries for "artifactsinv"	-Results were scattered all over the hard disk in different files, mostly in unallocated clusters

5 Conclusion

The results presented in the paper suggest the level of isolation and privacy provided by the tested techniques are sufficient for an average user. No traces should be found in common storage locations for any web browser activity if a user decides to work in any of these three modes. However, complete isolation does not occur, and significant amounts of data are dumped into the main memory (RAM) as well as in various files and unallocated clusters on the hard disk. This could help forensic examiners investigating a case where suspected malicious browsing activities were performed using these modes.

References

1. Sandboxie. http://www.sandboxie.com
2. Firefox portable. http://portableapps.com/apps/internet/firefox_portable
3. Bares, R.A.: Hiding in a virtual world: using unconventionally installed operating system. In: International Conference on Intelligence and Security Informatics, pp. 276–284 (2009)
4. Said, H., Al Mutawa, N, Al Awadhi, I.: Forensic analysis of private browsing artifacts. In: International Conference on Innovations in Information Technology (IIT), pp. 197–202 (2011)
5. Mrdovic, S., Huseinovic, A.: Forensic analysis of encrypted volumes using hibernation file. In: 19th Telecommunications Forum (TELFOR), pp. 1277–1280 (2011)
6. Oha, J.J., Leeb, S., Leea, S.: Advanced evidence collection and analysis of web browser activity. Digital Invest. **8**, 62–70 (2011)

Author Index

Alobaidli, Hanan   39
Baggili, Ibrahim   39, 207
Baier, Harald   170
Balan, C.   17
Breitinger, Frank   170
Brennan, Fergal   189
De Marco, Lucia   237
Dija, S.   17
Doyoddorj, Munkhbaatar   3
Ferrucci, Filomena   237
Gerhards-Padilla, Elmar   51
Gladyhsev, Pavel   147, 189, 223
Goel, Prachi   30
Gupta, Deepak   247
Iqbal, Asif   39
Iqbal, Farkhund   207
James, Joshua I.   147, 223
Kechadi, M-Tahar   237
Lambertz, Martin   51
Liu, Huajian   102, 170
Lopez-Fernandez, Alejandra   147

Marrington, Andrew   39, 207
Mehtre, Babu M.   30, 247
Peshin, Esti   119
Poisel, Rainer   67
Rhee, Kyung-Hyune   3
Rowe, Neil C.   86
Rybalchenko, Alexey   170
Rybnicek, Marlies   67
Shabana Subair, P.   17
Shosha, Ahmed F.   223
Steinebach, Martin   102, 170
Thomas, K.L.   17
Tjoa, Simon   67
Udris, Martins   189
Uetz, Rafael   51
Watney, Murdoch   130
Winter, Christian   170
Yannikos, York   102